W9-CTI-454

HOW I BUILT AN EMPIRE
&
GAVE IT AWAY

HOW I BUILT AN EMPIRE AND GAVE IT AWAY

BY

JOSEPH J. ZILBER

WITH

KURT CHANDLER

LIBRARY OF CONGRESS CATALOGING-IN-PUBLICATION DATA

Zilber, Joseph J., 1917-2010
　How I built an empire and gave it away / by Joseph J. Zilber with Kurt Chandler. — first Edition.
　　pages cm
　Includes index.
　ISBN 978-1-62600-040-7 (hardcover : alk. paper)
1.　Zilber, Joseph J., 1917-　2.　Millionaires—Wisconsin—Biography.
3.　Philanthropists—Wisconsin—Biography. 4.　Real estate investment—Wisconsin. I. Chandler, Kurt. II. Title.
　HG172.Z55Z55 2013
　333.3092—dc23
　[B]
　　　　　　　　2013014660

Printed by Burton & Mayer, Inc., Menomonee Falls, Wisconsin, USA

⊗The paper used in this publication meets the minimum requirements of the
American National Standard for Information Sciences—
Permanence of Paper for Printed Library Materials, ANSI Z39.48-1992.

CONTENTS

ACKNOWLEDGEMENTS

It was not as easy as I thought it would be to talk about my life. The difficult points were more complex, the bright spots harder to recollect. In this effort, I was helped by an extraordinary group of individuals. This list is not complete. I wish I could thank everyone with whom I ever came in contact, all those who contributed to the stories and the moments that lie within this book.

Special thanks, however, to Kurt Chandler, who sat with me for hundreds of hours, both in person and by video conference, to probe and prod, to filter and focus my thoughts over nine decades of history. After more than 60 interviews with me and with family members, friends, company employees, business associates, and community leaders, Kurt then compiled his notes and the transcripts of the audio sessions with me and put everything in some semblance of order, helping me turn my stories and ideas into the book that you now hold in your hands. His patience and perseverance were above and beyond. Any mistakes, errors, perceptions, or loss of memory are mine and not his. The events depicted are written the way I remember them, and for that I am solely responsible.

Thanks also to Marcy and Marilyn, my wonderful daughters, who refreshed my memory, clarified points of view, and occasionally disagreed on my perspective and viewpoint. I thank my longtime assistant and vice president, Mike Mervis, who pushed me to go in a direction that I had delayed taking. As always, he did what had to be done to make sure the end product would make me happy. Thanks also to Jerry Stein, my longtime employee and friend, as well as, Vice Chair and CEO of the company. I cannot thank him enough for the use of his journals, notes, and recollections, which provided us with a rough format to jog my memory and enhance my stroll through time.

To Mary Ellen McCormack Mervis, who took the words and stories and edited them down to manageable proportions and who utilized her considerable skills both as an English teacher and a dear friend, thank you. To Maria Domkowski, who set up the meetings, managed my time, greeted me daily on the video conferencing system prior to my meetings with Kurt, and provided the smiles and the incentive for me to continue, and who, most important of all, put in hours and hours of coordinating facts and information: I am forever indebted. I thank my senior management team: Jim Borris, John Kersey, Bob Braun, Steve Chevalier, Jim Janz, Art Wigchers, Bill Wigchers, Don Mantz, Jim Young, Sue Laabs, Jack Tsui, and other long-term employees who shared their memories about the events in this book, I thank you for your dedicated service, friendship, and input. Finally, to all of the employees who worked with me and for me over the years: thank you for allowing this old man's life adventure to be put down in print in the hope that the lessons learned, both good and bad, will enhance the lives of others and make their paths less difficult.

INTRODUCTION

On a late summer day, I sat with my daughters Marcy and Marilyn in the living room of our home in Milwaukee. Marilyn had found a cardboard box on a closet shelf, and inside the box were a bunch of check stubs, bank statements, and receipts dating back to the 1940s — my early days, by the numbers. As we picked through the papers, the memories rushed by . . .

I found a receipt from May of 1942 for $41, the monthly rent for the very first apartment that my wife Vera and I lived in.

I found a cancelled check to Mount Sinai Hospital for $9.15, partial payment for the costs of our son Jimmy's birth in 1946.

I found a yellowed contract for the first office building I bought, at 11th Street and National Avenue in Milwaukee. The down payment was $100.

Those checks and receipts made me think about just how things have changed over the years. I'm now in my ninth decade on this Earth and, believe me, I've seen changes of all kinds. There's not much that has stayed the same.

Poring over those old papers also moved me, and gave me the chance to look back to a marriage that lasted 61 wonderful years, to the joys of raising a family and the heartbreak of watching a son die too soon, and to the success of growing a company that took me to every corner of the country and made me wealthy beyond my wildest dreams.

Writing a book does that too. It forces you to concentrate on the past, to reflect and to take measure of your life. That's not something that comes easily for me. I'm usually looking for what's around the next bend. Even today, I'm thinking ahead to the future, eager to see what tomorrow will bring.

When I sat down to write this book, I began to think about all the stories I wanted to tell, and as I began to relive those stories, I thought about all the people I have met.

Through these stories and the people I've known run a common thread, weaving them together into a whole fabric. Life is not simply a journey through time and space. Life for me has been a series of events and interactions with all kinds of people, a rich experience of adventures (and occasional misadventures) that in context make up the person I am.

I started out as a builder of homes. I wanted to be a lawyer once upon a time, but no one would hire me when I got out of law school. So I became a builder, starting my own company, Towne Realty, in 1949. We built thousands of houses, entire neighborhoods, and over the years we expanded into office buildings, churches, nursing homes, car washes, retail stores, fitness salons, college dormitories, Florida condos, Las Vegas hotels. You name it, I've built it — a heat-generating plant in the Arctic Circle, a circular church designed by the irascible Frank Lloyd Wright, and 15 fake missile silos in a North Dakota farm field, made to fool the Russian satellites as they passed overhead.

My years have been filled with excitement and a passion for life. I traveled the world with Vera, took two companies public, tried and failed at early retirement (twice), and dealt with people of all kinds — from politicians to mobsters to one of history's most notorious serial killers.

I've also known tragedy. I grieved the loss of 11 construction workers who died when a building we owned collapsed in Florida, and I watched my only son die of drug addiction, a father's greatest sorrow.

As a businessman, I've been a risk taker. As a young and eager man, I started out with nothing and created a real estate empire that has endured for over 60 years, bringing me success and more wealth than I ever could have imagined. I'm still a builder today, and I'm still hard at work. While I've handed over the reins of my company to a fourth generation of leaders, I remain involved in the day-to-day management of my businesses.

Along with the responsibilities of running a company, I've taken a new and exciting course. In the twilight of my life, I've decided to give away my fortune. I will use part of it to rebuild the city of my birth, Milwaukee, and the remainder to help those who don't have adequate educational opportunities, suffer from spousal abuse, are addicted to drugs, are impacted by crime and its consequences, lack adequate housing, or can have their lives changed by someone having the guts to act on their behalf. Instead of holding on to what I've made in my lifetime, I've decided to contribute more than $100 million to the institutions and organizations I respect and admire, and to several well chosen community action groups in the inner city neighborhoods I knew when I was growing up.

As we roll along through life's adventures, we learn many lessons. Some are obvious, some are not. Some look plain and understandable, but end up not quite so clear. Some bring satisfaction and rewards, and some carry a huge amount of pain. If we're smart, those lessons will carry us forward to success.

What follows on these pages are my best recollections of a lifetime that's closing in on 100 years, and the lessons I learned along the way.

PART ONE

WITNESSING THE
AMERICAN DREAM

CHAPTER I

PENNY POKER

I had heard the words before in my 60 years as a businessman and real-estate developer: "A bad idea . . . too much of a gamble . . . way too risky." But I had taken risks many times; not crazy, shoot-from-the-hip risks, but calculated risks. I had built my company on *hundreds* of carefully thought-out decisions that turned into successful deals and projects.

"Joe, this really is not a good idea," one of my top execs said. "There's just no way this project can be successful."

I was outnumbered by my own managers, but I wouldn't take no for an answer. I had an idea to rebuild the abandoned Pabst Brewery into something special for my hometown. The owners of Pabst — Milwaukee's very first brewery, an historic landmark — had walked out on Milwaukee in 1996, just locked up the brewery and threw everybody out. Now, almost 10 years later, it was still empty, a blight on downtown Milwaukee, with many of the site's 13 buildings badly deteriorating. I wanted to bring the brewery back to life by buying it and converting it into a 21-acre urban neighborhood, with apartments and condos, restaurants and hotels, office space and college classrooms. Something unique. I knew it was the right thing to do.

My team of 12 senior managers weren't so sure. So I sent them over to the brewery one day to take a look at the place. It was a freezing, winter day, the temperature below zero. Wearing hardhats and carrying flashlights, they toured the Pabst, building by building, then returned to the office to talk about my plan. Sitting around the conference table, I could sense their uneasiness. No one wanted to speak . . .

On Sunday evenings, in the early 1920s, my mother and father sat in the back of their storefront grocery store where we lived, talking with my aunts and uncles. Every Sunday my parents invited the relatives over for dinner and a game of cards. They made sandwiches and brought out fruit, salads, and bakery from the deli counter. While my sisters and I tore around the house with our cousins, the adults sat around the kitchen table, eating, kibitzing, and playing penny ante poker. Now and then a bell rang above the storefront door, signaling the arrival of a customer. My mother would jump up from the table. Without skipping a beat, I'd slide into her chair and play her hand. "I'll play for you, Ma. Don't worry. I'll play your cards."

By the time I was six years old I could deal seven-card draw. I even won a few hands.

These are some of my earliest memories — living above our store in Milwaukee, playing penny poker for pocket change on Sundays. As I got older, I began to venture outside the neighborhood. I rode the electric streetcars everywhere, all around the city, to the theaters downtown, to the Lake Michigan lakefront. But it was the family grocery store that was the center of my universe. Lessons were learned, values were taught — values that stuck with me for the rest of my life, carrying me into law school and the world of business.

I learned from the examples of my father and mother. They were hardworking and humble people, Jewish immigrants who came to America from Kiev, Russia, around the turn of the century. They had married in Kiev when they were very young. This was the time of the pogroms, when Jews were persecuted in the Russian Empire. Millions of Jews fled the violence and mistreatment, and many came by ship to America to find a better life.

My father was one of them. Samuel Zilberbrand said goodbye to his young wife Sonia in 1898. When he landed at New York's Ellis Island, he shortened his last name to Zilber and traveled to Milwaukee, Wisconsin, where a contingent of Russian Jews had already settled.

Sam Zilber believed Milwaukee would be a fine place to raise a family. The city was growing, and the opportunities were abundant. But it took two years for him to save enough money to bring Sonia across the ocean. He bought a horse and wagon and went looking for work, loading produce, hauling trash. Whatever he could do, he did.

Sonia was 19 years old when he finally sent for her. The year was 1900. Sam and Sonia Zilber at last were reunited.

I was born on November 13, 1917, in a house at 9th and Vine Streets in Milwaukee. Three sisters came before me — Frieda, Gertrude, and Fannie. We moved a few years after I was born to the corner of 10th and Lee Streets into a house with a grocery store in front. Dad worked three jobs and Mom ran the store. There were times when she didn't take in more than $2 a day, working from 6:00 in the morning until 11:00 at night. It was hard going for them. My father would hitch the horse to the wagon and go to the markets before dawn to buy fruit and vegetables. Then, after hauling it back to the store, he would make his way to the local factories — companies like Nordberg Manufacturing and the Falk Company — to pick up scrap metal and then sell it to scrap metal dealers. He probably made just enough to feed the horse.

Our grocery was a typical storefront, 20 feet deep by 50 feet wide, with a big deli counter and a plate glass window in front that let the morning sunlight shine in. Three steps led up to the living space in back — a living room, a kitchen, and a bathroom — and on the second floor, two bedrooms. If there were hardships, my sisters and I hardly noticed. Our childhoods were happy times, and we always seemed to have what we needed.

Because I was the youngest, I enjoyed what I would call special privileges. I remember I had a bath once a week, and in those days a bathtub was like having a swimming pool! We didn't know anything better. As the youngest, I was given a bath first. After splashing around for awhile, I would hop out and my three sisters would get in — into the same bath water. My parents were trying to cut down on the hot water bill.

That bathtub was also used to make wine. I was the lucky one who got to stamp the grapes. My feet were blue for a month, and so was that tub. When the crushed grapes had fermented, my father would fill a dozen quart bottles with his moonshine wine and give it away to friends.

My father also raised chickens inside a pen in the backyard. He butchered them in the basement, and I would get to watch. He'd wring the hens' necks, drop the dead chickens into a barrel of boiling water, and then scrape away the feathers. In those days, you could buy chickens for 10 to 15 cents apiece.

My father was an enterprising young guy, and very energetic. His jobs didn't pay that well, but I saw how dedicated he was to his work. His work ethic made a strong impression on me. Years later, as a young man, I applied that same stick-to-it attitude to my own work as I made my way into real estate and started my own company.

Dad stood five feet, five inches and weighed around 160 pounds. He was a good man, kind and concerned for his family. I don't remember him disciplining me too often. (I guess he never needed to. I must have been such a good kid!) I never had a reason to be afraid of him, but I do remember one time I got into a load of trouble. I was standing at the top of the stairs in our house, and my sister Gertrude walked by below me. I had a clothespin in my hand. I don't know what got into me, but I flung it at Gerty and broke her glasses.

She started crying. "Oh, geez, now I've done it," I thought, and I scrambled upstairs into the attic and hid in a crawl space where nobody could find me. I must have stayed there for hours, petrified, afraid of what my father would do to me. He found me, of course, and he was not happy, I'll tell you. He wouldn't let me go to the movie theater that week. Going to the movies on Friday nights was my favorite thing to do, so that was serious punishment for me. Looking back, considering the cost of eyeglasses, I believe his justice was more than fair.

I've always remembered my mother as a beautiful woman. She was quite slender, with long, black hair, and very sensitive to the needs of others. Sadly, she had breast cancer when she was young and underwent a mastectomy. It was very difficult for her, I'm sure, but she recovered and lived a long and healthy life.

Mother also had a pleasant personality. She ran the grocery store, and all the customers were her fans. She treated them well, and they remained very loyal. In those days, nobody paid in cash. Instead, everybody had a running account at the store. My mother kept a list on the counter in the store. She wouldn't pressure anyone. Whenever they could pay, they'd come in and pay, and we never lost money on them. Everybody paid. It was an honorable way to do business with the neighborhood customers.

As a kid whose parents owned a grocery store, I had certain built-in advantages. For example, we had a whole showcase of penny candies in the store. Licorice sticks, chocolates — everything was a penny. Inside the display case, there were pink pieces of candy that my sisters and I called "winners." For a penny, you could reach inside a box and pick out one candy, and if you picked a *pink* winner, you'd get a nickel candy bar for free. All the grocery stores did this, and after awhile, I got pretty good figuring out where every pink candy was in every box at every store. I would take five cents and go store to store, searching for pink winners. I'd come home with five nickel candy bars for just five cents. Not a bad deal, and not a bad lesson. As I would see throughout my life, when making a deal, you're always trying to figure out an edge, whether it's negotiating the sale of a multi-million dollar hotel, or getting the best deal possible on five nickel candy bars.

Being the youngest kid also had its drawbacks, and a few humiliations. Once, when I was just a little tyke, my sisters decided they wanted to dress me up as a girl. They put me in a dress, placed a girl's hat on my head, and gave me a penny to go into our store and buy a piece of candy from our mother. They wanted to see if Mother would recognize me. To this day, I still don't know whether she knew who I was or not. She never let on, at least. But my sisters and I had a ball thinking we had faked her out with my disguise.

There was always plenty to do when I was growing up. I helped out at the store. I knocked around my grade school, Lee Street School, across the street from my home. It's funny. I remember the school, playing on the playground and all that, but I don't remember the classrooms. I guess that says a lot.

I also sang in the temple choir on High Holy Days. I had to practice every day after school for six months straight to be in that choir. My mother was very proud of me. "That's my son. That's my son," she would say to everyone in the gallery, and I would sing out, loud and clear.

As I got older, my horizons stretched to the downtown streets of the city. I gained a practical knowledge of the world, a street-smart savvy that would serve me well as an adult. Milwaukee was bustling in the years after World War I, as an economic boom swept through the land. The city's population grew, and new neighborhoods sprang up around its central core. Streetcars clogged Grand Avenue (now Wisconsin Avenue), the main drag, running east to Lake Michigan, and with near-ly all the streets paved, automobiles were everywhere. At night, electric signs and street lamps seemed to light up the sky. The city's manufactur-ing plants retooled their production lines after making armaments and supplies for the First World War, and began turning out everything from Evinrude outboard motors and Harnischfeger construction cranes to Allis-Chalmers tractors and Harley Davidson motorcycles. Prohibition put a lid on Milwaukee's famous breweries and beer gardens from 1920 until 1933, but to a boy my age, that didn't matter at all. Living just blocks away from the hubbub, with the newly constructed parks and the beaches of Lake Michigan, the city was an adventure land for any kid.

Meanwhile, the world was changing dramatically. Radio was a big thing. I remember listening with my father to the first Gene Tunney – Jack Dempsey fight in 1926. Tunney beat Dempsey to become the heavyweight champ and beat him again the next year in a rematch at Soldier Field. On summer nights, my friends and I would play baseball in the street in the light of my parents' storefront. We'd wad up a piece of newspaper and wrap it with string, and that would be our baseball. Somebody had a bat, and we made bases out of wood or scraps of cardboard — first, second, third, and home — and laid them out on the street, and that was how we played.

On weekends, I'd go to the lakefront with my sisters. Our parents had their first Ford, and they'd drive us, or we'd take the streetcar. We would meet our friends at Lake Park along Lincoln Memorial Drive, and hoof it to Bradford Beach. We'd swim there for hours, without a care in the world.

When I was eight or nine years old, I hawked newspapers. I hauled them in a coaster wagon from my house to the corner of Fond du Lac and Grand Avenue. The streetcar would stop, passengers would get off, and I'd sell them *The Milwaukee Journal* for three cents. I'd have to pay two cents back to the *Journal*, but a penny was my profit on each paper I sold, and that was a big deal to me at the time. That was good money. I would give my profits to my parents and spend the rest at the movie theaters.

There was one theater near our house, the Iris, on 14th and North Avenue. I'd go there every Friday night. Admission was five cents. I'd get a few pieces of candy from the store and walk over, mostly to see the cartoons and the Westerns. Those were the days of silent movies: Buster Keaton, Charlie Chaplin and Mary Pickford. Later on, I saw my first "talkie," *The Jazz Singer* with Al Jolson, at the Majestic Theater. It was like nothing I'd ever seen before. Magical. The actors came alive on the screen, laughing, talking, and singing.

When I was a little older, I would go to the Riverside Theatre, where they had all-day stage shows and movie matinees on Saturdays. It was a little more expensive, ten cents to get in, but I would spend the whole day watching vaudeville shows, movies, and newsreels. The Riverside was a beautiful theater, with chandeliers in the lobby and a balcony and box seats in the auditorium. I remember waiting between shows and staring up at the vast, curving ceiling, wondering how in the heck they'd painted it.

Years later, after I had gotten into real estate and was buying commercial properties, I bought the Riverside Theatre. In fact, I still own it today. It's hard to believe. I think back to when I was a boy, sitting in that very same theater. Who could have imagined that one day I'd actually own the place?

I remodeled the Riverside in the mid-1980s. It had fallen into disrepair, and I considered converting it into a shopping mall. I could've made quite a profit, but the theater was such a big part of Milwaukee's heritage, people didn't want to see it go. I decided to invest in its renovation. I wanted to preserve it for the people of Milwaukee. After the job was completed, I received hundreds of letters of thanks from people telling me how they used to go to the theater when they were kids, just like I had. It was very gratifying, and something that I often thought about when I purchased the historic buildings of the former Pabst Brewery in Milwaukee as a revitalization project, and when I designed my philanthropic initiative to rebuild the city's inner city neighborhoods.

When I first bought the Riverside as a young businessman, it was a big charge for me. I remember the day I told my father. We were at temple. "I'm going to buy the Riverside Theatre," I said to him. "How about that?"

"Why would you buy it? What do you need it for?" he asked me, puzzled by my news.

"It's a good deal, Dad, and the building is a landmark, a beautiful place."

"Okay, I'll come in with you on it," he said. "I'll buy it with you." I can't recall what I was going to pay for it, and I knew my father was being generous, but I didn't want him to take the risk.

"No, no, it's not *that* good of a deal," I told him. Fact is, my father had worked hard over the years to make a living. I didn't want him to get hurt by a risky investment.

❧❧ ❧❧ ❧❧

Changes were in store for the Zilber family. Some time around my 10th birthday, we moved to the West Side of Milwaukee and the neighborhood near Sherman and Washington Parks. Many middle-class Jewish families were moving into the Sherman Park area in particular as they worked their way up and became successful in life. I went to a brand-new school named Neeskara Elementary, five or six blocks from my house and just west of Washington Park. Washington was one of the biggest parks in the city, designed by Frederick Law Olmsted, the same landscape architect who designed New York's Central Park. It was a great place for a kid to hang out. There was a zoo in the park, with a monkey cage, a family of bears, a couple of elephants, and a huge lagoon where we'd go ice skating in the winter. The homes in my neighborhood were fairly new, built as housing expanded to the western limits of the city.

Most of the homes were craftsman bungalows, sturdy houses built with hardwoods and brick or stucco exteriors, but some streets were more exclusive, flanked by enormous homes that were owned by some of the city's wealthiest and best known residents: the Harley and the Davidson families; the Gettelman family, owners of the beer brewing company; and the Trecker family, co-founders of Kearney & Trecker, one of the largest machine tool companies in the country. Mostly the neighborhoods were made up of solid middle-class families, teachers and factory workers and salesman, people like my parents. When I first started to build houses, I could have built enormous homes for the city's wealthiest people, or smaller, sturdy homes for middle-class families. To me, the sturdy homes for middle-class owners were more important.

My father and mother opened a storefront grocery in the neighborhood, this one at 57th and North Avenue. It was in a two-story brick building that contained two apartments and a three-car garage in the back. My parents owned the building, holding a mortgage of $10,000. Again, as at our first family store, we lived upstairs. The latest thing at the time was selling ice cream cones. We had 10 delicious flavors. You could get one cone for 15 cents, or two for a quarter. That was a big deal. We advertised that with a big sign in the window.

My parents were doing pretty well in the new store. The neighborhood was growing, and they were always busy. But then the Great Depression hit, and everything was turned upside down. Nobody was working. Banks were closing. It was a very uncertain time. People didn't have any money to spend, and business at our store fell to almost nothing. When my parents couldn't pay the monthly mortgage, they were forced to close down the store. Again, our family packed up and moved, this time renting a duplex nearby at 47th and Garfield. It was a hand-to-mouth existence. Money was tight, and my father and mother had no choice but to get out of the grocery business for good. I'm sure it was devastating for them, as they had worked in the business since they had first settled in Milwaukee. They were able to get by with the help of family and friends. More often than not we had to take what was left on the shelves of our own store so we had food on the table. Things were not easy, but we all survived. Through my parents' hard work, somehow they made enough to help each of their kids go to college. They knew how important it was for us to get a college education.

I feel the same way. That's why Vera and I set up a scholarship fund years ago at Marquette University to help students pay their tuition. That's also the goal behind my new initiative to revive Milwaukee's inner city neighborhoods. If parents are able to gain a solid foothold in life — with good jobs and stable households — the chances that their children will succeed in school and go on to college are greatly improved. It plays out to the next generation, and to generations to come.

Despite the economic crisis of the 1930s, there were still plenty of good times in the Zilber home. My youngest sister Fannie was living at home when she got engaged. The wedding was planned for our backyard. Fannie was marrying a man named Bill Kesselman, and he had some kind of connection with the Milwaukee County Parks Department. On the day of the wedding, a county truck from the parks department showed up at the house filled with shrubs and flowers. We placed them all around the backyard for the ceremony. We had a marvelous time.

The Depression days were not always dark and bleak. I remember one amusing story: My dad had been down and out for awhile, but he found a job running a gas station in the neighborhood. On one Saturday afternoon, he had some other errands that he had to do, so he had me fill in for him. I must've been about 13 years old and I had no choice. I was his only son.

"You're going to have to take care of the gas station," he told me. "I'll be back as soon as I can." As soon as he left, a truck came rolling into the station.

"Give me 10 gallons, kid," the driver said to me.

Gas must have been about 12 cents a gallon back then. I put the nozzle in the truck and turned on the pump. Everything seemed to work okay. I pumped 10 gallons, watching the gauge closely as the numbers turned, and when it registered 10 gallons, I asked the driver for $1.20 — a lot of money during the Depression. He paid me and drove away.

Well, my dad finally came back, and the truck driver came back too — and he was mad.

"Hey, this kid said he put 10 gallons of gas in my truck but there's no gas in my tank," he hollered to my dad. "It's still empty."

My father blew a gasket. "What's the matter with you?" he said, glaring at me. "What did you do?" I thought he was going to kill me, but I couldn't figure out what went wrong. I had turned on the pump and thought I put 10 gallons in that truck. But somehow the pump had malfunctioned. Although the gauge showed 10 gallons going into the guy's truck, not a drop of gas went into his tank as it pumped. That was the end of my brief career as a gas station attendant.

It seemed like everybody was out of work in those days. Fortunately, my father still had connections with the factories where he hauled scrap metal. They were good to him. They wouldn't do business with anyone else, so my father was able to make ends meet. Ah, but those were lean years, all through the 1930s and up until World War Two.

Sometime in the mid-1940s, when I was in my 20s, I took my parents out to dinner at a nice restaurant. It was the very first time they had eaten a meal in a restaurant. I had returned from my stint in the Army, and I took them to a classy restaurant called the Boulevard Inn. I suppose we were celebrating my return home. My parents were in their 60s by then, gearing up for retirement. They had never enjoyed a quality, sit-down dinner in a fancy restaurant. They could never afford to splurge like this. My mother was thrilled. The waitress kept refilling her teacup. "I just loved that," she said to me. "I loved being waited on. It was a marvelous treat." My father didn't have many words to say. "It was very good, son," was about it, but I know they both enjoyed it. That was a great night for me.

As with most people who lived through those years, growing up as a son of the Great Depression prepared me for life in a unique way. I saw people go broke, and I learned the value of a dollar. I saw my father and mother pinch pennies to support their kids, and I learned not to be wasteful or spendthrift. That's the way I was raised, and it was a useful lesson as I navigated the world of business.

When I started my own company years later, I also came to understand economic cycles and saw how changes can come at any time, without warning. In nearly 70 years as a businessman, I've seen recessions come and recessions go; the latest one, beginning in September 2008, was nearly as deep and far reaching as the Depression of the '30s. Yet I never let the fluctuations stop me from following my instincts or taking risks when making a decision or a deal. I don't mean I took reckless crapshoots, but I took calculated risks knowing that there could be repercussions. It's exactly how I approached the Pabst Brewery project. As I always tell my managers, "Don't be afraid to take risks, but know the risk you're taking." It was a bit of practical wisdom I learned from my parents, and it helped me weather all the ups and downs.

❦ ❦ ❦

My school days were a challenge, I must admit. From grade school through junior high and into high school, I was never the best student. My grades were only fair and really didn't improve until I got to college. But my four years at Washington High School were some of the best years of my youth.

Washington was an outstanding school, and one of the largest in the city. There were always things going on. I had more independence in high school than ever before. It helped to have a little spending money, so I found a job. I worked at a big grocery store called Six Points, which was run by a guy named Fishkin. I did everything, from stocking shelves to bagging groceries. My folks had had a grocery store and I knew the grocery business. So at the age of 16, I was in pretty good demand as a worker. On Saturdays, it was my responsibility to drive the company truck and pick up goods. I made 25 cents an hour at the time, and when President Franklin D. Roosevelt raised the minimum wage, I got six cents an hour more. I was pretty happy with that six-cent raise.

Of course, like any high school boy, I always had my eye on the girls. Problem was, I didn't have a car. There was one boy in my class whose father ran a car dealership. This kid had his own new car, a convertible, and all the girls he wanted. I was envious at the time, and never really got that many dates. But as the saying goes, good things come to those who wait . . .

I graduated from high school in June of 1935. Like any teenage kid, I thought I knew it all, but life doesn't always reveal itself in ways that you expect. While I was at Washington High, a strange and profound coincidence had been unfolding without my knowledge. Little did I know that during all those years, a girl named Vera Feldman was living in my neighborhood. She had attended the same grade school and the same junior high school that I did, and then went on to graduate from Washington three years after I did. Later I found out that Vera Feldman also had a father named Sam who also was a grocer, and that when my family ran the store on North Avenue, her family had lived just two blocks away. I could never have guessed that one day Vera Feldman and I would meet and I would ask her to marry me.

It was the smartest thing I'd ever done.

※ ※ ※

"All right, let's take a vote," I said. "Who's in favor of buying the brewery?" I raised my hand.

I looked around the conference table. Not one manager had his hand up. The vote was 12 to one. But it wasn't over. I wasn't giving up. I was determined, and I was a risk taker, something I learned early on in my life while growing up in Milwaukee.

CHAPTER 2

THE JESUITS HELP ME GROW

My parents expected all four of their children to go to a good college. I thought about Harvard University, but it was out of the question; Harvard wouldn't give me a scholarship. I wanted to go to the University of Wisconsin in Madison, but I couldn't afford the cost of living away from home. So my next choice was Marquette University, a Catholic school in Milwaukee run by the Jesuits.

As a Jew, I had no idea what a Jesuit was. When I started at Marquette, the Jesuits pointed me in a new direction. They opened my eyes to a whole new way of looking at the world around me.

The Jesuits want students to change and grow as complete individuals, not just as scholars. They don't just teach someone how to practice law or how to become an accountant. That's only part of it. The Jesuits at Marquette University turn out graduates that are well educated, and also better people. They teach students to work at changing the world. The Jesuits have a deep commitment to the success and welfare of a community, and believe we all should be held responsible for improving our community. I liked that. I wasn't a Catholic, but I could relate to the Jesuits' point of view, coming from a big family and living in a community of Jewish immigrants that tried to look out for each other. That's something I learned in my own home, and something I could relate to at Marquette.

This sense of family at Marquette, and a feeling of being responsible for others, shaped the way I built my company and influenced my philanthropic plans later in life. Decades after I graduated, I gave back to Marquette University, the school that had given me so much.

❧ ❧ ❧

I was a business administration major at Marquette. As a freshman, I couldn't pull together the $15 tuition every semester, so I paid the university a dollar a week. I continued to work, bagging groceries and driving a truck for Mr. Fishbin's grocery store. I took another job at a county golf course in Greenfield Park as a starter, calling golfers to the tee box to begin their rounds. I'd get to the golf course at 5:00 a.m. and go until 5:00 p.m., or 6:00 p.m. in the afternoon. It was a weekend job, and I'd see the same people every Saturday and Sunday mornings. I remember one golfer. He was there every Sunday with three girls who were dancers at his nightclub in Milwaukee. They would close down the nightclub, have a little breakfast, and then drive out to the golf course to play nine holes. I was a young college kid. What did I know about nightclub dancers? But I'll tell you one thing, I sure did admire that guy. He was part of the best-looking foursome on the golf course.

I started at Marquette University in the fall of 1935. The campus was still suffering from the effects of the Great Depression. The student population was small, just under 3,500 students. Marquette had a long and prominent history. Named after the missionary and explorer Father Jacques Marquette, the school first opened its doors in 1881 as a liberal arts school for men. In 1909, it became the first Catholic university in the country to admit women students. The campus straddles Wisconsin Avenue in downtown Milwaukee about a mile from Lake Michigan. The double steeples of the Jesuit's historic Gesu Church and the spires of the gothic Marquette Hall — with its 48-bell carillon in the top of the tower — make the campus a recognizable landmark.

When I arrived, the university had colleges of liberal arts, business administration, engineering, journalism, and nursing and schools of law, speech, medicine, and dentistry. Over the years, it welcomed many world-renowned leaders to its campus, from General Douglas McArthur to Archbishop Desmond Tutu to Mother Teresa. On the basketball court, the Marquette Warriors (now called the Golden Eagles) became a national contender in the NCAA tournaments, thanks mostly to the school's most famous nonconformist, Coach Al McGuire.

When I was an undergrad, I got involved with a student publication called the *Business Ad Digest* as a staff writer and editor. I learned how to work with copy, but from the articles that we published, I also learned some of the fundamentals of business. Marquette was a great training ground for future Milwaukee business leaders. Years later, when I started a company, I was surprised to find out that a lot of the people I hired were Marquette grads.

I also became a pledge of a fraternity called Omicron Alpha Tau, one of two Jewish fraternities. I distinctly remember one thing that happened to me when I was a pledge. A fraternity brother named Leo Pinski was studying to become a dentist, and a girl was supposed to come and sit as his "patient" for his final exams. She was a girl who lived on a farm and needed a lot of dental work. Well, the girl didn't show, and Leo called me and said, "Joe, will you come in and sit? I'll do my dental tests on you." I was a new pledge, so I had to say I would.

So off I went to the dental school. Back then, all the procedures were done by hand. There were very few motorized instruments. Dentists would fill cavities by pounding gold foil with a small hammer. Leo did some procedures on me that weren't completely necessary but were required for him to pass the exam, so I spent two long days sitting in a dental chair. I was 20 at the time, and today, more than 70 years later, I still have in my mouth all the things he did to my teeth, the gold foils and everything else. I've had very little dental problems, all because I was Leo Pinski's volunteer guinea pig.

I later became president, or "chancellor" as they called it, of Omicron Alpha Tau fraternity. That is how I met Vera, the woman who would become my wife. Like all fraternities, we threw a lot of parties, most of them "smokers," social gatherings for men only. We also attended university "promenades," the equivalent, I guess, of a formal dance or a ball. Big bands from around Milwaukee played, bands like Steve Swedish and his Orchestra, and all the students danced. The promenades were hugely popular. Sometimes we had 500 or 600 couples at a place like the Eagles Ballroom, a famous concert hall a few blocks west of campus.

At one of the fraternity parties, a girl named Vera was invited, accompanied by a guy who happened to be a friend of mine. I saw Vera across the room and said to myself, "Now there's a girl I'd like to marry." So the next day I asked my friend if it would be okay with him if I took her out. He said, "Sure, go ahead." So I asked her out. Her name was Vera Feldman.

Because I was the chancellor of Omicron Alpha Tau, I was invited to several formal dinners held by different fraternities. Vera and I spent maybe an hour or two at each fraternity's affair. One of the dinners was at the Schroeder Hotel (now the Hilton City Center) in downtown Milwaukee. We went with five other couples. The girls were in long gowns and the guys wore tuxedoes. It was a very big deal. One of the guys at our table noticed that the waiters were coming out of the kitchen with bottles of champagne, one after another, waiter after waiter. "Watch this," he said with a grin. He took his napkin, threw it over his arm, and went into the kitchen. Two minutes later, out he came with a bottle of champagne for all of us.

Vera and I had no way of knowing it at the time, of course, but I would buy that hotel, the Schroeder, 30 years later. Our oldest daughter Marcy would hold her wedding there. Many times in my life, a real estate property would come full circle.

When we met, Vera was 17 years old and I was three years older. She was going to the University of Wisconsin-Milwaukee, at the time called the Downer State Teachers College. She transferred to Marquette two years later so we could be at the same school together. While she was studying, she also worked. Her father had a grocery store and she used to help out. Vera was on the Marquette debate team, the only girl on the team. She had an excellent mind.

We hit it off pretty well on our first date. In fact, Vera never again went out with that friend of mine who had taken her to the frat party. I'd never had a girlfriend before. She'd never had a boyfriend before. When she got home that night after our dinner together at the Schroeder Hotel, she told her parents the same thing I had been thinking when I first saw her. "He's the man I want to marry." That was the start of our lifetime romance. From that point on, there was no question that we would get married one day. I'd take her to movies and hayrides out in the country, or we would ride the streetcar on Wisconsin Avenue and walk up and down the city streets and window shop. Those were our first dates. We didn't have to do anything special. We were together, and we were in love.

❧ ❧ ❧

I received my undergraduate degree in business administration in 1939. In my senior year, I had decided to go to law school at Marquette. At that time, a student could begin law school in his last year as an undergrad. With a business degree, I could have become an accountant when I graduated. But there wasn't much in the way of jobs at that time. I figured there would be greater opportunities if I graduated with a law degree.

I was a much better student in law school. I joined the editorial board of the Marquette Law Review, and then served as its advertising manager, getting my first taste of sales as I sold ads in the publication. I finished law school in 1941, graduating first in a class of 53. Then I tried to get a job. I wanted to go to work for one of the big firms in Milwaukee to gain experience. So I went to Miller, Mack & Fairchild, one of the most prestigious firms in the city. I asked them to take me on as a staff attorney, but they said no. They wouldn't hire me. My dad, who had very little resources, gave them a call and said, "Look, I will pay you a few dollars a month and my son will work for free if you put him on." They still said no. Maybe it was because I was Jewish, I don't know.

My father had been working with Nordberg Manufacturing Company, hauling away their scrap metal for years. He was one of their favorite employees, so he said to them, "I need a job for my son. He just graduated from law school. He's a lawyer." So they gave me a job in the plant. My new job required quite a bit of skill. With a ball peen hammer, I tapped a metal punch against a piece of steel at one specified spot, over and over and over. I would make the punch mark so that the tool and die worker would know where to drill into the steel. Well, I couldn't get the hang of it. All of my punch marks were off, and finally they said to me, "Go home, go home. You're costing us money." I was out of work.

It was 1941. Here I was, a college graduate with a law degree, and I needed a job. By sheer coincidence, I ran into a guy who worked for a Milwaukee real estate company called George Bockl Enterprises. This guy was moving quickly up the ladder in the company and suggested I talk to Bockl about work. Sensing an opportunity, I walked into George Bockl's office one day and asked for a job — and he hired me on the spot. That began my life in real estate.

I didn't know a thing about real estate. I was fresh out of law school, and the last thing I expected to be doing was working in a real estate office, but I needed a job. Taking a job with Bockl was an opportunity to get started. I figured I could pick up a little business experience. At the time, I never imagined real estate would become a lifelong profession that would last more than 60 years.

In short order, I saw that working for George Bockl Enterprises was another kind of school for me. In law school, I had learned contracts, torts, commercial law, constitutional law — I learned everything about the law, which was great. However, it was clear to me at the time that I wasn't going to make a living practicing law, so I gave real estate a shot.

As it turned out, working with George Bockl became as important to my education as law school.

CHAPTER 3

FIVE-DOLLAR CLOSINGS AND CLEAN LATRINES

George Bockl had a small real estate office on Vliet Street selling Milwaukee residential properties. In the early 1940s, he had 10 salespeople working for him. I worked as a "closer," closing deals at $5 a close. That doesn't sound like much, but we had three or four closings each week and I was making a weekly salary of $15 to $20, a fair sum for those days.

I spent every day in the office — weekends included — watching George operate. I would sit in a chair next to his desk while he was on the phone with a savings and loan company, trying to get a mortgage for a homebuyer. It would sometimes take hours for George to work out a $3,000 loan. He'd have to get mortgage insurance for the customer, or he'd have to negotiate points. George was absolutely tenacious, and he would eventually get the loan. He refused to give up. When he was on the phone with an S&L, he would not let that loan officer hang up. He'd keep pushing and pushing until the guy was tired out and finally gave in to George's terms.

George Bockl was an immigrant from Russia. When he was 12, George and his mother had escaped into Poland in the dead of night in a hay wagon and then made the trip across the Atlantic, crammed into a ship bound for America. Once here, they were reunited with George's father in Milwaukee, where his father had been working.

After graduating from college, George formed his real estate company. Eventually he moved into commercial real estate, purchasing several historic buildings in downtown Milwaukee that he worked to preserve and renovate. When it came to real estate, George was a visionary. He was ahead of his time on concepts like "condo-izing" and converting unused commercial properties. He made a practice of "recycling" old buildings in order to save valuable materials and energy. It's something that I later adopted in my own business.

In the early days with Bockl, people didn't make much money. This was still at the tail end of the Depression. It was also around the time that I had met Vera. I wanted to get married in the worst way, but I had promised my father I wouldn't get married until I made at least $50 a week. My father said, "My God, that'll be a long way off. I wouldn't worry about a wedding yet."

I didn't handle too many actual sales. I mostly closed deals. Eventually, to supplement my income, I became a salesman. One day I got a call from a fraternity buddy of mine whose parents wanted to buy an apartment building that Bockl Enterprises had listed. This was the family of Leo Pinski, my fraternity brother from Marquette dental school who used me as the guinea pig so he could pass his final dental exams. Bockl owned a 24-family building, with two- and three-bedroom apartments. We were selling it for $22,500, and Leo Pinski's parents were interested in buying. I set up an appointment to show them the building, and Vera came with me. I remember that the weather was freezing, but she waited in my car while I showed the property. Thankfully, Leo's parents liked the place and decided to buy it. I ran out of the building to tell Vera. She was happy I had made the sale, of course, but even happier to get out of the cold.

I made a commission of $225 on that deal — which satisfied my promise to my father. Vera and I were married on February 1, 1942. After the wedding, we spent what was left of my $225 commission on our honeymoon.

❧❧❧ ❧❧❧ ❧❧❧

By the time we were married in 1942, World War II was already underway in Europe and the Pacific. Japanese warplanes had bombed Pearl Harbor just two months earlier, and the first American forces had arrived in Great Britain, prepared for battle.

A month after our wedding, I joined the Army, reporting to Fort Sheridan, Illinois, one of four Recruit Reception Centers in the country. One day I called home and my mother answered the phone.

"What are you doing, Joe?" she said.

"I'm cleaning latrines," I told her.

"You're doing what?"

"I'm cleaning the latrines," I repeated.

There was a short pause, and she said, "I've got a son who's a lawyer and he's cleaning latrines?"

I regretted telling her that for the rest of my life.

Army life was different than anything else I'd yet experienced. I had a rough start, but eventually I adjusted. The country was at war, and people did what they were ordered to do, no questions asked. The military had its own way of doing things. Your commanding officer told you what to do and when. It didn't matter if you had a law degree or who you were. You took orders. Nothing else mattered.

I didn't go overseas. Instead, I completed basic training at St. Petersburg, Florida, and was then assigned to an intelligence group at Bartow Army Air Base, just outside of Winter Haven, Florida. A few months after my transfer to Bartow, my daughter Marcy was born. I made it back to Milwaukee on leave. When Vera went into labor, she called her doctor and he picked us up and drove us to the hospital, flying through the stop signs because he knew the baby was coming fast.

When we got to the hospital, I went to the waiting room. There was another young man sitting there. I said hello to him and sat down, and in two minutes, the nurse came out. "You've got a baby girl," she said to me, smiling. The guy sitting next to me couldn't believe my luck. "I've been waiting here for 24 hours," he said, "and still no baby."

We named our daughter Marcy, and while she was still an infant, Vera and the baby moved from Milwaukee to Florida. We rented a cottage on Bartow Army Air Base. Marcy wasn't even a year old, and she quickly became a little star on the base. Everybody loved her. She became the base's mascot. Every Friday night, I'd invite the sergeant and couple of corporals to have dinner with us. Vera was an amazing cook, and she would go to the butcher shop and get something for "the boys." The butcher would never accept her food ration points because he knew she was cooking for the troops.

The air base was used as a training field for pilots. The B-26 Marauder, a twin engine bomber, and P-51 Mustang fighter plane flew out of the nearby MacDill Air Field in Tampa. One of my duties at the air base was to evaluate the performance of the aircraft. I wasn't a pilot, but I would test the systems of the planes — the weapons systems, the navigation systems, the engines — and compare the findings to the specs we had on German and Japanese aircraft, Japanese Zeroes, for example.

We would match up how they handled, how fast each of the planes was, things like that. I was doing intelligence work, gathering as much information as possible for American pilots. Knowing what our planes were capable of doing — and what the enemy's planes could or couldn't do — was useful. We wanted our pilots to have every possible advantage.

Although I didn't see combat, I came pretty close to getting killed on that Florida air base. I was a corporal by then, and one day we were standing inside this one-story building that looked out onto the airfield. A row of P-51s were lined up in front of us. Somehow the weapons mechanism of one plane went berserk and one of the guns started to strafe the building. The plane was empty; no one was onboard. But the guns just kept firing, shattering all the windows in the barracks and sending everyone scattering. We all hit the deck, and fortunately nobody was wounded.

❧ ❧ ❧

I was on active duty a year and four months, and discharged in 1943. I moved Vera and Marcy from Winter Haven back to Milwaukee, and we got an upstairs apartment in a duplex on 39th and Capitol Drive. I went back to work for George Bockl, selling real estate so we would be able to pay our $45 a month rent.

After the end of the war, Bockl came up with a new idea. In some Milwaukee neighborhoods, particularly on the South Side, there were properties where two houses had been built on one lot, one in the front and one in the back off an alley. They were known as "Polish flats" because the neighborhoods were home to large groups of Polish immigrants. The houses at the back of the lot were small, usually nothing more than a bedroom and a kitchen and bathroom.

The war was coming to an end, and soldiers were returning home and looking for a place to live. Veterans could buy starter homes on the GI Bill with no down payment through the Veterans Administration. George would split the properties and sell the back house for very little money. Many of these we sold to veterans. It was a great way for people to own a house for a mortgage of only a few thousand dollars.

George Bockl had any number of ideas like this. He was creative and fiercely determined to become successful. He taught me all about perseverance, and he taught me well. After working for him for just a few years, I started coming up with my own ideas, my own insights on what it took to make a business deal successful. It was something George called my "x-ray business vision." He told *The Milwaukee Journal* years later:

> Joe thought in three dimensions. He was a fearless type of guy. Some fellows are scared. They might have a lot of ability but they're scared. Joe would plunge ahead fearlessly. . . . He surpassed me. His business sense is a fast fox trot. Mine is a slow waltz.

George Bockl's morals and ethics were impeccable. He was a mentor to me, and one of my best friends. Working for George, I learned business principles that would stick with me for the rest of my professional life: how to negotiate a fair deal, how to build a team, how to build partnerships, how to be a decent boss.

My time working with George Bockl was a tremendous learning experience, another rung on the ladder, another step in a young man's education. I was feeling confident, armed with a viable business experience and furnished with a strong set of moral and ethical values that had been passed on to me by Bockl, the Jesuits, and my parents.

I was also feeling restless. I was ready to take what I knew and put it into practice in my own particular way.

CHAPTER 4

A CHURCH ON EVERY CORNER

George Bockl was a tutor to me — and I was a quick learner. I never would have guessed that soon after I went to work for George my life would be changed forever.

In my years at George Bockl Enterprises, I learned the business basics, and I studied real estate. However, no matter how many times I asked George, he would not pay me a fixed salary. I wanted a certain amount each week, guaranteed. He insisted that I was earning more in commissions, but now that I was married and a father to boot, raising a family on only commissions was just too chancy. I needed a steady paycheck.

In the end, George wouldn't give in, so I decided I had to set out on my own.

I took all that I had learned about real estate from Bockl and I asked another salesman who worked for him to join me — an older gentleman named Herman Eisenberg. We opened an office called Federal Realty at 24th and Vliet Streets in Milwaukee, with Herman's wife Ruth working as our secretary.

Eisenberg and I had an angle: every Saturday night, we would get the Sunday newspaper and scour the classifieds, looking to see who was selling a home. We'd circle the ads and go out at 6:00 a.m. on Sunday morning, knocking on doors and negotiating with homeowners on a deal to purchase it. The cost of these properties usually was negligible. Many of them were run-down homes that we called "khalupas," a Yiddish term for an old, broken-down house. We'd secure a loan, and have our small crew of workers fix the places up. Then we'd sell the properties and make between $300 and $500 per home. That was pretty good money for us.

There came a time, though, when I wanted to build new homes. I believed I could create a quality home from scratch. I knew there was a backlog of demand for new housing, and with the VA guaranteeing loans, it was easy for homebuyers to get financing. I was ready to jump into the home-building business. My partner Eisenberg thought it was too risky. He was getting up in years, close to 70 — it seemed old at the time — and he didn't want to make the leap into a new construction company. So after a few years in business together, we decided to split up.

The way we split up was very simple. Federal Realty owned a total of 12 houses at the time, all on the market, all unsold. They were listed for three, four, five thousand dollars apiece. We wrote the amounts on little slips of paper, each with an address on the bottom, and dropped them all into a hat. Herman and I then each drew six slips of paper from the hat. We added up the amounts, and the guy with the highest amount paid the other guy the difference. It was a fair split, and would be a fine way to split up a business even today.

Herman wanted to hold on to the name Federal Realty. "Well, what am I going to call my company?" I said to him. The two of us were eating dinner at the Wisconsin Hotel in downtown Milwaukee, sitting at a table along a window. Across the street was the Towne Theater, and next door the Towne Hotel. "Joe," Herman said, looking out the window. "Why don't you take the name Towne? That would be a wonderful name." And that's the way Towne Realty was born.

That was in 1949, and from that day on, I was on my own.

The timing couldn't have been better. The housing market was booming. Millions of young veterans were buying homes under the GI Bill with guaranteed loans. From 1944 to 1952, almost two-and-a-half million World War II vets bought homes with Veterans Administration loans. I was an Army veteran myself, and I realized that real estate would be a lucrative field, one that I could excel in.

As the young owner of a brand new real estate company, the first thing I did was put up a new house. I went out and got a loan, paid $900 for a lot, and hired a construction crew. I ordered a prefabricated home, a "prefab," made by Gunnison Homes, a subsidiary of U.S. Steel Corporation. It was a terrific little house at 37th and Fairmount in Milwaukee — still standing today, as a matter of fact — and I was sure I could make some money. I sold that house for $5,950 — and lost $100. It seemed like the end of the world, but there was an important lesson to be learned: You cannot build just a single house. You've got to build in volume if you're going to be successful.

It was easy to borrow money. So after losing $100, we built a 400-house subdivision for our next project. I looked at pieces of land — usually farmland right at the edges of the city limits, close to sewer and water lines — and I'd make an offer to the farmer. If he accepted, I let him keep his farmhouse and we'd develop the lots around it. We'd keep the corner lots for churches, offices, and retail, and sell the interior lots with finished houses on them.

These prefab homes sold for $6,900 on up to $7,500. As we grew, we built about 200 to 300 of them in a year. These were by no means trailer homes. They were well-built, one-story houses that came in 10 or 12 different sizes and several styles—colonial, Cape Cod, and ranch. The smaller homes were about 1,000 square feet with two bedrooms and one bath, but they could go as large as four bedrooms with two-and-a-half baths. Nice homes.

The houses were built without basements, so cement slabs had to be poured in advance. The way they were assembled was quite a process. The houses were delivered to the lots in sections by trucks. Everything was finished, inside and out, and ready to be assembled. We wanted to put them up in a hurry because of our costs. So I would get there at about 5:00 a.m. and the house would arrive at 5:30. We would unload the sections from the truck, and the construction crew would piece them together. In the winter months, I'd get up before the sunrise, go out to the lots, and sweep the snow off the cement slabs before the houses arrived.

Gunnison Homes was the first prefab outfit to come along. The company was started in the early 1930s by Foster Gunnison, who worked with a group of architects and engineers to design moderately priced houses made on an assembly line in Cincinnati and shipped by truck around the country. Towne Realty soon expanded throughout southern Wisconsin, building prefabs by National Homes, Great Lakes Homes, and Harnischfeger. At the beginning, it took us maybe a couple of days to put up a single home, but after awhile, the crews got much faster, and I said, "All right, when you finish a house you can take the rest of the day off."

Then one day I noticed they were going home at 2:00 in the afternoon! Well, then I had to tell them "Okay, you've got to do *two* houses a day per crew." On some days, they were able to do just that. It was amazing. They were putting them up as fast as we could lay the concrete slabs. We were able to accomplish an awful lot in those days, and we made good money doing it.

Most of the homes that we built and sold were new houses constructed on site from the ground up, "stick homes," as we called them, because when we framed out the houses, the 2-x-4s from a distance looked like wooden sticks rising vertically from the ground. At our peak, we built 1,000 of these homes a year, most of them on one-time farmland northwest and south of central Milwaukee. We had our own construction crews, dozens of crews. We would hire electricians and plumbers on contract to wire and plumb the houses. Everything else was done by Towne Realty-hired crews.

A couple of years after starting out, we began a third type of home construction. We bought an old factory in Cudahy, a suburb just south of Milwaukee, and started manufacturing houses inside the plant on an assembly line. The factory at one time had been an aircraft assembly plant that another builder had converted to a home-manufacturing site. We took it over and started Towne Manufacturing. We hired carpenters and roofers, plumbers and electricians, tradesmen of all sorts who would build the homes from scratch inside the factory. A railroad track ran through the center of the plant, and as the workers started at one end of the track, the houses came out fully finished at the other end.

First, the studs were erected and the floors were laid. Then the roof was framed out and the basic mechanical systems were installed — the furnace and heating ducts, the plumbing. Next, the windows and doors were installed. The roof was shingled, the interior walls were drywalled, the siding was hung, the electrical wiring was connected, and a fully completed house stood at the end of the line. People didn't even realize they were factory built — and they really weren't like most factory built homes.

These also were "stick built," framed from the bottom up with 2-x-4s and 4-x-8s, good lumber, and much stronger than the trucked-in modular prefab kits that came in pieces — walls and ceilings and floors. In a lot of ways, our factory homes were better than houses that were constructed on site because they were built inside the plant and away from the elements. No one else in the country was building homes this way.

During its heyday, Towne Manufacturing had around 50 people working at the factory, sometimes turning out one full house in a day. Each house was loaded onto a flat bed trailer. At 3 a.m. we'd truck the house to a lot. The electric company would cooperate with us by raising the power lines that hung over the city streets, and down the road we would go with our houses.

At the sites, the basements had been built, and we'd fit the houses right on top of the foundation, the entire house intact. The next morning, the neighbors would wake up and drive by on their way to work and say, "What the heck is this? There's a brand new house standing there." Incredible.

When the expressways were built in the late 1950s and early 1960s, however, it became impossible to truck the houses under the overpasses, and so that was it for the plant. In their day, they were the best houses money could buy, the sturdiest construction, all union made. We sold thousands of them, starting at $9,950 with the lot, a very reasonable price. Because of the volume we were doing, we bought our materials at the manufacturer's price, so we were able to sell our houses cheaper. It was a wonderful way for young families to get their start.

I worked very closely with five or six savings and loans at that time. They were the lifeblood of the company. After I bought and subdivided the land, I'd go to a lender for a construction loan to put in improvements — the sewer and water — and to erect the homes. When we sold a house, we paid off the loan for that particular lot and the buyer would get a mortgage. The whole process became a well-oiled machine.

We also listed real estate. As I did with my partner Eisenberg, I'd scan the classifieds of the newspaper every day, looking for homes that were for sale. Whenever I'd see a for sale ad I liked, I'd have my salesman rush out and make an offer to the homeowner. If the homeowner accepted, we'd give him a down payment, and we'd have a listing. Towne Realty held public meetings at our office every Sunday morning at 10 a.m. We'd advertise in the paper. Anyone could come. Our salesmen would be at the office, waiting to meet potential customers, then they'd show them our listings and take them out to the homes. There wasn't a multiple listing service back then, and we hustled to have the most listings possible. The more listings, the more homes we sold.

Towne started out with three or four salesmen, and in just six or seven years, we had a team of 35. One of my first sales managers was Paul Melrood. I met him at a Jewish War Veterans gathering. He was on stage, performing a comedy show or something. Paul had been working in sales for a toy manufacturing company. He was imaginative and outgoing, so I offered him a job on the spot, and he took it.

At that time, Towne Realty was the first big real estate developer to sell a home with no down payment. One of our developments was on the South Side of Milwaukee, a big piece of land in the shadow of a factory. The development was a goldmine for our sales staff, as Paul tells it:

> We didn't even have a model. We had a tent, and we laid out all the floor plans on tables inside the tent and took orders. It was unbelievable. The potential buyer would give us a $100 deposit to hold a house, we'd process them and send them to a savings and loan for a mortgage. Those buyers who bought houses did very well because they got in on the ground floor with nothing down.

The salesmen were getting $200 a house in commissions, good money back then. These were easy deals to make, and Melrood started out with a bang. In his first year, he sold 90 houses. That's almost two a week. He was good with promotions, too. He came up with the idea of Five Percent Down to Anyone. We called it "5PDTA," and it became a big slogan in Milwaukee — "Five Percent Down to Anyone." He also sent letters to accountants, pitching our homes as investments, as rental properties that could be used as tax shelters by investors. We ran ads in the newspapers, on the radio, on billboards, and business just took off.

By 1954, we were one of the largest residential builders in the state of Wisconsin, putting up prefabs, building factory houses, and constructing single-family homes on site in subdivisions we developed. Most of those homes are still standing today, entire neighborhoods south and northwest of downtown. I can drive through the city and see them, hundreds and hundreds. I used to take my family on Sunday drives when my children were young, and I'd give my oldest daughter, Marcy, a penny for every Towne Realty sign she saw along the street. She made a killing, 30 or 40 cents every week.

It was easy to sell a house in the '50s. But it turned out it was even easier to sell a church. We had a guy working for us by the name of Milan Jursik. He was a salesman par excellence. He could sell anybody anything. One day Milan met a guy who wanted a church. I gave him the go-ahead and he took it from there. He started selling custom-built churches. He would go out to the subdivisions we were developing on the South Side of town, where Towne Realty was buying acres and acres of farmland.

After the land was subdivided, Milan would find a corner lot that was larger than the regular lots, and we would put up a 3,000 square foot, wood-framed church, many of them with brick exteriors. We sold them for as low as $15,000. Some were custom built on order for neighborhood congregations. We'd put a steeple on the top, whatever they wanted.

As the word spread that we were in the church building business, we began to sell them "on spec." At the time it seemed like there were ministers all over trying to build churches. Sometimes it was a minister looking to start a new church. Sometimes it was the pastor of an existing but older church who wanted a new building for his congregation. The congregation would put a couple hundred dollars down, and we would carry the balance under a land contract; they'd make monthly payments, and we held the deed. Remarkably, everybody paid off the churches, we never lost a dime. After all, these were ministers we were dealing with. Over a period of six years, we built 30 or 40 churches.

❦ ❦ ❦

As Towne Realty grew, I built a solid team of managers and salesmen, talented and ambitious people like Paul Melrood and Milan Jursik and others like Jack Weiss, Harold Melman, Parker Rosevelt, Joe Belin, Jack Levin, and Sol Gellman, who became experts at what they did. Real estate was a very good business career choice. A fellow named Dan Tishberg was my first general manager, and later became a trusted business partner and good friend. Danny had graduated from Marquette University Law School a year ahead of me and married a girl named Lala Stein. The Stein family owned a furniture company, and Danny worked for his father-in-law. I knew Danny from school and asked him several times to come and work for me, but he kept turning me down.

I finally convinced him that he would do better in real estate than in the furniture business, and he came over to Towne. It wasn't long before I took him on as a partner. The company then was small enough where we worked together on everything — locating properties, building houses, selling, securing loans. Later on, Danny took charge of certain divisions within the company as we diversified, and in the 30 years that we worked together, we became best friends.

Danny Tishberg was a hail-and-hearty fellow, a happy-go-lucky kind of a guy. He made friends easily, and in those days we needed friends. He was extremely outgoing. I was more of the quiet guy. We spent a good deal of time together, professionally and socially. Years after I started Towne Realty, we moved our offices into a new building. Every Friday afternoon, Danny and I would have cocktails in my office with two business associates, Alan Flugrat and his partner, Fred Brenner. They ran a heating company and did a lot of business with us. We started with cocktails at 5:00 p.m., then we'd go out to dinner together, usually at Karl Ratzsch's, a well-known German restaurant in town. After dinner we'd go to the Milwaukee Athletic Club to play cards. We played gin rummy. And we drank.

That went on for years and years. We were all so close that Fred Brenner's doctor came to us one day and told us that Fred had a terminal illness. His doctor didn't want to tell him, so trying our best to relay the news with the utmost sensitivity, we told him during one of our Friday night dinners. His response came back to us — "Well, if I die, I die." After all that anxiety and worry, though, Fred didn't die. Fortunately, he lived for many years after that, and we all remained good friends.

When we started this card club, the other three guys used to drink pretty much. I used to have one or two drinks. By the time we disbanded maybe 15 years later, I'd have to call Vera and have her open the garage door. I'd get home at about 2:30 or 3:00 a.m. and just drive the car into the garage, and she'd put me to bed. She was a wonderful wife. That's how we did a lot of business back then, just four guys getting together after hours.

Danny and I sometimes used our contrasting personalities and differing styles as a tactic for negotiating a deal. We could play the classic "good cop, bad cop." We would go into a meeting to negotiate a contract, and Danny would be a tough SOB, always driving a hard bargain. I'd be the schmoozer, willing to compromise and make concessions. Danny was the wheeler dealer, and I would close the deals. Sometimes it was the other way around, and I would be the hardliner. It depended on who we were negotiating with and what the deal was.

Danny was sociable and flashy. He liked expensive cars. When he began making serious money, he bought a Rolls Royce. He also liked to dress well and became a real clothes horse. I remember there was a clothing company in Chicago that sold fine Italian clothing. The Italian manufacturers would send discounted suits that they couldn't sell fast enough to this place in Chicago. So every year Danny and I drove to Chicago and bought three or four suits apiece, plus sport jackets, dress coats, things like that. We'd get them for probably a third of the original price. Those suits in those days were $1,000 suits, and Danny and I paid maybe $300 a piece. I still have some of them in my closet today. I was able to wear nice clothes thanks to Danny Tishberg.

The two of us played golf every week, always with people who did business with us. Danny's first wife, Lala, and my wife Vera were the best of friends. They did everything together — spent time at a country club we joined, traveled together. Danny and Lala moved into a home about a block away from ours.

Danny also liked to gamble, and that got him into some trouble. I remember one afternoon when he walked into my office. "Joe," he said, "there's a couple of very large guys out here who want a quarter of a million dollars from me, and they say if I don't give it to them they're going to break my legs." I could see two giant thugs standing in the doorway to his office.

"What for?" I asked him.

"Something about some money I owe to a big casino out in Vegas," Danny said. He looked a little nervous, and he was missing the big happy smile he usually wore.

"Well what do you want me to do?" I said.

"I could use a quarter of a million dollars, Joe."

So I wrote him a check and the two bruisers disappeared. But some time later, the Internal Revenue Service showed up, and they had a few questions for me.

"Mr. Zilber, we see you gave Daniel Tishberg $250,000," they said, "but the problem is, Mr. Tishberg did not report the money as income."

"It was just a loan," I said. "In fact, he still owes me that money."

With some quick and careful explaining on my part, the IRS went away and Danny came out of it okay. It wouldn't be the first time he would get in trouble with gambling, but that was Danny. He was my partner and my friend.

As I built the company, I recruited people who I believed would be well suited for Towne Realty. Sometimes it was just chance that they came to work with me at Towne.

Sometime in 1957, the accountant for Towne Realty left to serve a stint in the Army, and so I called my personal accountant, Phil Siegel. "I'm in trouble, Phil," I said. "I need a bookkeeper over here right away." Phil said, "I'll send you my best man." He gave Jerry Stein a dime and Jerry used it to take a bus to our office. Jerry was still in college at the time, a junior at the University of Wisconsin-Milwaukee, studying accounting. A professor had lined up his part-time job with Phil, and Jerry had just started on the day that I phoned. Jerry, today a retired vice chairman of my company, still remembers that day:

"Phil Siegel said to me, 'Jerry, go up to Towne Realty at 53rd and Burleigh. Tell 'em you're the bookkeeper. Make believe you know what you're doing, and I'll stop by the next day and try to explain to you what you should do.' So I went to Towne Realty and they put me in the basement at a small desk in an office the size of a closet. A month or two later, some guy came downstairs. He needed a shave and he looked at me and said, 'Who are you?' I said, 'I'm Jerry Stein, the bookkeeper. Who are you?' He said, 'I'm Joe Zilber. I own the place.' That's how I met Mr. Zilber."

Our accountant eventually came back from the Army, and he said to me, "I've got this kid at a desk downstairs doing bookkeeping. We're only paying him 95 cents an hour. I think we should keep him." So we had Jerry Stein working on a whole variety of things, from making deposits and collecting rents to leasing apartments and fixing toilets. Jerry became invaluable to us. He went on to get a law degree while working for us, and stayed with me for more than 50 years. We worked together for so many years that when I started a sentence, he was able to finish my thought. We were on the same wave length. Jerry eventually replaced Danny Tishberg as CEO. Smart and dependable, Jerry played a critical role in the company's success. At Jerry's 50th anniversary party in 2007, I told him, his wife Louise, his family, and friends how much he meant to me and the company. I said in part:

> I felt that it was important that our salute to Jerry Stein and his 50 years of service should focus on all the things that Jerry has accomplished for Zilber Ltd., for our community, for our faith, and for his family. I felt it was entirely appropriate and fitting that this evening be devoted to providing a very special look at this man that I know so well and for me to take this opportunity to simply say to Jerry . . . thank you. Thank you for everything you have done. Thank you for your leadership. Thank you for your guidance. Thank you for helping us recruit members of an organization that is without a doubt the finest of its kind in the country... no, in the world.
>
> I'm sure by now most of you have seen the ad that I placed in this morning's *Milwaukee Journal Sentinel* which was our way of thanking Jerry for the critical role he's played in the growth and success of Zilber Ltd. in a very public way. Quite frankly, I wanted everyone to know what I have known for years . . . Jerry Stein is the very best at what he does. There is no one like him. There will never be anyone like him and I have been fortunate to have him at my side for the past 50 years.

❧ ❧ ❧

In the first decade or two of Towne Realty, I found people to work with me from all walks of life. One salesman, Jack Weiss, was selling clothing in the basement of Boston Store, a downtown department store. Another salesman, Harold Meldman, was managing a retail furniture store, and eventually became my sales manager. Another guy, Parker Rosevelt, ran our sales office in Madison before coming to Milwaukee to oversee the sale of existing homes. Once people joined our group, they seldom left. For years, Towne Realty did not have a personnel department because there just wasn't any turnover.

Joe Belin was one of my original employees. He was an expediter with the company, the man who keeps tab on the subcontractors — the carpenters, the plumbers, the electricians — so the construction schedule remains on track. When he was young, Joe was in the U.S. Navy at Pearl Harbor when it was attacked. Immediately he was called into combat duty. I had known Joe Belin since we were kids and living in the same neighborhood in Milwaukee. Joe's father worked in a factory in the garment business. Once a week, I would deliver groceries in my coaster wagon from my family's grocery store to the Belins' home two-and-a-half blocks away. They bought $3.50 worth of groceries every week. They were one of our best customers.

Later on, in the early days at Towne, Joe worked as a salesman for a while. Once, we put up a home on Milwaukee's south side, a prefab made by U.S. Steel. Joe was working an open house on a Sunday. Those prefab homes were erected on a slab of concrete, and the kitchen tiles were glued right to the concrete. It was the dead of winter, subzero temperatures. It was so cold that a couple of the floor tiles were coming up in the kitchen. So for the entire open house, Joe stayed in the kitchen, standing in the same spot all afternoon, his feet on the floor tiles that were peeling up.

Joe went on to head our hotel division. He and I also started a poker club with 11 guys that played every Monday night. Years later, he relocated to Hawaii with his wife Shirley and ran our Hawaii office. When Vera and I moved to Hawaii, we moved into the same Honolulu apartment complex that the Belins lived in. I knew Joe Belin my entire life, and he remained my dear friend.

One of my first partners at Towne Realty was Don Margolis. We had an agreement where I would put up the money for a lot and the construction of a home, and Don would build the house. We first got together at a meeting of the Jewish War Veterans. He was also an attorney, and he stayed on as an associate of mine until 1956, when he started his own company.

I remember one time Don and I were approached by an immigrant from Poland who wanted to sell his home and buy another house from us. His English was not very good. Don and I spent hours with this fellow, going over the deal again and again, until finally he said he understood and signed the purchase agreement. The next morning, this man called Don in a panic, saying he couldn't go through with it. So I tore up the contract and let him out of the deal. Why not? It was the right thing to do.

Jack Levin ran the Towne Manufacturing factory. He was an engineer, and a great, great negotiator. Because of our volume, we had a manufacturer's agreement with our suppliers. Manufacturers were given a different price scale than the average builder, so our prices were about a third less. Jack was able to buy lumber, shingles, kitchen sinks, and all kinds of materials at the manufacturer's price. You'd walk into his office and he'd have boxes of faucets and doorknobs all over the place. The pricing worked out very nicely for us. It gave us an edge. Even today we have some of those same agreements for appliances and plumbing fixtures.

For years, Sol Gellman was a designer with us. He was Towne Realty's chief designer and then took over as head of planning. I first met Sol at my parents' corner grocery store when we were kids. We went to the same kindergarten, and in 1957, he came to work with me at Towne. He was there when we were building the subdivisions, the nursing homes, the student dormitories. He was there for it all.

Once in awhile, though, some of Sol's drawings did not work. He once figured the measurements for wall-to-wall carpeting that turned out be six inches short around the perimeter of the rooms. Another time he designed two windows that came together at a corner of a building that didn't have a support to hold the glass in place. (We changed the design, of course, before construction began.)

Sol Gellman was a remarkable man. He always had an idea, and he was always thinking about something new. He could make the most beautiful drawings. Whenever I ran into him in the office, he'd have a design rolled up under his arm. He'd unroll it for me and say, "Here, take a look at this." He was an idea man, and he was with me for nearly 60 years.

Several key office staff stayed with me for a long while, too. I found two of my best after hearing they each had retired from local financial institutions. Both of them were already in their early 60s, and I asked them to join my company as office temps. This was in the early 1950s. One woman named Bessie Loyda stayed with us until the late 1960s when she retired from Towne. She was hardworking and very efficient, lovingly known as "Bossy Bessie."

Then there was Leone Henricks. Leone was hired as a bookkeeper to work for us temporarily for just six months in 1952. She stayed until she was 93 years old. Leone would be the first employee in the office every day, arriving at 7:00 a.m. In her later years, I would send a taxicab in the morning to bring her to work and then another to take her home at night. She worked on an old adding machine, but her accuracy was one hundred percent. Finally, after living on her own until she was in her late 90s, she retired to an independent living facility.

For her birthday, I bought her a custom-formed electric wheelchair. On the back hung a license plate that read, "Leone's Lincoln." She drove that thing up and down the corridors of the place. Leone lived to be 103.

My mother-in-law Sadie Feldman was also one of those first employees at Towne Realty. Her husband Sam had passed away from tuberculosis when he was in his 60s, so Sadie came to live with Vera and me. She worked every day at the office. She handled all the utility bills from the properties we owned, and she watched every penny that came in or went out. If something was off, Sadie would find it and take care of it. She'd come to me and say, "You know, Joe, this is wrong. You're paying too much money here. Somebody's not watching." When it came to money, if you made a mistake, Sadie was going to catch it.

One of Sadie's responsibilities was locking up the office at night. She would go around to everyone's office at the end of the day and turn off all the lights. She'd walk by the offices, reach inside along the wall, and turn off the lights. She'd open the bathroom doors and turn off the lights. More than once, there would be a guy sitting quietly at his desk working — or sitting on the john in the men's room reading the paper — and suddenly everything would go dark. Sadie decided when it was quitting time and off went the lights, no matter who was still there, or what you were doing.

Another one of my secretaries was a woman named Hildegard Malecha. Oh, God, what a gal. She was my secretary for I don't know how many years, second to none. Hildegard was a German import, a flamboyant young woman who came to the United States as a war bride. She loved spending money at Milwaukee's German restaurants and wore a charm bracelet with charms that represented the history of her many male conquests.

Hildegard was quite the character. She would entertain businesspeople who came to meet with me at my office. Hildegard set up my appointments by the hour, and I was always running late, so sometimes people had to wait to see me. Next to my office we had a lounge, with a sofa and tables and a bar, and Hildegard would sit my appointments in the lounge and offer them a drink.

I remember one guy came in from New York for a deal we were working on. It was 10:00 a.m., and Hildegard offered him a cocktail. He said, "No, no. No drinks in the morning." She came back 15 minutes later and again he said, "No thank you, it's too early." Finally he succumbed to a drink, and then another. By the time I got to see him, I couldn't do any business with him at all. He came all the way from New York for nothing. That was Hildegard, always the perfect hostess.

In 1976, I hired Kim Treis as my secretary. She too, was a wonderful secretary. I had known Kim's father. He was also in real estate, and we had done a few deals together. Before she came into my office for a job interview, she talked to her father to get the lowdown on me. She recalls:

> I saw the ad in the newspaper, and I called my father. "Dad," I said, "I'm thinking about going over and interviewing with Mr. Zilber for this position. What do you think?" And he said, "I think it's a great idea." I said, "Well, I've always been pretty intimidated by the name Joe Zilber. He has an awesome reputation, but what is he really like?" Dad said, "Joe's just a normal person. He has been successful because he never takes himself too seriously and he loves what he's doing. Joe Zilber is the most loyal employer in the world if you're loyal to him. So if you work hard, you will be rewarded. If you don't, you'll be out the door."
>
> So I did the interview, and I got the job. After just a few weeks, I could see that my father was absolutely right. Mr. Zilber is very down-to-earth. I mean, if you met him somewhere and started talking to him, you would never imagine the man is who he is and has done all that he's done. He can get along with anybody.

Kim Treis was with me through a lot at Towne Realty. She saw partners come and go. She saw the sale of our public company and hundreds of the other deals I made. She knew my wife Vera and our children and my sisters, and she was there through many of my personal changes as well — through the celebrations and the misfortunes, the joys as well as the sorrows. Kim is a wonderful, wonderful person. She retired after 32 years as my secretary. I missed her from the very first day she left.

All these wonderful people became like family after awhile. That was something I nurtured and encouraged right from the start. When I hired people, I looked for talent and drive in their personalities, sure, but I also made a point to ask about their personal lives — their background, their education, their families, their marriages.

This was long before "family values" became a popular phrase. I wanted to know what a person's morals were, what a person's character was, what made a person tick. It was important for me to understand how my employees would fit into the Towne family. I don't think it's a coincidence that in the years I've been in business, all of my senior managers have been married, and none has been divorced.

As my company expanded and diversified, I built my staff and partnerships with the belief that I would be working with these people for the rest of their professional lives. That has indeed been the case. Some have stayed with me for 30, 40, 50 years or longer. Today the company is as large and widespread as ever, reaching coast to coast. Yet we're still a family.

CHAPTER 5

THE SMARTEST WOMAN
IN THE WORLD

I always thought I was pretty smart — until I met Vera Feldman. In our 61 years of marriage, I became convinced that she was the smartest woman in the world. Not only was she bright, but she also had an amazing spirit. She was gutsy and she was adventurous.

Vera Feldman was born on October 31, 1921, in Decatur, Illinois, but grew up in Milwaukee near Washington Park. The park was a green anchor to the city's expanding West Side, an area that was becoming the center of Milwaukee's Jewish community as families, including my own, moved into new neighborhoods west and north of the park.

Vera's father, Sam Feldman, emigrated from Lithuania just after the turn of the 20th century, settling in Ontario, Canada, and then moving to St. Louis. Sam met Sadie Blank in St. Louis, and the two were married in 1919. Sam worked for a housewares supply firm, LB Price Mercantile, and got promoted in 1928 to a regional manager position, based in Milwaukee. The Feldmans moved into one of the many new duplexes being built near Washington Park. The neighborhood was tight knit and friendly. As Vera would describe it years later:

> It was a lovely neighborhood. It was like one family. When we moved into the neighborhood, people came over. They brought us bakery, they introduced themselves.... You just had good neighbors. Nobody was suspicious of anybody, everybody cared about each other. They were just good people.

Vera's father eventually lost his job when LB Price closed down its Milwaukee operation, so Sam took another position with the company in Indiana, but the relocation didn't go well, and the Feldman family moved back to Milwaukee a few months later. Vera's father and a partner opened a fruit store and then he became the proprietor of a grocery store. It was the same type of business my own father was in. It was on 56th and Burleigh Avenue, just three blocks from where I would open the offices of Towne Realty years later. Small world.

It was an amazing coincidence that the Feldmans first Milwaukee home, the duplex on 56th Street, was just two blocks from my parents' grocery store. Even more remarkable is the fact that Vera and I went to the same schools at the time — Neekskara Elementary, Steuben Junior High, and Washington High School. For awhile, as a boy, I went to the same temple as the Feldmans, Temple Beth El on Sherman Boulevard, where Vera attended Sabbath school.

These incredible twists of fate weren't apparent to me until years later, but I'm sure our paths crossed without us knowing it many times as we were growing up, and I am absolutely convinced Vera and I were destined to meet.

❧ ❧ ❧

Vera and I got married in 1942. By then, I had gone to work for real estate broker George Bockl. The wedding was held in a hall on Prospect Avenue in Milwaukee. Prospect Avenue is Milwaukee's "Gold Coast," a mix of historic buildings and high-rise buildings overlooking Lake Michigan. Many years later I would buy that very building on Prospect in a commercial real estate deal, partly because we were married there. I remember so well the day of the wedding. Everything was prepared and everyone was gathered in the hall. Except me.

I was at the train station to pick up relatives who were arriving from Chicago. The train was behind schedule, and they had to hold up the wedding ceremony until I got there. Oh what a scene! Everyone was waiting for me. It turned out to be a fantastic day, one of the best memories of my life. I still have the suit I was married in. I bought it off the rack for $29.50, and it came with two pair of pants. It's a beaut, and someday I'm going to be buried in that suit.

When Vera and I became engaged, I was living at home with my parents while working for Bockl. My three sisters had already married and moved out. So after Vera and I got married, she moved in with me. My folks gave up their bedroom for us and stayed in a smaller bedroom. I thought, isn't that something? What a generous gift.

After the wedding, Vera and I took a honeymoon to New Orleans. I had bought a new car when I was in law school, a blue 1941 Plymouth, for $400. So we loaded up the trunk with suitcases and hit the road. Our first stop was Memphis, Tennessee. We stayed at the Peabody Hotel, a premier historic hotel. The accommodations were more lavish than any place we had ever seen. On our first night we went dancing in the Skyway Lounge, a ballroom and restaurant on the top floor. We danced and danced, and then had dinner. I remember our waiter, his name was Willie. After our meal, he came over to our table with a sheepish grin.

"Sir, I'm sorry," he said, "but I gave your check to a gentleman at a different table. It was a mistake and I could get in trouble. I apologize, sir, but . . . would you mind taking his check?"

"It all depends," I joked. "Was his check more than mine or less than mine?"

"His check is less than yours," he smiled.

"Okay, I'll take it." The entire bill was probably $3 or so, and I gave Willie the difference between the two checks in a tip.

We had a terrific time that night. Richard Himber and his Orchestra were performing, and they played a tune called "All the Things You Are." From that time on, it was our favorite song. It became very popular, recorded by Frank Sinatra, Jo Stafford, and Ella Fitzgerald. Whenever we heard it we would think of Memphis.

From Memphis, we drove to New Orleans. We walked for miles around the Crescent City, and ate at the old southern restaurants in the French Quarter. We had a great time, and from that point on, New Orleans became our stopping-off place for the ocean cruises. For years after, we sailed on the same cruise ship, a small but beautiful ship named the *Stella Polaris*. It was owned by the Bergen Line in Norway, and when it was first launched in the 1930s, it had been very famous for its resemblance to a royal yacht.

During World War II, the Germans seized the *Stella Polaris* and used it as a recreation vessel for crews of their U-boats, but after the war, it was returned to Norway and reconditioned as a cruise ship again. The *Stella Polaris* had accommodations for 200 passengers, with six decks, a gymnasium, a café, stained glass windows, teak deck floors — the very best of everything.

We took our first trip on the *Stella Polaris* after the war. There were parties all the time, but for some reason, we were not invited. We thought we'd been snubbed because we were so young. On our next trip, I planned to make an impression. Vera and I arranged to host the very first party of the cruise and invited everybody on board, including the captain and crew. Well, from that point on, whenever we sailed the *Stella Polaris*, we were invited to every single party.

Ocean cruises became an ongoing pleasure for us. Vera organized each trip, making a point of booking one every year, sometimes on the *Stella*, sometimes on other ships. In the early years, we sailed out of New Orleans, and later out of Florida and New York. We traveled all over the world — the Mediterranean, the Caribbean, Europe, Africa, Asia. I don't think there was any place we didn't see. You might say it was our extended honeymoon.

⁂ ⁂ ⁂

When I was discharged in 1943, Vera and I moved back to Milwaukee with our daughter Marcy, who was just a year old. We rented a place on the North Side of the city at 39th and Capitol Drive. It was a two-bedroom duplex and we were upstairs. Rent was $41 a month, the gas and electric bill was $1.67, and the cost of a postage stamp was three cents.

Our son Jimmy came along on December 9, 1946, and not even a year later, on October 24, 1947, Marilyn was born. That winter, it snowed so much we were stuck in the house for a week. Nobody could drive, and finally I had to take a sled to the store to buy a gallon of milk for the kids. We had quite a houseful in that two-bedroom duplex, and I knew we had to move.

I found a bigger place, a single-family home, in the North Shore suburb of Whitefish Bay. It was the first house that we owned, purchased on the G.I. Bill, a two-story with a long driveway and trees in the backyard, and right across the street from Cumberland Elementary School. The kids were at the playground all the time. I was a young man starting out in business, and I worked long hours in those days, but occasionally I did find time to spend with the kids. Marcy remembers those days like they were yesterday:

> I remember the whole family playing board games after dinner. We played Canasta, and we played Monopoly a lot. My father loved that game. He would try to get all the houses and hotels. He would make us stay up and play until late, until he won. I guess real estate was always his natural talent.

We took the kids to Florida during spring break nearly every year, driving from Milwaukee to Miami. Sometimes Vera's mother, Sadie, would come along. It was quite a carload. On one trip, we stopped along the highway at a place called Pickin' Chicken. They served homemade Southern fried chicken.

After we all finished eating, the waitress gave each of us a bowl with a slice of lemon in it. "What is this?" the kids asked. "Is this soup or what?" Vera said, "No, no. It's for washing your hands. Dip your fingers into the bowl and wash your greasy hands." Of course, this made the kids laugh. They had never heard of such a thing: Why would you wash your hands in a bowl of soup? From that point on, whenever we drove to Florida, we always made sure to stop at Pickin' Chicken, mostly for the "lemon soup."

There was also a more serious lesson to be learned on our trips. In those days, the South was still very segregated. You could still see bathrooms that were labeled "Whites Only." The kids didn't understand, and when Vera and I explained that some gas stations and restaurants didn't allow blacks to use the same restrooms as everyone else, they were confused. "That's not right. They shouldn't do that," Marilyn said one day. But that's how things were back then. Fortunately, things changed, but change came slowly.

In 1948, the state of Israel was formed. I was 31 years old at the time, and I wanted to support the new nation. A meeting was called by members of the Milwaukee Jewish community at a downtown hotel, and as people praised the birth of Israel, I stood up and in a shaky voice made a pledge to contribute $10,000 to the new nation. That was an awful lot of money then, and people looked at me with surprise. I could almost read their minds: "Who is this little guy who says he'll pledge $10,000? Who is this kid?"

Here I was, a young businessman with a wife and three small children, saying I would give $10,000. I didn't know where I would get that kind of money, but it was important to me, and somehow within the next few months, I made good on my pledge. That contribution to Israel marked the beginning of a lifetime commitment by Vera and me to the Jewish state.

Our membership at the Brynwood Country Club became another connection to Milwaukee's Jewish community. Brynwood was just 10 minutes from our home, and members often held fundraiser dinners to support Jewish projects and programs. It also became a comfortable place to relax and socialize. There were restaurants, tennis courts, a golf course, and a swimming pool. The kids learned how to swim at Brynwood. Brynwood was like a second home to Vera, and the club was helpful to me for business. I played golf a couple of days a week with clients, and we spent a lot of time with my partner Danny Tishberg and his wife Lala.

We also got to know Max and Mary Kohl and their family. Max was a Polish immigrant who opened a corner grocery store on the South Side of Milwaukee and built the first supermarket chain in the city, Kohl's Food Stores. He also built a national chain of department stores. Max and Mary had three sons and a daughter. Sid and Allen became real estate developers, and Herb became the owner of the NBA's Milwaukee Bucks and a United States Senator. I worked on several projects with Max and his sons over the years.

At the club, Vera got involved in planning parties and social events, and she sang and acted in some of the talent shows and skits. She was very outgoing and could be a real ham sometimes. She loved to socialize, and loved to tell jokes. Usually her jokes were pretty racy. What can I say? Vera could be very entertaining. In fact, she performed on a radio program for a short time. A DJ in Milwaukee who called himself "Fritz the Plumber" had a daily show on the station WYLO.

Fritz was a corny character with a thick German accent. When he appeared at public events, he dressed in bib overalls, a derby, and a big bushy mustache. Fritz played polka music on his show. With huge communities of German and Polish polka fans in Milwaukee, Fritz was a big hit. His show went on for 40 years, and eventually Fritz the Plumber was inducted into the International Polka Association Hall of Fame.

One day Fritz got sick and couldn't do the show. Somewhere along the line, the station manager had met Vera and apparently liked her sparkling personality, so he asked her to fill in for Fritz. "Why not?" Vera said, and a star was born — "Fritz the Plumber's wife."

She really played it up, putting on polka songs and faking a German accent. She even threw in a few unscheduled plugs for Towne Realty when she was on the air. Vera did the show for a full week while Fritz recuperated from his illness, and she got tons of fan mail. The listeners loved her, and when Fritz the Plumber returned, they wanted his "wife" to come back, too.

❦ ❦ ❦

Some years later, as Towne Realty began to grow and business took off, Vera and I built our dream house, and what a house it was. We had been living in a nice home in Whitefish Bay on Lake Drive, a tree-lined street that runs parallel to Lake Michigan's shoreline, when I discovered a property across the street on Lake Park Court. The street was a cul-de-sac, and there was an empty lot facing the lake. I called the guy who owned the land and he said he was going to build on it himself. I said, "Well, okay, but if you don't, let me know."

Six months later I called him back, and he said he had decided not to build on it, but his son wanted to put a house on the lot. Again I said, "If he doesn't, just let me know." A few months later I called him again, and this time he said his son did not want to build on the lot after all. "Well then, I'd like to buy it from you," I told him, and he agreed to sell it, finally. "You can have it at exactly my cost. Just contact my attorney. His name is Charlie Goldberg."

I said, "How about that. Charlie Goldberg is my attorney too." So we let Charlie Goldberg work out all the details. The asking price was just under $100,000, and I paid it. I worked harder to get that lot than just about any business deal I'd ever done. I kept at it and kept at it because I knew it was something Vera really wanted.

Vera worked closely with the architect on the floor plan. She designed most of the house and decided on all the materials and products. She did a beautiful job. It was a two-story home, with a circular driveway. The exterior of the first story was lannon stone and the second story was wood shakes. We had five bedrooms, three bathrooms, a living room, den, dining room, laundry room, and big, big kitchen. In the back of the house, you could look out at Lake Michigan from an enclosed porch that was heated by radiant heat. We built steps to the lake, 152 steps going down to the beach. It wasn't bad going down, but most people had to stop to rest along the way up. But, oh, the parties we had along the beach. It was a marvelous spot.

The house included materials and designs that nobody had tried before. Instead of the traditional wall paint, we used thick wallpaper that you could paint on. For a new house, it had everything. At the time, Towne Realty had gotten pretty big. I was doing a lot of building, so there were all kinds of tradesmen who wanted to help with that house, to impress me, I guess, and sell me on their workmanship and on their products.

For example, the three biggest drywall companies in town came to give me a demonstration of their products. Everybody used plaster then, but they wanted to build the walls with gypsum board instead. They wanted to show that this product was good. "If people know we used gypsum drywall on Joe Zilber's own house, we'll be able to sell it to other customers," they said. This was one of the first houses with gypsum drywall, which later became known as "Sheetrock."

Well, they put up the first layer, a half-inch thick, but it didn't work. It was wavy and buckled as they installed it. So they put a second layer over it, and again no good. By now, the walls were thick and heavy with two layers of gypsum drywall, so before they put up another layer, we had to add an extra crossbeam to the basement foundation just to hold up the walls of the house. As it turned out, the third layer was a success. It was even and it looked great, so we ended up with drywall that was an inch-and-a-half thick. It turned out to be an especially sturdy house.

Our home became a real party house. We had dozens of celebrations — employee parties, family parties, and parties with our Brynwood friends. Vera put everything she could into those house parties. They were unforgettable. They became social events, as my long-time secretary, Kim Treis, remembers:

> Vera Zilber also knew more about parties than anybody I've met. She knew how to do the best catering, the best hors d'oeuvres. Everything was beautiful and elegant. She was the perfect hostess, and very gracious. When you were invited to one of the Zilber parties, you went because you didn't want to miss it for anything in the world.

Sometimes Vera would invite celebrities. Hollywood actors Lorne Greene and Rita Moreno were guests in our home. One year we hosted a party for Golda Meir, who served as the Prime Minister of Israel. Like my parents, Golda Meir was born in the Ukraine and immigrated to Milwaukee, where she was raised. She was certainly an exceptional woman.

Another time we hosted a fundraising party for the United Jewish Appeal, and Eleanor Roosevelt was our houseguest. We held a huge reception for her, with local dignitaries attending and police escorting her to our home. The children were young, but they remember meeting Eleanor Roosevelt. Marilyn recalls:

> We greeted her at the door, and my dad said to her, "Come on in and let's sit and talk." I was eight years old, so this would have been around 1955. I sat on the floor with my sister and my brother, playing a board game. She was very friendly.

It was a very special occasion. We introduced Mrs. Roosevelt to our friends and took pictures of her with the kids. After the event, she asked if we had any more of these dessert rolls that we had served so she could have them the next day. She liked them so much that she wanted them for breakfast. So we fixed up a bag for her to take along. She was a woman of great importance, yet very approachable.

Vera once hired a professional instructor to give dance lessons to our friends in our kitchen. Our friends came over every week to learn the rumba and all the other latest dances on our big kitchen floor. I tell you, a lot of people learned how to dance in that house, myself included.

At the time, Vera's mother, Sadie, had been living with us. Sadie was also working at Towne Realty as one of my secretaries. Her husband, Sam, Vera's father, had passed away and so we made a place for her in our home. Sadie was the happiest lady I knew. I never saw her in a down mood, not once. Vera's great aunt stayed with us for a while, too. We always made room for family. But eventually, after Marcy and Jimmy went off to college, we decided to sell the house; it was now too big for us. It was a shame. We enjoyed that house immensely, but we didn't need all that room.

The house was so well known within the community — maybe because of all the parties we threw — that we didn't need to advertise. By word of mouth, we attracted three interested buyers. They all wanted the place, but instead of accepting the highest offer, Vera and I said, "Let's pick the one we think will be happiest here."

As it happened, we picked the buyer who wasn't able to pull together enough money to pay for it. Still, Vera and I thought that he and his wife would be happy living in our dream house, and we gave it to them anyway. We sold it on a land contract, where we kept the mortgage and they paid it off over time. They continue to live there today.

❧ ❧ ❧

Like everyone who has children, home life changed as the kids grew up. Our two oldest, Marcy and Jimmy, graduated from Whitefish Bay High School and went off to college. It was my dream that my son Jimmy one day would take over my business. Jimmy was as quick and sharp as a whip, and he worked with me at Towne Realty for many years. However, my dream would never be realized as his life, due to drug addiction, sadly spiraled out of control.

Marcy graduated from the University of Wisconsin in Madison, moved to London for a few years and then to Vancouver, where she lives today. Our youngest daughter, Marilyn, attended Woods Schools, a private boarding school in Langhorne, Pennsylvania, for children with special needs. It was an excellent school, probably one of the finest in the country for kids who have developmental challenges and need individualized care.

With our children gone from home, Vera and I moved to the East Side of Milwaukee. We moved into a unit on the twenty-first floor of Prospect Towers, an apartment building overlooking Lake Michigan that Towne Realty had constructed and owned for many years before selling in the late 1970s. We combined two units and turned one of the units into separate living quarters for Vera's mother, Sadie.

Vera and I both continued to enjoy traveling — Vera in particular. For a time, maybe four or five years, we spent a good amount of time in Jamaica, where we leased a condo. There was a nonstop flight from Milwaukee to Jamaica, which made it easy to fly back and forth. Vera would stay at our Caribbean home for part of the winter, and I would fly down on a Friday and back to Milwaukee on the following Monday.

It was nice to get away. Every weekend we chartered a sailboat and went sailing for the day.

As Towne Realty expanded, Vera and I began vacationing in Florida. Towne was developing high-rises on the Atlantic coast — Cocoa Beach, Cape Canaveral, the "Space Coast." In later years, we bought a condominium along the water that Towne had developed in Cocoa, Florida, called Oleander Pointe. Much like she had designed our lakefront house in Whitefish Bay, Vera had a wonderful time planning and decorating our Florida home.

One day when we were in Florida, Vera decided she wanted to buy a boat. So we drove to the marina at South Cocoa Beach with two of our closest friends, Jack and Brenda Bennett. Jack worked for Towne Realty running our Florida office. He and I looked at one particularly beautiful boat, a used boat that a doctor had traded in. It was equipped with all the electronic gear you would ever need. I thought it would be a great choice. But Vera wasn't interested.

"Let's look at that one," she said, pointing instead to a larger, brand-new boat.

It was more expensive, of course. "We really ought to think about this used boat," I told her, eying the doctor's trade-in. "I think we could get a good deal." But Vera wouldn't have anything to do with it. "I don't want somebody else's troubles," she said.

We must have looked at two or three more boats, and Vera kept going back to her first choice. She was growing impatient with me, so she went into the marina to place a phone call to one of my financial assistants, Bob Braun.

"Bob, I want to buy a boat," she said to him. "But tell me, do I have enough money?"

"Vera," said Bob, "I think you could buy the whole marina if you wanted."

After that, I gave up the fight and Vera made the deal.

Vera named her boat *Marenda*, combining the names of her daughters Marcy and Marilyn and our friend Brenda Bennett. It had everything — twin inboard engines, room to sleep five people — and even outfitted for fishing. In the years that she owned the *Marenda*, Vera was the captain. It was her boat and she was proud of it.

Vera was like that, strong-willed and independent. She was a woman who knew what she wanted, but she was also very genuine. She didn't put on airs and wouldn't stand for people who did. I'm sure that came from the way she was raised. Vera loathed anyone who was pretentious or flaunted wealth or social standing. She could see right through people like that.

Throughout our marriage, Vera brought about a lot of opportunities within our social life — the parties, the traveling, the country club skits. She also kept me grounded as I pursued my profession and built my business. When I went tearing off on something — the latest, biggest deal — she brought me down and made me remember that there was more to life than my business, more to life than just *me*. It was hard for me to recognize that. I was an ambitious and hard-driving guy, but if anyone could keep me in check, it was Vera. She was my foundation, and a true partner.

PART TWO

FULFILLING THE AMERICAN DREAM

CHAPTER 6

LIZ TAYLOR, COLLEGE DORMS, AND THE FATHER OF THE BRIDE

I never met Liz Taylor, but I paid a million dollars to show one of her movies in a theater I owned. Unfortunately *Cleopatra* bombed in Milwaukee and we lost a bundle. That was typical of the theater business. Popcorn was about the only thing that made us money. Still, I had a good time through it all.

Towne Realty built houses, thousands of them, but as we grew, we built other things too — college dormitories, nursing homes, supermarkets, parking structures. We bought and sold hotels, office buildings — and a chain of movie theaters. At one point, we were one of the largest holders of commercial real estate in Wisconsin. We were risk takers, always looking for the next best deal. Sometimes it paid off, sometimes it didn't.

The theater business was a risk, that's for sure, but it was an opportunity I couldn't pass up at the time. In the late 1950s, Towne Realty bought several office buildings in downtown Milwaukee. The first was the Carpenter Building on the corner of 6th Street and Wisconsin Avenue. I bought it on spec, figuring we could fix it up, and that's what we did. We renovated it, and it turned into a profitable investment.

On the street level was a theater, the Wisconsin Theater, which we leased to 20th Century Fox. Fox was the owner of a national chain of theaters and ran 11 in the state of Wisconsin. The Wisconsin Theater opened in 1923 as one of the first "movie palaces" in the city. Back then it had a stunning, two-story lobby, with a marble staircase, dazzling chandeliers hanging from a gilded, coved ceiling, and a 75-foot electric sign on the outside of the building. By the time the chain took over, the

Wisconsin Theater had seen its best days pass by, but it was still one of the city's more popular places to watch a movie.

Next door in another building I owned was the Strand Theatre, a smaller theater with around 2,000 seats that wasn't really built for movies, yet it was also one of the more popular first-run movie houses downtown. The manager of these two theaters was Al Frank. Al was the rep for 20th Century Fox, and he did a terrific job. I liked him a lot. Fox informed us one day that they were going to sell their Wisconsin theaters to an outfit in Indiana. So I called them up.

"Look," I said. "I rented *you* the theaters. I didn't rent them to somebody in Indiana. The least you could have done was call me to see if I would buy the theaters."

They said, "Well, we didn't know that you would be interested in buying 11 theaters."

"Well, if Al Frank would run them for me, I would buy them," I told them.

"We're going to close on the deal for the theaters on January 1, and if the buyer changes anything, we'll let you know."

Came January 1 and I got a call from 20th Century Fox. "Our buyer wanted to make a change in the contract that we didn't like," they said. "Do you still want to buy them?"

"Give me an hour," I said, and I called Al Frank to see if he would run the 11 theaters. Al said, yes, he'd be my partner, and he stayed with me at Towne Realty for the next 30 years. I called Fox back and told them we had a deal: Al Frank would run the movie houses with his brother Nick, and I would have a check delivered to Fox's agent that afternoon.

"How do we know that your check will be good?" they asked.

"Of course it will be good. Call my bank, Marshall & Ilsley's Northern Bank, and ask for Mr. Bud Franke. He's the president and he'll tell you."

So I hung up the phone with the 20th Century Fox guys and immediately called Bud Franke. "I'll be right over with a deposit to cover that check," I told him. "I just have to stop at my savings and loan to get the cash, but I'll be there."

"Okay," he said, a little nervously, "I'll be waiting."

My check was delivered to the Fox representative, who promptly called Bud Franke.

"I have a check here from Mr. Zilber," the Fox rep said to Franke.

"Well," said Franke, "if it's Mr. Zilber's check, bring it over and I will certify it." Northern Bank certified my check — before I arrived with the mortgage papers and the deed and my cash.

Meanwhile, I had gone to the savings and loan, put up four or five buildings for collateral, and within a couple of hours, I had the funds. I drove over to Northern Bank to make the deposit. Bud Franke was outside of the bank, pacing up and down the sidewalk, sweat pouring from his forehead.

"Relax, Bud. I told you I'd be here, and here I am. What's to worry about?"

Everything was fine and the deal went through without a hitch. But I thought to myself, "How many bankers would do this for a customer?" Northern Bank was one of the first of many banks that Towne Realty worked with; it became our lead bank, and I did business with Bud Franke personally for many more years, with the two of us becoming very good friends.

With that deal I ended up with 11 movie houses, and eventually I expanded my chain to include a total of 27 all around the state — Green Bay, Stevens Point, Wausau, Fond du Lac, West Bend, Kenosha, Racine. In Milwaukee, we owned the Strand, the Palace, the Paradise, and the Wisconsin Theater. At the peak of our operation, we averaged 60,000 admissions a week.

I bought the theaters in January, and right away we made money. *The Ten Commandments* with Charlton Heston as Moses was one of the first movies we showed, and it was a huge hit. "My God, this is great," I thought. "This is wonderful." Then came April, May, and June, and the theaters weren't making much money. We weren't selling any tickets. Or popcorn. I later realized it was a business that was seasonal. Business fell off during the warmer months because there were more outdoor activities for people to participate in. We showed some great movies, and the blockbusters helped keep us in the black.

In 1959, while Vera and I were on a cruise ship, I got a phone call from Al Frank.

"Joe," he said, "we can get *Ben-Hur* for the Strand Theatre."

"That'd be great, Al. *Ben-Hur* should be a good picture."

"The thing is, we've got to advance the studio a million dollars."

"A million dollars? How long will it take to get that back?"

"About 12 months."

"Twelve months? Usually we show pictures for two weeks."

"Joe, this'll be a hit for a long time. You should take this. It'll be a good one."

We had a big, black tie opening, with a spotlight shining into the night sky and hundreds of people lining up on the sidewalk. And lo and behold, *Ben-Hur* ran for 18 months. We made our million back, and a lot more.

Next came *Cleopatra*, with an all star cast: Elizabeth Taylor in the lead role, Richard Burton as Mark Antony, and Rex Harrison as Julius Caesar. There were high expectations that it would be a monster hit. Again, the studio wanted a million dollar advance.

"Sure, go ahead, give it to 'em," I told Al Frank.

But the critics were not kind to Ms. Taylor. The movie was excruciatingly long — over three hours — and "Cleopatra" opened to bad reviews and low box office sales. We never recouped our million dollar advance.

Shortly after, someone came along who wanted to buy nearly all of the theaters, and that was fine with me. We got out pretty fast. I didn't know the theater business, but it was fun while it lasted. Al Frank did a good job for me, and he stayed on with the company and ran other businesses for us for a long time.

Years later I became a theater owner again when I purchased the historic Riverside Theatre in downtown Milwaukee. The Riverside was one of the city's premier theaters. As a boy, I spent hours and hours there, watching vaudeville shows and the first "talkies" to come to town. I still own the Riverside Theatre. It doesn't show movies, but it remains one of the most popular entertainment venues in town.

I got another bonus out of being in the theater business. When I was negotiating the deal for the chain with 20th Century Fox, I met with an attorney named Art Laun, who represented Fox. Art worked at the Milwaukee law firm of Quarles & Brady at the time. When we were putting together the contract, I saw how he worked. If there was a change that needed to be made to the agreement, he went to his office to rewrite the language and come back in just five or 10 minutes with it all worked out. During our negotiations, I mentioned that I was also a lawyer, a graduate of Marquette Law School. "I never lost a case," I told him.

"That's because I never had one. I never practiced law." It was unbelievable how smart and efficient Art Laun was. I was so impressed.

After we finished the deal on the theaters, I asked him if he would represent Towne Realty in the future. He agreed and became our chief outside counsel for the next 30 years, in the process mentoring many young lawyers at the company. Art had a free and easy style. Art was the kind of guy who would be the first to take off his jacket when he was in the office. He drove a Cadillac convertible with whitewalls instead of the dark sedans that attorneys typically drove. Art Laun became a very dear friend. He was another example of how, over the years, with a little bit of luck and a lot of instinct, my staff and I were able to find and recruit enormously talented people.

❧ ❧ ❧

As we sold off the theaters, Towne Realty began buying office buildings in downtown Milwaukee. In fact, one of the buildings, the First Financial Building on Water Street and Wisconsin Avenue, we bought and sold three times over the years. It was a property that we thought could make money for us, whether we owned it and leased it or sold it to another investor. We purchased these downtown properties because they were good deals. The Commerce Building, the Wells Building, the Bankers Building, the Lewis Center, the Strauss Building, the Empire Building, which would one day become the home to our corporate headquarters — these were majestic, landmark office buildings, 12 floors, 14 floors, with marble staircases in high-ceilinged lobbies, and ornamentation on the exteriors that you just don't see on buildings built today. Over time, they had become neglected, and their vacancy rates rose to 50, 60 percent. The owners had given up on them, but where they saw lost investments, I saw missed opportunities. We would buy the buildings at a discount — saving some of them from the wrecking ball — renovate the interiors, and rent them at a cheaper square footage price than new office buildings went for in downtown Milwaukee. With a facelift, these grand old buildings became good deals for lease holders.

To manage the buildings, I hired a man named Al Sweet, who was at the time a door-to-door vacuum cleaner salesman. Al became our leasing agent. He was an honest man, and very smart. He learned that federal governmental agencies were looking for office space, and he learned that a governmental agency can't rent office space on its own. Each agency is required to go through the Government Services Administration, the GSA. If the Social Security office in Milwaukee, for example, needs office space, the GSA finds the space and puts together a lease.

Al Sweet got to know how the system worked, and we ended up leasing to the Department of Commerce, the National Labor Relations Board, the Federal Housing Authority, even the U.S. Marine Corps. We took these empty buildings and the GSA signed five-year leases and 10-year leases at very good rents.

We also rented to a long list of private companies, from Standard Oil to Merrill Lynch, from Ford Motor Company to Scandinavian Air Lines. We had dozens and dozens of tenants. Again, we'd fix up the interiors of these buildings and rent them for maybe 10 dollars less per square foot than it cost to rent in a new building. That made all the difference in the world for those tenants. The vacancy rate dropped very quickly, and at one time, we were the largest holder of commercial office space in the city.

I remember one building that I bought a few years later that worked out especially well, both for us and for the seller. We wanted to buy the Clark Building, once the headquarters of the Clark Oil Company, on Wisconsin Avenue in downtown Milwaukee. Clark Oil began as Clark's Super Gas. It grew into the largest independent oil refiner in the Midwest, with about 1,500 gas stations.

The founder of the company, Emory Clark, had died and the building was owned by his estate, which was made up of young family members. In our negotiations with the seller to buy the building, we ended up being $250,000 apart. I went to the attorney of the estate and I asked him, "How old are the beneficiaries?"

"They're young people, young kids," he said. "They have got to have the $250,000."

"What are they going to do with all that money?" I said.

"We'll invest it in something else," he said.

"I'll tell you what I'll do. Instead of $250,000, I'm going to give you $1 million. And I'm going to give it to you in a 30-year, zero-coupon bond." This was a government bond of some kind. So in the end, that building cost me $87,000 for the bond that I bought, not the $250,000 they wanted. And 30 years out, those Clark kids got a million dollars. It was a good tactic, one that I used many times to buy properties.

❊❊❊ ❊❊❊ ❊❊❊

The key to buying real estate is having someone to loan you the money. Money is the true raw material of any real estate business, and I had a great relationship with the savings and loan associations in Milwaukee. They provided Towne Realty with huge amounts of capital through the years.

In the early days when we were building homes, I could call up the president of First Federal, for example, which was the largest savings and loan in the state, and ask for a loan. I knew the presidents of all the associations. I cultivated those relationships. We had drinks on Friday night, we played cards once in awhile, and I took them golfing at Brynwood Country Club.

So when I was going to buy a building, I would ask them, "Will you loan me the million-and-a-half dollars?" We negotiated back and forth, sometimes on the golf course or at the poker table. In those days, I could get close to a 100 percent loan. So if someone had a building for sale that I wanted, I could say, I've got a lender who'll give me 100 percent of the purchase price, and the seller would get very interested.

As we moved into larger commercial real estate transactions, we began to move away from savings and loans and expanded our relationships with banks to finance these larger projects. Banks lend money at lower interest rates because they don't do as much work on a real estate deal. Unlike a savings and loan, they don't sell insurance policies to their borrowers. They don't run the title company that issues the title policies and things like that. So it was cheaper to go to banks than it was to go to savings and loans.

We had one bank that was our primary lender for awhile, Northern Bank. Northern was once the fourth largest bank in the city and had been bought by the Marshall & Ilsley network in the late 1950s. It has always been my belief that it is better to have good relationships with many different banks at once. It's better to borrow a million dollars from 10 banks than $10 million from one bank, because I feel if you only have one bank and anything happened on a project, then they could close you off. I never wanted to be beholden to one bank.

We were good to the banks. We never stiffed a bank. That was always a prime concern of mine, that you never, ever stiffed a bank. Even if we had to take funds from one pocket and put it into another, we made our payments. We were good to the banks and they were good to us. Even in the worst times, we would go to them and say, "Hey, don't make us pay you back right now because we just can't, we're short, but stick with us. We will pay you." And we always did.

Here's another lesson in banking: The more money you've got, the less you need to borrow at the high rates; the less money you've got, the more you borrow at the high rates. I decided very early on that I never wanted to borrow at high rates. I wanted to try to get everything at the base rate. In order to do that I had to convince the lenders that a Towne Realty project would be first rate.

We would put together a pro forma that, for example, would show we needed a million dollars for a project, but when the project was finished, it would be worth a million two or a million three, so we would have $200,000 or $300,000 worth of equity in it. If I was starting with a 100 percent loan, I would say to the lender, "Now wouldn't you rather loan 100 percent to someone who is going to pay you back than 80 percent to someone who won't pay you back?" So that began the whole basis of "relationship banking," which means you get money because you know the bankers.

After awhile, I began to look for banks in cities other than Milwaukee. There was a law firm in Chicago by the name of Friedman & Koven. They represented the Hilton Corporation, and when we built the Hilton Hotel I got to know Billy Friedman. We took a liking to each other, and Billy knew everybody, not just everybody in Chicago, but people in hotels and banks all over the country. He was a true big shot. He introduced us to the First Chicago Bank, to Pioneer Bank, and to the Cole Taylor Bank, and they began to make loans to us. He then introduced us to the Mercantile Bank of St. Louis and Bank of Boston, which ultimately merged with Fleet Bank.

Billy Friedman was a fine attorney, and I eventually hired him as an outside attorney for Towne Realty. He also sat on our board of directors. Here's a little joke about him: Billy used to tell me these stories, amazing stories about business deals around the country. I began to wonder how he knew all these people who were involved in those deals, or how he was involved himself. I couldn't believe how connected he was.

Over time, I noticed that whenever Billy would tell me a story, it was also in *The Wall Street Journal*, the same details, the same scenarios. I began to understand that he was taking credit for the deals *The Wall Street Journal* had reported. How much of the story was real and how much an invention of Billy's I'll never know. Quite a storyteller, Billy was one of those one-of-a-kind finds made over the years.

A third type of lender that we used was an insurance company, such as the Northwestern Mutual Life Insurance Company in Milwaukee, or Continental Insurance Company, also known as CNA, in Chicago. These insurance companies could make direct loans at a lower cost than banks because they were looking for large projects and their cost of funds was very cheap; they had all the premiums coming in and they weren't paying out big dividends. I threw in a little twist with the insurance companies and said, "Let's do projects as a joint venture." They lent us money at a lower rate, and I gave them 50 percent of the profits. Early on, I met the president of Northwestern Mutual Life, Fran Ferguson. We decided we would become 50-50 partners. He supplied the funds and we supplied the work. NML got interest, plus they got an equity kicker for their money.

This was right about the time we acquired a piece of the construction firm called the Woerfel Corporation. Woerfel, a huge Midwestern company, started back in 1917. Over the years, they built huge projects in the Milwaukee area, including the Schroeder Hotel, the Northwestern Mutual Life building, *The Milwaukee Journal* building, the Milwaukee School of Engineering, the annex to the Milwaukee County Courthouse, and an addition to St. Mary's Hospital. I believed that teaming up with Woerfel could lead to large third-party construction projects for Towne Realty. Woerfel had bonding authority. That simply meant that if we came in as the lowest bidder on a project, Towne Realty, through Woerfel, could give our client a completion bond or a security bond, guaranteeing that the building would be finished. If it wasn't, we would have to give the down payment back. Woerfel Corporation had this bonding authority, which allowed us to do jobs we couldn't otherwise do.

By 1964, we bought out all the other investors in the company and owned Woerfel 100 percent. With Woerfel as our construction arm, and Northwestern Mutual Life as an investor partner, we began building apartment buildings. Lots of them. The first was Quarles House, a high-rise apartment building on Milwaukee's Prospect Avenue. Next came Lake Shore Tower on Milwaukee's South Side, right on the Lake Michigan bluff. After that, Prospect Towers, another high-rise on Prospect Avenue. We owned and managed the Prospect Towers, and I lived there for some time with my family. A few years later, NML also became a partner when we began building student housing projects.

These were big days for Towne Realty. We were building big projects and acquiring big properties. We had come a long way from the "stick houses" that we built in our factory in the early '50s. Like a real life game of *Monopoly*, we began buying hotels. The first was a 40-room place called the Chalet Motel, just north of Milwaukee on Port Washington Road. Danny Tishberg and I put that deal together. It was the start. We ran it for awhile and then sold it. We then bought the Plankinton Hotel on the corner of Michigan and Plankinton Avenue in downtown Milwaukee. That was a large hotel, and we ran that hotel for many years. Danny's children were married at the Plankinton.

We bought another in Benton Harbor, Michigan, and another in St. Louis — the Statler Hilton — as well as The Milwaukee Inn (now the Comfort Inn & Suites) in Milwaukee on Cass and State Streets. All of our hotels became our Hotel Division, headed up by Al Frank, the same fellow who had run the theaters for me.

My favorite hotel, though, was the Schroeder at 6th Street and Wisconsin Avenue in Milwaukee. This was where Vera and I had our first date when we were in college. So, of course, there was a sentimental value to the Schroeder. From a businessman's point of view, I thought it was a good hotel, and well worth what we paid for it — $4.5 million for the hotel in 1964.

My God, I thought, it couldn't be built for four times that. We fixed it up, enlarged the convention area, and built the Crystal Ballroom on the fifth floor. The hotel was massive; when it was constructed in 1928, it had 811 rooms. I believed we had a really good investment, but as it turned out, we couldn't make any money running it.

The Schroeder was quite a grand hotel, though. When I bought the Schroeder, my daughter Marcy was engaged to be married. Because we had put so much into remodeling the hotel, in just three weeks time, there were rumors that I had bought the hotel just for the wedding, but that was not true. It was an investment for us. We did put a lot into that wedding, and my God, it was a fabulous wedding, the wedding of the century — 500 people, with one waitress for every table. We used the entire hotel, nearly every room in the place.

There was just one snag: the manager of the hotel reversed the order of seating. He seated all of the children in the front rows near the stage, and all the adults, the "important" people — the parents of the bride and groom, all of our relatives, all of my business associates — in the back next to the kitchen. I couldn't believe it. I was so angry, but nothing could be done.

Still, it was a marvelous day. Marcy's groom, Michael, was from England. After the ceremony, Michael's father made a toast to our family and our country. He stood up raised his glass and, in a very animated and jovial way, said, "I give you the President of the United States." Everybody laughed and drank champagne. Well, I came right back with a toast to his country and his family: "I give you the Queen of England," I joked, and everybody laughed and drank. It was a wonderful wedding.

Ultimately, we decided the Schroeder Hotel was too big for us to run. We needed to put a "flag" on it, meaning we needed a national operator. Six months after we bought it, we were introduced to the Sheraton Corporation, and we entered into a management contract with them to run the Schroeder. It was renamed the Sheraton Schroeder Hotel.

The Sheraton sent in a young man named Mark Flaherty to manage the hotel. I liked him, he did a fine job, and after awhile, I asked Mark to manage all of our hotels. He became the head of our Hotel Division, another excellent young addition to the Towne Realty family.

In time, we got out of the Sheraton hotel, and out of hotels altogether. It was not the best business for us. Each hotel we bought for a different reason, and in the long run, they weren't profitable. Like other businesses we got into in coming years — and there were dozens — hotels too often served as distractions. Like any other business, we had to make the right decisions at the right time. Hotels were not a bad business for Towne, but they weren't great. In the end, they were not pure real estate, the business that Towne Realty was founded on, the business we did best and returned to again and again.

When we realized that the Schroeder wasn't making any money for us and decided to sell it, we began negotiations with the Sheraton Corporation. I took our attorney Billy Friedman to New York with me to meet with Ernest Henderson III, the son of Sheraton's co-founder. The negotiations weren't going so well, and finally, at 2:00 a.m., we came to a stalemate.

"To hell with it," I said to Henderson. "I want nothing to do with you anymore. That's it." I walked out of the room. When I looked back, Billy was walking after me.

"Billy, what the hell's the matter with you?" I said to him in the hallway. "Get back in there and make the deal." It was a negotiating tactic I had used often.

So Billy went back into the room and sat down with Henderson and made the best deal we could get, which wasn't really very good. Fact is, we were lucky to sell it for four-and-a-half million dollars — the same price we had paid for it. After putting in so much cash to remodel the place, we ended up losing money on it. Ah, so it goes.

In the early '70s, we began building a Motor Inn on the South Side of Milwaukee, and then three more in Nevada — in Las Vegas and Reno. That grew into some major hotel projects, including Circus Circus, the Las Vegas Hilton, and the Palace Station, which opened up a whole other division in the company.

In Milwaukee, at 26th Street and Wisconsin Avenue — not far from the Schroeder Hotel — Towne Realty had built a high-rise hotel for Hilton. We owned the building, and they leased it from us. The hotel later was taken over by the Holiday Inn Corporation. To accomplish the transition from Hilton to Holiday Inn, it was necessary to send two letters simultaneously — one to Hilton terminating their lease to the property and the other to Holiday Inn accepting their lease. The letters were prepared, sealed in two envelopes and taken to the post office to be sent registered mail.

But that evening, we all began to worry whether we had stuffed the right letters into the right envelopes. A mistake would have killed the deal because Hilton didn't know anything about our plans with Holiday Inn.

We marched down to the post office and, after about an hour of pleading with the postmaster, we got permission to go through thousands of pieces of mail. Frantically we dug and sifted and sorted until we finally found our two envelopes and ripped them open. All's well that ends well — the right letters had been placed in the right envelopes after all, but what a crazy night.

❧ ❧ ❧

There was something in the air in the 1960s. Change was everywhere — on college campuses especially. Things were very different than when I was a student at Marquette University.

Along with our partner, Northwestern Mutual Life, Towne Realty thought building college housing could be a lucrative business, certainly more lucrative than owning movie theaters. I was introduced to a fellow in Madison, Wisconsin, named John Borman, who was running a management company, managing student housing units at the University of Wisconsin. At the time, student housing usually was nothing more than simple residence halls — tiny, single rooms usually for two roommates, with a common bathroom at the end of the hall. The residence halls were divided either as boys' dorms or girls' dorms. That was it; that was the dormitory picture.

To his credit, John Borman believed this was not the way college students in the '60s wanted to live. Instead, he thought students wanted apartment-like settings. Borman and our architect came up with a new design, a unit that had a modest-sized living room, with a bedroom to the left and a bedroom to the right and a kitchen in the middle — a private apartment that would be geared toward upper classmen and built off campus. The concept was cutting edge.

I was not new to student housing. Towne Realty had built several apartment buildings and a dormitory in Madison called Carroll Hall, the first luxury dormitory at the University of Wisconsin. It was right on the shoreline of Lake Mendota, really a higher grade dormitory for the students.

So, with John Borman, we began building some of these new apartment building dorms — The Haase Towers, The Regent, Allen Hall, Kent Hall, University Courts. We decided they would be coed, making them especially attractive to the students. Borman was highly respected in Madison. He was politically well involved, and very well connected with the University. He did an excellent job, and eventually he began to take us into other college towns. We built a student housing project at the University of Wisconsin in Oshkosh, the University of Wisconsin in Platteville, and the University of Missouri in Columbia.

The Missouri project proved to be more challenging than most. We had a devil of a time with the city of Columbia's Zoning Board. To satisfy the Board's requirement for parking at a dormitory we were building, we ended up buying a former Knights of Columbus office building with a huge parking lot behind it.

Trying to make lemonade out of lemons, we decided to renovate the three-story office building and rent it out as off-campus apartments. Things were moving along. We remodeled the interior and hired a drywall sprayer to paint each apartment with white paint. Our young accountant, Jerry Stein, was in Columbia, working on one of his first real estate deals.

When Jerry went in to inspect the work, he discovered that everything had been painted. I mean everything. From the windows to the light fixtures, the toilet seats to the kitchen sinks — everything was white! The drywall sprayer hadn't bothered to cover up anything in the rooms. He hadn't taped anything off. He simply went in, put on a face mask, and turned on his spray machine.

Unsure what to do, we sent Jerry to a hardware store to buy 100 utility knives, and we offered the first week's rent free to any college student who would scrape off the excess paint in his or her apartment.

Problem solved. We had our parking spaces for our dormitory and an apartment building that actually did quite well for us.

In fact, that deal led us to a relationship with the Mercantile Bank in St. Louis, which brought in more deals than I could have imagined. That's a perfect example of how business goes sometimes. The majority of the deals I've done in my life have grown out of another deal. I hardly ever start from scratch. One thing leads to another and then another and then another. I might work on a deal with a partner, and then expand on that deal with someone else. It's like a game of cards. You might be dealt three of a kind and then, who knows, you draw another pair and you end up with a full house.

CHAPTER 7

NO SHOES, NO WORK, AND THE BOGUS SILOS

Working with the government can be a crap shoot. It took me 10 years to find that out. In the process, I got involved in a few once-in-a-lifetime projects that sometimes made my blood boil but were never, ever dull.

We began to bid on military contracts in the early 1960s. Our country was still in the midst of the Cold War, and the Space Race with the Soviets was going full throttle. There were plenty of government projects across the country.

Our introduction to military work was more or less a coincidence, another case of meeting someone who I believed had some drive and some potential to succeed at Towne Realty. I was vacationing with my family in northern Wisconsin. We were at a resort, sitting outside on the deck, taking it easy, and I kept hearing this guy's name coming over the resort's loud speaker: "Phil Akwa, please report to the office for a repair. . . . Phil Akwa, please go to the boat house to help a customer. . . ." Phil Akwa do this, Phil Akwa do that.

I said to Vera, "Who is this Phil Akwa?" I looked him up that day and he told me he was a college student, an engineering major, who was working at the resort for the summer. He struck me as a bright and ambitious young man, so I said to him, "Look, when you get out of school, come and see me and I'll make sure you get a job."

Phil graduated as an engineer and eventually found a job in Milwaukee, working on government contracts, expediting construction projects. He worked, for example, on the design and construction of the jetways at

Milwaukee's airport, General Mitchell Field. Phil apparently remembered meeting me at the resort in northern Wisconsin, and he called me one day to tell me about a government job in Florida. Another outfit had gotten a construction contract at NASA's Cape Canaveral, as it was known at the time, now called the John F. Kennedy Space Center in Cape Canaveral.

This outfit was looking for a partner to help with the work and the financing. They needed bonding for the project, and that's something we could provide through the Woerfel Corporation, the construction company Towne Realty had acquired. So we signed on to the Florida job.

The project was the construction at Cape Canaveral of the Vehicle Assembly Building, a giant aircraft hanger where NASA assembled its launch vehicles. These were the vehicles used in the Saturn and Apollo space programs of the 1960s, enormously powerful rockets that propelled space capsules through the atmosphere and into orbit. The Apollo project later sent men to the moon. After each vehicle was assembled, it was transported on railroad tracks in an upright, vertical position to the launch pads several miles away.

The Vehicle Assembly Building was massive. When it was first constructed, it was one of the tallest buildings in Florida and one of the largest by volume in the entire world. NASA expanded the building over the years and still uses it today. It was so massive, in fact, that clouds would form inside the structure.

When the building was finished, my partner Danny Tishberg and I were given seats at the space center to watch a liftoff. That was really something. The spacecraft was secured to the gantry, and when the rockets ignited, the ground rumbled and our seats shook, and slowly the vehicle lifted out of the gantry. The light from the rocket engines lit up the sky as bright as the sun. It was unbelievable. I was very proud to be part of that project.

We did dozens of jobs for the military over the next few years. Phil Akwa was an idea guy and he would try anything. The government would issue a Request For Proposal and Phil would call on the best engineers in the country to figure out if we could do a job. If he decided it was possible, we would bid on it.

Another extraordinary project was the construction of Intercontinental Ballistic Missile (ICBM) silos in North Dakota. With our partnering construction company, the Woerfel Corporation, we built over 25 ICBM launch sites on a piece of empty land outside of Fargo, each silo made out of concrete and steel, with a launch mechanism inside.

We had just about completed the 25 silos when I got a call from the Department of Defense, arranging for me to meet with a colonel who was overseeing the project.

"We want you to build 15 more," he said to me.

"Well, okay. We can do that," I told him. "Are you going to give us a change order, or should we submit another separate bid?"

"No, we just want you to build the holes," said the colonel. "We want empty silos, with no control center or launch mechanism inside. Just the holes."

"Just the holes?" I couldn't understand why.

"We want you to build 15 holes and put lids on top, so they'll look like active ICBM launch sites from above," he explained. "As the Russians send their satellites over, Russia's military command will think we have additional missiles in the ground."

The Pentagon's plan was to outfox the Russians. So we cleared the land and built the 15 decoys. In the end, we'd completed 40 silos, some that were armed with ICBMs and some that were simply empty holes. I remember when we had finished, the colonel took me down to the bottom of a silo. I got on my knees and prayed: "I hope to God they never have to use these." Thankfully they never did, because I honestly didn't believe they ever would have worked. They're all dismantled now, demolished, and that's fine with me.

From there, we built a heat-generating power plant in Point Barrow, Alaska, the northernmost point in the United States. Point Barrow is at the very northern edge of Alaska, bordered on three sides by the Arctic Ocean. That natural gas-powered plant supplied all of the energy to heat the city of Barrow. It was a difficult project because you could only get a marine barge into the port for six or eight weeks in the summer because the Arctic Ocean froze for the rest of the year.

We had to load materials onto barges in San Francisco and Vancouver and had only a very narrow window of time to deliver the materials to Point Barrow. If you missed that window, you could not get a barge through the frozen sea. It was quite a challenge, but we got it done.

Phil Akwa was also our engineer and partner on a number of highly sophisticated communication systems. One of those was a radio navigation system in the mountains of Hawaii. The project was known as the Omega Station in Haiku Valley, not too far from Honolulu on the island of Oahu. The station has a long and interesting history, dating back to World War II. Following the attack on Pearl Harbor, the U.S. Navy constructed the original station in 1942 and 1943. It operated as a giant, very low-frequency antenna system and allowed radio communication with Navy ships across the Pacific.

The communication station was deactivated by the Navy in 1958, but in the late 1960s, the military issued a Request For Proposal to redesign and reopen the station as part of a series of nine Omega transmission systems around the world. Towne Realty got the contracts to build several, including the one in Hawaii.

And what a job it was. We built support towers that were anchored in concrete on the side of the mountains; then we ran the thickest, heaviest cable you can imagine between the towers. The cable ran in a horseshoe shape, 7,200 feet around Haiku Valley and elevated 3,200 feet in the air at some points. We needed helicopters to pour the concrete. When we were finished, the government asked us to clean the entire cable. "Clean the cable?" I thought. "How in the world do you clean a cable that's 3,200 feet in the air?"

Well, we had to be innovative. So we went to Neiman Marcus, of all places. And "for the man who has everything," we bought a hot air balloon. We had it delivered to the mountain. The balloon operators inflated it and took it up to 3,200 feet, then swung around the valley, cleaning the cable with a big piece of cloth as they went.

It was one hell of an operation. When all nine stations were up and running, the United States and its allies in South America, Europe, Asia, Africa, and Australia could track ships and submarines around the globe. The Hawaii site was decommissioned sometime in the late 1990s, but a staircase built in 1942 to haul equipment up the mountainside is still used by tourists. It's known as the "Stairway to Heaven," and it takes two hours to climb the 3,992 steps to the top.

We were also awarded a contract to build a desalinization plant in Trinidad, a Caribbean island nation off the coast of Venezuela. The plant was designed to remove salts from sea water to make it suitable for drinking and irrigation. The technical aspects weren't that difficult, but the project turned into a cultural Catch-22 before we even started. The Defense Department informed us that, according to U.S. law, all construction workers had to wear shoes on the job as a safety requirement. It was in our contract, like wearing safety glasses.

However, in Trinidad, people went barefoot all the time. Workers didn't like to wear shoes. You couldn't get *anybody* to wear shoes. It's just how they lived in Trinidad at the time.

We thought and we thought, and finally, we came up with something: to satisfy the government, we gave all the workers one pair of shoes. They tied the shoelaces together, hung the shoes around their necks, and went out to work. That solved the problem. The workers were "wearing" shoes, and the terms of our contract were met. Everybody was happy.

❧❧❧ ❧❧❧ ❧❧❧

We continued the military contracts with Phil Akwa, providing him with construction bonds. We'd make a few bucks on one, and we'd lose a few bucks on another. This went on for four or five years. Phil was a good salesman. He could get the jobs, and if you can get the jobs and get them done right, everything is fine. We were relying totally on Phil to complete these projects, and after awhile we felt a little vulnerable in that position. We wanted more control over the contracts.

So we decided to part company with Phil and take a different direction. Instead of the high-profile projects like the missile silos or the navigation systems, we focused on what Towne had done from the beginning — housing. We renewed some of the relationships we had made with the federal government and began to bid on military housing projects on bases around the country.

At that same time, the military had begun upgrading its housing. By then, the draft had been eliminated and there was a volunteer Army. The Army's shoddy housing conditions didn't make for a very good selling point when trying to sign new recruits. There hadn't been any new housing since pre-World War II. So the military went to Congress and got appropriations to build new housing.

These projects were all new construction. There were a few conversions, but the conversions were a sham. The military would raze an old barrack but save one wall, and under the guidelines, they could call that single wall an existing building. The Pentagon could get funds from Congress to rehab existing buildings easier than they could for new buildings. So the military would tell Congress it had a 500-unit building that needed to be rehabbed, but in fact, they would tear down everything except one wall to satisfy the requirements, and then built a new structure around that wall.

Partnering with the government is not an easy thing to do. Frankly, it was sometimes hard to find our way through the bureaucratic maze. Simply getting paid often became a tug of war between the military and us.

Sometime in 1974, we found a guy named Jack Bennett. My partner Danny Tishberg was running our military housing projects, and he began to search for a replacement for Phil Akwa. We had a contract to build barracks at Fort Hood, Texas. So we phoned the chief of the Army Corps of Engineers out of Fort Hood. "Who's the best contractor you ever worked with?" we asked him, and he told us it was the Centex Corporation, one of the biggest home builders in the world. They had worked on four projects at Fort Hood. So we asked for the name of the best people with Centex, and we were directed to Jack Bennett, who lived in Miami, Florida.

Jack was reluctant to talk to us. He had been with Centex for 20 years and had built 30,000 houses for them. He wasn't looking to leave, but I was persistent. I thought we had found the right man for the right job at Towne Realty, and I knew I could bring him on. Jack tells a good story of how I signed him on with us. He recalls:

> I got a phone call from a manager at Towne Realty, and he said, "You know, we've got a $22 million job at Fort Hood, and we understand you would like to do the job for us.'" And I said, "Well I don't know where the hell you got that idea? Because I got a $100 million job right here that I'm right in the middle of, and I don't figure I want to quit."
>
> So I thanked him for calling, and about five minutes later the phone rang again and it's another guy from Towne Realty, Danny Tishberg. Danny comes on like he had known me 100 years, and he got me talking. He said he would be in Miami in a few days and he'd like to see me. I told him that would be a waste of his time, but he gave me his phone number anyway.

Well, I thought about it for a little bit and I called Tishberg back. I said, "All right, I'll tell you what. I can fly to Milwaukee next Saturday afternoon if you want to meet." And he said, "Okay, we'll send you a ticket and have somebody pick you up at the airport."

I got into Milwaukee, and was taken to a meeting with all these guys from Towne. They were bouncing questions off me right and left, and I said, "Hey, now wait a minute. You guys get me up here and you evidently know something about me, but I don't know squat about you folks. So why don't you tell me something about you all. For starters, do you have any money?"

And that's when Joe Zilber started talking. "You know, it depends on what day you ask," said Joe. "Some days I have money, and some days I don't. Let me make a phone call to the president of my bank. You can ask him." Now, this was 9:00 p.m. on a Saturday night, but he called the guy at home, the president of the Marine National Bank, and this guy talked to me very wide open, saying, "Yes, Towne Realty has been in business since 1949 and they have fought their way to the top, and they're true people and they believe in fair play." The more I talked to Joe Zilber, the more I liked him, and we ended up shaking hands on the deal. I joined up with him that night.

Jack was a pro. At Fort Hood, he put up 921 units in 15 months. From there, we sent him to Arkansas to build 100-plus units, and then Hawaii to build 477 units. In many ways, military housing was good for us, because this was at a time when interest rates were sky high and everybody in the residential housing market was going bust. So we had this alternative — the military business — which at the time looked very good to us.

Around this time, we bid on 11 military family housing projects across the country and got eight of them, which is a pretty good average. But we got caught with our pants down. There was no way we expected to win all these contracts, which totaled around $350 million. In a 24-month period, we scrambled to meet our deadlines. We built for the Air Force in Ogden, Utah, the Army at Fort Riley, Kansas, and the Navy at its shipyards in Philadelphia. We went all over the place, building family housing units: from Fort Riley, Kansas, to Fort Drum, New York; from Grand Forks Air Force Base in North Dakota to the Strategic Air Command (SAC) airbase in Blytheville, Arkansas; from Peterson Field in Colorado to the Great Lakes Naval Base in Illinois.

With all these military housing jobs pending, I really needed to staff up. Towne Realty had formed a joint venture with two Milwaukee architects, Jordy Miller and George Waltz, the principals of Miller-Waltz Architects. We called the partnership TMW, and it became our vehicle for military construction for many years, but I needed a top rate construction man to work with Jack Bennett and manage the projects. Jordy Miller introduced me to Don Mantz, who managed construction operations for a design and construction firm in town.

Don's firm, Stevens Construction, had partnered with Towne on a couple of senior residential homes and nursing homes. He was a straightforward guy, and I knew he'd be up for the challenge. Don accepted the job and brought in Bob Kiesl, one of his colleagues from Stevens Construction, to do the estimates and bidding. Bob was a perfect fit.

The volume was great — 3,000 military housing units within 24 months — but so were the headaches. When you're dealing with the military, the problems never end. We were constantly trying to get the government to approve change orders so we could get paid. While we waited, we had enormous interest costs on money investments.

There were hundreds of change orders. Here's how they would work: say we had to change the dimensions of a bedroom window in 1,000 units. And say each replacement window cost $100 more. We would request a change order for the difference in price ($100,000 total) and bill the military.

The costs, however, could be negotiated between the engineer at the base and the contractor, and then had to be approved by the contracting officer of the base. So what started out as a normal, routine change order could get way out of hand. The change orders got to be so numerous that we had millions of dollars in outstanding payments that the government had not approved.

On one job at the Philadelphia naval yards, we ran into unsuitable soil conditions and couldn't begin digging the foundation for a huge housing development, so we filed a change order to redo our design plans and increased cost. We argued with the military for months and months about footing design and building design. The officers at the base wouldn't approve our change order, so we had to go up the ladder and file the claim with the Pentagon. It took a year or two after the job had been completed to collect our payment.

On another project, this one at Fort Hood, Texas, the Army Corps of Engineers wanted to add a patio and walkway at one building. It was a small amount of work; labor and materials were no more than $5,000. But the Army delayed for weeks; they had all kinds of reasons. It would have cost us thousands of dollars on legal fees to pursue a claim, so finally we just went ahead and did the work. "You have your patio and walkway at no additional cost, thank you very much," we told the Corps.

Sometimes it was so bad that it got to be a joke. I remember to settle one claim, we sent Danny Tishberg and a team of our attorneys to negotiate with the Army on a bunch of change orders. Danny and the lawyers were supposed to be there for a half-day meeting and ended up staying for three days. Tishberg had to take the guys to a department store so they could buy a change of socks and underwear.

On a few projects, things were simply beyond our control. That was the case at Fort Riley, Kansas. Our contract was to build 1,000 homes for the Army Corps of Engineers. It was a good job and we were well underway. The units were built in sequence, as if we were moving down an assembly line. We were at about unit 600 in our building starts. The first 200 had been turned over to the government and were already occupied. We were moving through the project, moving down the line, doing quite well, when one day we ran into a little challenge: we took a direct hit by a tornado.

The twister hit the project at about unit 400, right in the middle of the operations. Two multi-family buildings were actually lifted off their foundations and dropped into a ravine. Fortunately, not a single person was injured, but because the tornado hit the project square in the middle, we had damage of varying degrees going each way.

All in all, 400 units needed to be repaired or replaced. Don Mantz did a superb job of getting the project back on line. He set up a team to document the damage, file insurance claims, and complete the work. When all was said and done, the Corps was happy, we got paid for what we did, and, most importantly, no one was hurt, just damage to empty buildings.

Around this same time, Towne Realty had started building high-rise condos on Florida's Atlantic coast. As it turned out, Jack Bennett was ready to start another military housing job in Texas, but I gave him a call. "Jack, you're going to Florida," I told him. "Why not," he said, and he got on a plane, rented an apartment in Cocoa Beach, and took over a seven-story condominium project we had begun called Windward East. He finished that and was about to go to Texas, but just before he left, he called me and said, "Why don't we build another one on the land next door?" So we put up another seven-story condo, this one called Wind Rush.

Thirty-five years later, Jack Bennett and his wife Brenda are still with me in our Florida office on the Space Coast. I consider them both very close friends. Jack's two sons, Maath and Kohn, are also with the company. Maath serves as a vice president of Benko Construction Company Inc., the construction arm of our company in Florida, and is the director of all construction activities. His brother Kohn is a vice president for Homes by Towne and Towne Realty, and is the manager of the Florida Division.

All in all, many of the jobs were exciting projects. I would get calls from Army generals who were supervising the missile silo project, or fly to Cape Canaveral to watch the launch of an Apollo rocket, but in the course of time, military family housing became a losing operation for us, and we stopped bidding on contracts. It had run its course.

Don Mantz and Bob Kiesl thought they had reached the end of the line at Towne Realty. Recalls Don:

> We worked on the military projects for a couple of years and then, quite honestly, Bob and I thought it was time to move on and may-be start our own company. Joe and Danny came back to us and said, "Good idea, but we would like you to do it as part of the Towne fam-ily. We will provide you with the financial resources necessary to get into construction projects." Joe listened to our dreams and he sup-ported our efforts, and the Kiesl and Mantz team then became KM Development. Almost immediately we started building projects.

KM Development built everything from nursing homes to hotels to retail stores. Bob Kiesl passed away many years ago, and I miss him terribly. Don is still with me today. He was the ground floor manag-er when we started our Arizona operations and continues to head KM Development. He's a down-to-earth guy, and very confident. He knows what he wants, and you cannot sway him.

As with Jack Bennett's sons, the sons of Don Mantz and Bob Kiesl joined the Towne family, too. Kevin Mantz developed a passion for ar-chitecture, watching his father put up buildings. He now manages our architectural department. Kevin Kiesl (yes, another Kevin) had a passion for construction and a solid work ethic, like his father's. He worked his way up to the top of our Arizona division, and is now the senior manager of our Arizona operations, based in Phoenix.

The Bennetts, the Mantzs, and the Kiesls are just three of many examples of how the Towne family extends to second and even third generations. I've always encouraged these kinds of family ties. They create a bond that opens up new opportunities to our employees and in turn strengthens the company.

CHAPTER 8

DRUG STORES, AND
10 MILLION DAWN DOLLS

Deals are all about relationships. The more people you know, the more deals you make. You meet one person, and that person introduces you to someone else, and then that person introduces you to someone else . . . it's like links in a chain, one connection to the next to the next. That's how deals come about; that's how partnerships are made. As the old saying goes, it's who you know. But it's also how *well* you know a person. Some people make very good partners and some do not. The trick is to figure out before you form the partnership exactly who is who.

In 1957, my brother-in-law Bill Kesselman and I purchased a building in Milwaukee that was once a hospital and turned it into a nursing home. We called it the National Convalescent Hospital. Bill was a pharmacist. He was married to my youngest sister, Fannie, and the two of them owned a drug store in town. Bill knew quite a bit about health care.

At the time, I sat on the board of directors of Mount Sinai Hospital in Milwaukee, so I was familiar with health care issues, too. Gradually, the 252-bed National Convalescent Hospital filled to near capacity. A few years later, Kesselman and I began purchasing and leasing more health care facilities in Milwaukee — four homes for the mentally challenged, one home for the mentally ill, another for children with behavioral problems and learning disorders, two facilities for neglected kids — and a nursing home in Fond du Lac. By early 1968, we had 10 facilities.

I persuaded Lowell Spirer, the administrator of Mount Sinai, to leave the hospital and run our health care division. Lowell had been in health care a long time and was top notch. He had been president of the Milwaukee County Association of Nursing Homes.

These types of homes traditionally had been dreary places. Residents were given just the basic care and the bare necessities to live on, and often they stayed until they died.

Around this same time, the federal government had put into place publicly funded health care programs for elderly, handicapped, and low-income Americans who couldn't afford medical treatment or retirement centers. A national debate eventually led to the signing of a law in 1965 by President Lyndon Johnson that created Medicare and Medicaid. Under federal Medicare, and state Medicaid programs, people were given government aid to pay for nursing home care and other health care centers.

Things were changing, and Bill Kesselman and I thought nursing homes would be a good area to get into, both from a humanitarian point of view and as a business. By 1968, we had 744 available beds and space for another 279. Nursing homes were needed badly. The government estimated there was a shortage of 250,000 beds for convalescent care.

The larger we grew, the more people I needed to hire, of course. Soon we had more than 400 employees working at our nursing homes. Towne Realty was starting down the road of diversification, a road that would take us into all different types of businesses in the coming years. I had no way of knowing where that road would take me before leading back to pure real estate.

As I've always done, I followed my instincts when hiring new employees and putting together partnerships. One such example is a fellow I hired named Guy Smith, whom I discovered in a restaurant, of all places. Every Saturday morning I would take four or five of our guys around to the sites we were developing. We'd start the day by meeting for breakfast. One morning we went to an International House of Pancakes. We walked in and noticed there was just one person working in the place, a young guy. He seated us, took our order, went into the kitchen to prepare our food, brought it out to our table, refilled our coffee cups — the whole thing.

"Where is everybody? Where are all the other employees?" I asked him as he gave me the check. "The cook didn't come in today, and the waitress is late," he said. "I'm the manager, and I've got to take care of the business."

He was young, about 28 years old, and I could tell that he was a go-getter. So I said to him, "I'll tell you what you do: you come to my office on Monday morning and I'll give you a better job." He came to the office bright and early on Monday. We talked, and I gave him a job. I hired him as an assistant administrator in one of our nursing homes. He knew nothing about nursing homes, not a thing, but over the years, Guy Smith worked his way up to become the president of our entire nursing home company. He was an outstanding manager and built a tremendous team.

As Towne Realty got larger, the company's business became more demanding of my time and attention. We were expanding our health care division, building college dormitories in Wisconsin, Missouri, and Michigan, and taking military contracts in Florida, North Dakota, New York, and beyond. More and more it was necessary for me to spend my time traveling. I was out of town every week, flying from state to state, project to project, sometimes making three, four, five stops in a day — Milwaukee to Madison, to Champaign-Urbana, Illinois, to Columbia, Missouri, to Ann Arbor, Michigan.

It was very difficult to get in and out of some of these smaller cities by commercial airline. So, with my partner Danny Tishberg and whoever else I needed to take along, I would charter a small plane out of Milwaukee's Timmerman Field. We chartered the same plane and the same pilot everywhere we went, starting out early in the morning and making a giant loop. It was a cost-efficient way to travel and do business, but flying with just one pilot could be dangerous.

❧ ❧ ❧

One day I got the crazy notion to retire from my job. I thought it was time to step away from a company I had run for 20 years. I had turned 50 and was living comfortably. Life was good, so why not take a breather, I thought. Maybe I could find something else to do and turn more of my attention to Vera and our kids.

I wanted the young up-and-comers at Towne Realty to have a chance to make the decisions. I believed that if I didn't get out of the real estate business, the young guys would never have a future. I wanted to show them there was an opportunity to move forward and excel. So I decided to get out. I named Dan Tishberg president of Towne Realty and

Jerry Stein executive vice president. I was confident they wouldn't screw things up too badly.

My retirement lasted all of two weeks. There was no succession plan in place, and my sudden absence came totally out of the blue. It really shook up the company. I quickly saw that I couldn't just walk out abruptly.

On a personal level, I also realized I couldn't stay away. I didn't want to leave the business behind. Even in the two weeks I was gone, I missed the game — the meetings, the phone calls, the traveling, the day-to-day negotiations. I started calling Danny and Jerry three or four times a day, checking on the deals they were making, second guessing their decisions, trying to run things from the outside.

Finally they said, "Listen, Joe, come on back. This retirement thing just isn't working out." So I said, "Yeah, you're right. I'll come back." It was unrealistic to think I could hang it up. Running the business was part of who I was. It was in my blood. I needed to work.

That was the last time I considered retirement. Even today, in my ninth decade on Earth, I continue to work. I'm on the phone every day with my guys. When I'm at my home in Hawaii, I've got a daily scheduled tele-conference call to my office in Milwaukee, checking on the latest deals, asking about my employees. It's what keeps me going.

So I went back to work as Towne Realty's chairman of the board, leaving Danny in place as president of the real estate business while I concentrated on the health care facilities with Bill Kesselman. We had 10 homes at that point and they were going pretty well. I could see how we could grow the health care division even larger, expanding it nationally.

One day I had a brainstorm: why not set up the health care properties as a separate company and take it public? I had always wanted to have a public company, but was never willing to do it with Towne Realty. Real estate had so many ups and downs that I thought if we ever went into a really deep recession, I'd have to crash the company, it would go under. I could never take Towne public, but the nursing homes were a different story. There were growing opportunities in the health care field, and the timing was right to try a public offering.

We contacted our attorney Art Laun to take us through the long and complicated process. Art had been a good friend of mine for years. I first met him when I bought the movie theaters. He represented the seller, 20th Century Fox. Art prepared a prospectus and all the other necessary legal documents. Our 10 health care properties were incorporated and placed into a holding company, which we called Unicare Health Services Inc.

We also put into motion a plan to build and lease four more nursing homes in Wisconsin — in Milwaukee, Madison, and Fond du Lac — and buy a couple of buildings in Milwaukee that we would convert into two group homes for neglected children. We acquired a 250-bed nursing home in Dallas, Texas, in order to give the company a national scope and make it more attractive to investors. All these additions would enlarge our bed count to nearly 2,100 beds at the time of the public offering.

We registered with both the federal and the state governments. We got permission to offer the prospectus and we offered stock to the public. Unicare went public on July 25, 1968. The stock came out at $10 bid and closed at $28 to $30 a share. In just five months, its value shot up to $208 a share, after splitting four to one. It was amazing. For awhile, my partners, Bill Kesselman and Danny Tishberg, and I were unexpectedly very wealthy — at least on paper.

I was growing the company with an excitement and passion that took me back to my early years, when Towne Realty was building and selling hundreds and hundreds of homes. With Unicare, it was all about acquiring new businesses. Typically when we found a seller, we would issue Unicare stock instead of cash for the purchase. This allowed us to buy properties essentially without borrowing any money.

All the expansion was done with public money, and in those days, the stock market was hotter than a pistol. The nursing home industry in particular became a darling because it had this new source of revenue — the federal government. So we began adding more nursing home beds to our portfolio, and in that first year, Unicare's stock went up every time we announced another acquisition.

On the first anniversary of the public offering, Unicare stock sold for a high of $27 per share. In coming years, the value stabilized and leveled off, as the rapidly expanding health care field got more competitive and profits shrank, but that first year was a real rollercoaster ride as the stock soared and fell.

Running a public company comes with a lot of regulatory baggage. It seemed like we were filing SEC documents every day. I talked to my attorney, Art Laun. Art suggested that I hire an in-house counsel to guide us through the bureaucracy. He recommended a lawyer in town who had graduated from Marquette Law School, my alma mater. His name was Jim Janz, and he had experience in real estate as well as doing some securities work. Jim is still with the company today. He is a wonderful person, a family man, a true humanitarian and a good friend. He recalls first coming onboard:

> Art Laun was absolutely certain that Joe Zilber, Danny Tishberg, and Jerry Stein just weren't cut out to be regulated. Art said to them, "You need someone to help you with all the red tape that comes with running a public company." I was with the Foley & Lardner firm at the time. I didn't know anything about Joe, Danny, or Unicare for that matter, but I met with Joe, and when you first meet Joe, you know he's a straight shooter and you believe in him.

> This was one of the most important decisions of my life, but Joe convinced me that joining him would be more rewarding in every way. So it didn't take much for me to decide to join Towne Realty. I think we met in September and I joined them in October 1969. I went to work right away on Unicare matters.

The company grew into the health care field very strongly. We negotiated with numerous groups to lease space in the nursing homes to physical therapists and other care providers who could work with residents. Soon we began to buy and build nursing homes across the country — from California to Florida, Illinois to Nevada, Minnesota to Indiana, Missouri to Virginia, Texas to Wisconsin.

In our first year, from 1968 to 1969, we increased our capacity from 744 beds to over 7,000. Our revenues in that year jumped from $2.8 million to $13.8 million. We were doing all right.

In the go-go years of our expansion, we also bought smaller nursing home companies. One group of developers in Indianapolis called Braniff Corporation, for example, had started building 40-bed nursing homes in small communities that didn't have any long-term care for seniors. We acquired 50 percent of Braniff as a silent partner. Their facilities were brand new, and the partnership worked very well for us.

We also acquired a group of facilities in California from a gentleman named Irv Kahan and his family. The Kahans were fascinating people, Jewish immigrants from Hungary. Just very entertaining characters. They could've been a vaudeville team. The stories they told were remarkable. Irv was a Hungarian refugee from the Holocaust, a survivor of one of the death camps. He had lived a terrible life in Eastern Europe, but somehow got to America with his family — his wife, his three sons, his brother-in-law, his sister, and another brother-in-law. With his three boys, he opened a series of skilled care nursing homes. They built the homes in the California suburbs.

As an aside: the Kahans' English wasn't very good. They were hard to understand. Whenever we negotiated with them, they never had to leave the room to talk, but merely switched to Hungarian and talked among themselves. Each of their nursing homes was managed by a member of their family. To manage a nursing home in California, you were required to pass a written examine to get a license. Irv and his son Andy passed the exam without any difficulty. The other members of the family weren't as successful.

On the second attempt to pass the test, Irv went along with each family member. While the exam was in process, Irv talked out loud in Hungarian. The exam moderator would ask him to be quiet and Irv would say, "The only way he can understand the question is if I say it out loud." The moderator conceded and Irv continued to recite the question in Hungarian — while, unknown to the moderator, also giving the answer. Eventually everyone in the Kahan family passed the exam.

When we met Irv Kahan, he was talking about taking his company public. He needed capital. Our Unicare stock was viewed as very valuable. So we told him, "Why don't you join the Unicare family? We'll form a joint venture, 50-50. You'll own half, we'll own half. You'll take your half in stock, and you'll make money on the stock." At the time, Unicare stock was rising by more than the value of the nursing homes because of all the leverage you got in public stock. So we formed a joint venture with the Kahans.

But not all the deals went smoothly. Here's one example: the Kahans wanted to open a nursing home in Las Vegas because they liked going to Vegas to do a small amount of gambling. So they built a nursing home in Las Vegas in which we were a part owner. In those days, Vegas was a come-and-go town built on tourism. We soon found out that nobody retired in Las Vegas. Nobody was born there, nobody died there, and nobody went into a nursing home. So our brand-new nursing home was sitting empty. We couldn't fill it.

Fortunately, we were introduced to a developer who said he knew of a group of doctors who might want to buy the building and turn it into a hospital. Las Vegas needed another hospital at that time. So we closed the nursing home — no one was living there anyway; we had about two or three beds occupied out of a couple hundred and we were losing a fortune — and sold the building to the doctors. To this day, it operates as Valley Hospital. When it was first opened years ago, television producers used the building for some exterior shots for the soap opera *General Hospital* and the series *Vegas*.

In what turned out to be one of the strangest deals in Unicare's expansion, we bought two facilities in Miami. In the negotiations, it was agreed that we would get a third nursing home in Virginia at no charge as part of the deal, a facility called Kings Mountain Nursing Home. Nothing is ever free. Kings Mountain Nursing Home turned out to be one of the biggest headaches in all the years we operated in health care.

It had problems and liabilities from the past that we didn't know about, and ultimately the place was closed, but we learned an important lesson: you get what you pay for. From that day on, everyone agreed that "free" was not what we were looking for the next time we bought anything.

On the lighter side, I remember the trip to Florida to work out the deal as kind of comical. Danny Tishberg and our nursing home administrator, Lowell Spirer, had gone to Florida to check out the Miami facilities. They liked what they saw and called me to come down and take a look. I contacted Phil Siegel, our treasurer, and asked him if he would like to go. Phil had never been to Florida and was anxious to go. "When are we going?" he asked me, and I told him. "In one hour." So Phil rushed home, grabbed a suitcase, filled it with clothes, and met me at the airport.

We got into Miami at 5:00 p.m. and went straight to the sellers' office to complete the contract. We worked until around 2:00 a.m., and then took a taxi to our hotel, the luxurious Fontainebleau along the Gold Coast in Miami Beach, right on the Atlantic. As we shuffled off to our rooms, I told everyone to meet back in the lobby at 8:00 a.m. to catch our flight back to Milwaukee. At 8:00 a.m. sharp, Danny, Lowell, Phil, and I stood at the front desk to check out. Because Phil was the company's treasurer, he said he would pay the bill. But when he looked at the bill, he saw that Danny, Lowell, and I had been charged $75 apiece, while he was charged $105. "Why is my room more expensive than everyone else's?" he asked the clerk, and the clerk told him, "You had an ocean view."

Phil looked at me and grumbled. He was in his hotel room from 3:00 a.m. to 8:00 a.m. and never even opened the drapes. So much for Phil Siegel's first trip to Florida.

In the 15 years of Unicare's expansion, the company grew to include 145 homes across the United States and just over 10,000 beds. As we grew, one of our Milwaukee nursing homes inevitably got some bad press in the local newspaper. We had no one in place to respond, and I realized we needed to bring someone on board to handle our public relations. We no longer had the luxury of operating as a private company. So I called up Mitch Fromstein, a friend of mine who ran a PR and marketing firm in town. He assigned a young guy named Mike Mervis to see what the problem was. Mike today has a clear recollection of how we handled this:

> I had called the state regulators and the staff people at the nursing home. Then I went over to the facility. After walking through the building, and inspecting it top to bottom, I drove over to Towne Realty to meet with Joe Zilber and Danny Tishberg. They were holding one of their regular Saturday morning meetings. I gave them my report, telling them that things at the nursing home were not what they should be. "You have no security and you're understaffed," I said to them.

> Danny and Joe didn't believe it. So I said, "Okay, let's drive over there." We walked into the nursing home, and it was still nearly deserted. "We've got to do something," Joe said, and he did. He replaced the administrator, added more employees, and tightened up security operations. That's how Joe operates. When he sees he's wrong, he acts.

Before working for Fromstein, Mike Mervis had been in the radio business in Milwaukee. He was thinking about moving to Boston to accept a job in the radio business again. "You come over and talk to me before you think about leaving," I said to him one day. So he came over to the office and we sat down together. "What do you want to go to Boston for? I'll tell you what: why don't you work for me instead?" I pulled out a yellow legal pad and we worked out a deal.

Mervis turned down his radio job in Boston, and he's been with me ever since, working on marketing, public relations, and governmental relations. He's now vice president and the assistant to the chairman of the board, helping me with whatever we need to get done. Mike is as loyal a person as I possibly could know. He is my right hand. He's like a son to me, and I trust him implicitly.

❧ ❧ ❧

With all the deals I had done over the years, I could be a real character sometimes, but I was a crashing bore compared to one partner I had, Phil Cohen. Now *there's* a character.

I had first met Phil when I was a kid. I knew him in the Boy Scouts and at Temple Beth El in Milwaukee. Phil Cohen was in the toy business. He was the owner and founder of Wisconsin Toy and Novelty, a company that sold toys to union members in Wisconsin and Michigan at Christmas. Just after the holidays, sometimes right on New Year's Day, Phil would buy huge surplus inventories from the big toy manufacturers, companies like Hasbro and Mattel. Sometimes he would wait until after the national toy fair in February. Phil remembers:

> I'd get a call from Mattel, and I'd buy anything that they had left — overruns or toys they were discontinuing. I worked with one guy at Mattel named Lou Silverman. We called him "Captain Closeout." He worked in a suburb of L.A., and I would travel out there and he would show me samples. I might buy 100,000 items — a toy car or something. I'd pay $2 for each item, knowing I could probably get $4 for each one when they were sold.

Phil would have the merchandise trucked to an old Sears warehouse in Detroit and then sit on it. He'd take off for the summer and play a lot of golf. As the holiday season approached — October, November and into December — Phil would start searching for abandoned grocery stores or vacant shopping center space in Wisconsin and Michigan — Milwaukee, Kenosha, Detroit, Flint, Lansing, Pontiac — and sometimes Chicago. He'd open stores in these spaces — from November 15 to December 31, just for the holiday season — and sell toys at a big discount to union members and their families.

Phil's genius was timing. He had to know what price to set so it would sell by the holidays. As Christmas got closer and closer, he'd mark it down and mark it down until it sold. What he couldn't sell, he sold to discount chains — Toys "R" Us and Target and companies like that.

The concept really came about by accident. The workers at the Allis-Chalmers factory in Milwaukee were on strike one year around Christmastime. The union asked Phil if he could sell toys wholesale to union members, and Phil agreed. They had people standing in line for an hour in a snowstorm waiting to buy toys for their kids.

After the strike was settled, Phil made the same deal with other unions all over Milwaukee. Union members would shop at his stores because they knew they were getting a bargain that no one else could get. So they would load up on toys for everybody they knew. It was a great marketing strategy.

The unions loved him. In fact, the United Auto Workers talked Phil into doing the same thing with pharmacies, because they felt their workers were getting ripped off on prescription drugs. Phil opened three pharmacies in Milwaukee, and soon expanded into Kenosha and Detroit. He made that work, too, sticking strictly to prescriptions for union members and forgoing things likes cosmetics and toothpaste and all the other products that had such a high markup. Soon Phil had a chain of 20 stores, which he called Union Prescription Centers, and that's when I decided to try to get him to bring his businesses into Unicare.

After going public, Unicare began to venture into other types of businesses using public stock in our negotiations. Phil Cohen's pharmacies looked especially compatible with Unicare. I figured, if we merged with Phil, we could open a pharmacy in each of our nursing homes. It's what they today call "a good synergy." So I met with him and laid out my idea. He was open to a merger, but only if I acquired the toy company, too.

"But I don't want a toy company," I told him.

"Buy it anyway, and then in a year or two I'll figure out how to get us out of it," Phil said.

I agreed, and Phil and I began negotiations to merge his companies into mine. We arranged a meeting over lunch one day at the Milwaukee Athletic Club in downtown Milwaukee. Things weren't going too well in the negotiations. Phil got up to use the men's room, and I followed him in. "Phil, let's work this out," I said to him. "Let's settle on a price."

Standing at the urinal in the men's room we came up with a price we both could live with. The rest is history, as they say. From that day on, we began a partnership that developed into a lifelong friendship. Years later, at Phil's retirement party, we gave him a urinal from that club as a gift. I think he still has it stored somewhere in his garage.

After reaching an agreement with me, Phil Cohen came into our offices to finalize the deal. The closing ran late into the evening, and everyone was getting hungry. We ordered some food from a restaurant across the street. The food arrived, and the only person with money in his pocket was Phil. To this day, he complains about it. "I signed away all my business for a bunch of paper (Unicare stock) and I ended up paying for dinner besides," Phil says.

After Unicare bought Union Prescription and Wisconsin Toy, Phil Cohen became very much a part of our company. He went on to sit on our board of directors. He retained a 10 percent ownership interest, plus Unicare stock. The whole operation did very well — for us and for Phil Cohen.

Still, he likes to remind me that I never gave him a bump in pay. "I worked for Joe from 1968 until 1989 and never once got a raise," Phil says. "My deal was I was going to get $150,000 a year and 15 percent of the pretax profits over a million dollars." Phil takes me to task once in awhile for being a relentless negotiator. "He was hard driving and shrewd," he says. Phil could be just as shrewd. The ownership interest he received turned out to be exceptionally lucrative for him.

Phil lived quite a glamorous life in those years, flying across the country on business trips, wheeling and dealing — something he looked back on as he passed his 90th year: "I would fly first class wherever I went. I had an apartment in Detroit, and an apartment in New York, top location, 38th floor. I had a car and a chauffeur, and I'd go out to all the best restaurants. My expense account was more than anybody else's in the company, and it never was questioned. I remember I used to hand Unicare's accountants a grocery bag filled with all sorts of receipts. Drove them crazy."

Union Prescription Centers grew to the point where we had more than 100 pharmacies in 14 states. We filled millions upon millions of prescriptions each year. With the unions, we supplied customers with flu shots and bought two fully equipped vans to travel through the area checking people's blood pressure. I later hired Al Frank, the manager of my theaters, to run Union Prescription.

Although I initially didn't want to buy Phil's toy company, it worked out very well. It was a good partnership. I would finance the purchase of closeout toys, and Phil would sell them. Wisconsin Toy and Novelty became the largest closeout toy company in the United States.

A typical deal was the one we made with the Topper Corporation, a giant in the toy industry. Topper was known for making the Johnny Lightning toy cars and Dawn Dolls, a family of six-and-a-half-inch fashion dolls similar to the Barbie Doll line. Dawn Dolls were number one on the toy hit parade for awhile. The Dawn Doll was a star, with different hair colors and hair styles, different outfits and friends with names such as Angie, Gloria, Longlocks, and Jessica.

But Topper had over-produced the line. They made far more than they were able to sell. We bought the entire inventory of Dawn Dolls, 10 million of them. The inventory purchase was one of the largest ever made.

We hadn't expected to own so many toy dolls. In fact, between the clothing, wigs, accessories, and dolls themselves, we figured we almost had more pieces than the number of children in the country. I thought, how in the heck are we ever going to get rid of them? But we did. We sold them all, every last Dawn Doll we had. Just as I had learned years ago, there's always a deal waiting to be made.

CHAPTER 9

THE ART OF MAKING A DEAL

It's been said that I would rather make a deal than eat. I wouldn't argue with that.

I've made deals with a handshake and with the flip of a coin. Actually, I've settled pretty many with a coin. Once we were buying a building in Atlanta, and I couldn't settle on a price with the seller. We were off by $25,000. "Okay, we'll flip a coin for it," I said, and I won. Sometimes it works out. In fact, I don't think I've ever lost.

Many times the deals I put together are done over lunch or dinner, but I never carry a legal pad or notebook. I just sketch out the details on whatever's available — a napkin, or a placemat, or something — and hand it over to my senior managers to decipher and then write a contract. Jim Young, my general counsel, once laminated a placemat that I had used to draw up all the fine points of an agreement I'd made.

Jim had a heckuva time reading my scribbling, as he vividly recalls: "I asked myself, 'What in the world did Joe agree to?' We needed to formalize the deal, but we couldn't understand the writing on the placemat. Of course, Joe is absolutely no help because he's off making another deal. So I looked through the ketchup and the mustard stains and the gravy to find one-liners that Joe had put onto the paper, and to find initials so we could figure out who approved what. Some of Joe's best deals are made through this kind of documentation. It's confusing, but it works."

Not all of my deals end up working out, of course. They're not all good, but they average out. The college dormitories worked great. The movie theaters, not so great. I figure if seven out of ten deals turn out good, you're doing okay.

After forming Unicare, we began to diversify, moving into drug stores, toys, and more nursing homes, while Towne Realty continued with its theaters, dormitories, hotels, and other real estate projects. Unicare was in an acquisition mode. Anyone who came to us with what looked like a good business we considered buying. We were a public company and wanted to maintain the value of our publicly held stock, which we used to purchase new businesses. So I had my eyes open for companies that turned a profit. We acquired a medical laboratory, for example, which, in later years, developed a new method of doing blood tests.

We also were on the cutting edge of the fitness center craze in the late '60s. I had heard about a company called Fair Lady Figure Salons, which were high-end, high-style fitness clubs for women. Customers would buy memberships and had exclusive access to Fair Lady exercise programs, as well as whirlpools, steam baths, and massage rooms. Members worked out in fashionable exercise outfits, sweating off the pounds on treadmills and stationary bikes. After looking at this chain of clubs — two in Milwaukee and another in Madison — we decided to buy the company. Fair Lady became part of Unicare.

Opening new salons turned out to be quite expensive, and we never made a lot of money with the Fair Lady salons. We sold the chain after only a year. But as always, one thing led to another, and soon after we acquired the chain, we got a call from John Borman in Madison. I had worked with John a few years earlier to build student housing units, and now his daughter had gotten interested in physical fitness. She'd heard about a place in Madison called Elaine Powers Figure Salon and was thinking about buying a franchise.

I contacted the owner and founder of the fitness centers, Richard Proctor, a chiropractor in California. Proctor had started his first center in Santa Rosa in 1964, combining a dieting system with exercises for women — "figure contouring" is how he described it — something that seems pretty run-of-the-mill by today's standards. Back then it was a revolutionary idea, coming on the heels of the Weight Watchers program and predating *Jane Fonda's Workout Book*.

Proctor's concept caught on, and he grew the company into a chain of 300 franchised salons from coast to coast. The company ran an ad that offered a four-month program with unlimited visits to an Elaine Powers salon for $7.50. Some shops offered weight loss guarantees. For example,

Elaine Powers guaranteed that a woman who wore a size 14 dress would fit into a size 10 within four weeks, or she would receive six months' free membership. A woman who was a size 16 was guaranteed to be a size 12 within five weeks. A size 20 would be a size 14 in seven weeks, and so on. You get the idea.

As part of Unicare's plan to expand, I thought I'd pay a visit to Proctor, so I flew to Sacramento. Unicare was in the health care business, starting with our nursing homes, and we were looking for health care deals. Elaine Powers salons seemed to fit our strategy.

In a matter of weeks, a deal was struck. In September 1970, Unicare became principal owner of Elaine Powers salons across the country — the largest fitness salon system in the nation — with approximately two-thirds of the units owned by the company and the rest franchised. Eventually we introduced Elaine Powers' "Sensible Eating Formula": a 250 calorie meal replacement product sold in individual food packages. Meanwhile, Richard Proctor remained on as chairman.

Once again it was a thread of a past relationship that led to another deal. Like so many things I've done, there was a tie-in, a connection that spun me in another direction. In this case, John Borman had led me to a student housing project in Madison, and then he became a franchisee of Elaine Powers with his daughter. Before you know it, we had a multi-million dollar deal and fitness centers around the United States.

By the way, there was never really an "Elaine Powers." The name, invented by Richard Proctor, was a fictional character, like Betty Crocker.

The Elaine Powers chain was going great guns. At one point in the 1970s, we hired fitness guru Joanie Greggains to represent the Elaine Powers Salons. Joanie was the star of the nationally syndicated TV show *Morning Stretch*. She was also the author of a string of best-selling exercise books and produced fitness videos long before cable television and DVDs were popular. She was based in San Francisco, but audiences all around the country knew her and tuned in to her show. She would lead TV viewers through fast-paced exercise routines with the bouncy rhythms of rock music playing in the background. Joanie was the Jane Fonda of her time, an absolute dynamo, blonde and attractive, and the perfect choice for putting a public face on our company and promoting Elaine Powers on a national scale.

As we continued to diversify, a wide range of opportunities came our way, many of them not in the health care field. We changed the name of the company to Unicare Services Inc. to reflect our diversification. We owned a chain of small video rental stores, for example, called Video Exchange. We never expanded the business. We had a chance to be the first Blockbuster Video, but we missed it.

We decided to try the restaurant business. A guy named Duane Moen was a tenant in our company headquarters in downtown Milwaukee, 105 West Michigan Avenue. He ran a restaurant on the ground floor called the Sveden House. From time to time, I would get lunch at his restaurant, and Duane and I would talk business. The Sveden House company was based in Minneapolis, and Duane ran the Wisconsin franchises, with four restaurants in all.

"Why don't you join up with us as a partner, and we'll expand?" I said to him, and he did. With Duane Moen on board, we opened up two more Sveden House restaurants.

Sveden House was a smorgasbord restaurant — "all you can eat" for $3.99. The food counters were set up so that the salads were the first course, next were the soups, then the pasta salads and potato salads, things like that, followed by vegetables and mashed potatoes with gravy. At the very end of the counter was the meat. The idea was, you wanted people to fill up on salads and veggies and potatoes so they wouldn't have much room for the meat dish. The meat, of course, was the most costly to the restaurant.

The strategy didn't always pan out. Our customers knew a good deal when they saw it. Truck drivers would come in for lunch or dinner and go straight to the carved beef, bypassing the salads and the Jello and the vegetables. I used to stand there in the restaurant and get aggravated watching them empty the meat tray, but what could I do? And then there were the senior citizens. We created what we called a "Golden Agers Club," which allowed customers 62 and older to buy a dinner at reduced prices on Monday and Tuesday nights.

The idea backfired. Some members of the Golden Agers Club would come in carrying big, plastic-lined purses, or sometimes empty plastic bags. They would fill up their plates, go back to their table, scoop the food into their purses, and return to the counter for seconds and thirds. It became an under-the-table take-out (literally!) for these folks. Finally we hung up a sign: "Take all you want, eat all you take." Duane Moen used to go around with a ruler, tapping on the tables and reminding the customers: "Don't forget our slogan," but it seldom helped.

Sometimes they would smile and nod, but most of the time they just glared at Duane and he moved on through the restaurant. Between the food-hoarding old ladies and the starved-to-death truck drivers, our profits were quickly eaten away, so to speak, but such was life. Eventually we ended up selling the restaurants.

Duane Moen led us to another contact, and another business deal. Duane's brother was a pilot who flew a businessman named Ben O'Dell and his partner from site to site in their dealings. Duane viewed Ben O'Dell as a golden goose. Everything he did made money. Duane said, "You guys ought to just meet him." So my executive VP Jerry Stein and I arranged a meeting. O'Dell told us he was starting a truck wash franchise and he was looking for capital. He had plans to open three franchises in Wisconsin, and he called each of them Truck O'Matic. Remember, these were the days when franchises were a hot thing. The word "franchise" would always get our attention.

O'Dell was persuasive. As he explained it, there's no way to wash a semi-truck unless you've got a stepladder, extension hoses, and a lot of brushes. It's just a lot of trouble to wash a truck. So O'Dell took a regular carwash, enlarged it, and designed a machine that would clean a semi-truck or a bus. He considered the concept to be cutting edge, and he claimed it was going to knock the socks off everybody in the trucking world. After all, there were 20 million trucks and busses on America's highways at the time. The market was untapped. So we went into business with him.

Jim Janz, then our administrative vice president, had close dealings with O'Dell. He still talks about him:

> Ben O'Dell was a lay preacher. He held Wednesday night prayer meetings at his home and was a member of the Fellowship of Christian Athletes. The Milwaukee Brewers would invite him to do the pregame prayer meetings in the Milwaukee County Stadium clubhouse. He looked like he was this good, honest, cared-about-everything guy. So we wound up with the Truck O'Matics and a car wash chain O'Dell

developed called Sir Waxer. Both companies were part of Unicare. We hired people to sell franchises, and we paid to have the machines manufactured, but the businesses didn't make money. The royalties never quite caught up with the operating expenses.

❦ ❦ ❦

Sometime in 1978, Phil Cohen, my toy company and pharmacy partner, got a call from a businessman he knew in New York City named Sam Osman. Osman, in his early years, had been a pushcart peddler on the lower East Side of Manhattan. In the 1950s, he started a company called Job Lot Trading, a discount store that sold closeout merchandise. Osman sold thousands of brand name items that he had salvaged from unsuccessful sales promotions, government auctions, and bankrupt companies. "Our business is other people's mistakes," Osman once said. From tools, earrings, and candy bars to fishing poles, golf clubs, and cosmetics — you name it, Job Lot sold it.

With the success of Job Lot, Osman opened up another store nearby and called it The Pushcart. The construction of the World Trade Center in 1967 forced him to move to a location just off Wall Street, where he combined his two stores into one, Job Lot/Pushcart.

When he called Phil Cohen, Osman had health problems and wanted to sell his company. His business partner had died, and his partner's two sons had taken their father's place in the business. Sam knew they did not want to run the business, and he wanted to sell out so that his estate would not have to deal with the two sons after he died. Sam thought Phil Cohen might like to buy Job Lot/Pushcart.

"Sam was a terrific merchant," Phil remembers. "He calls me one day and he says, 'Phil, why don't you buy me out? I have cancer. I'm not going to live a year.' So Joe Zilber, Jerry Stein, and I went to New York, and over dinner we made a deal. It was a fantastic deal. We basically paid for Sam's store with Sam's own money — with all the money we made from Job Lot/Pushcart after we bought it. Sam had been doing $12 million a year. During the holiday season, we used to have to close the doors and let people in 10 or 15 at a time because it got so busy. We would have $100,000 days, and we were open seven days a week."

Job Lot turned into a fantastic business for us. It was very well established in New York, way before Wal-Mart came on the retail scene, and eventually we expanded with more stores in New York and New Jersey. People knew they could get good deals on anything. It was like an enormous bargain basement store actually, but it was a huge store — two stories, 11,000 square feet. There were carts and bins everywhere, filled to the top with merchandise. Hershey chocolate bars, for example. We would buy tons of them and sell them for 25 cents on the dollar. They would be gone in a few days.

I remember, around Christmas one year, a businessman came into the store and said, "Hey, I've got a problem. I ordered four hundred pounds of sausages from Germany and by mistake they sent me four *thousand* pounds of sausages. Now I've got thousands of sausages and don't know what to do with them all." We said, "Okay, let's see if we can sell them. Here's what we'll do: We'll take some of the sausages and display them in a cart at the cash register. We'll sell them for a $1 a pound, and we will give you 50 cents a pound. If those sausages sell within a half-hour, we'll buy all of them from you."

Sure enough, they went in 10 minutes and we bought all four thousand pounds of sausages. That's the kind of a store it was. We would buy anything — candy bars, brassieres, books, power drills, shoes, calculators, sunglasses, wrenches, work gloves, boxes of macaroni and cheese. Anything and everything.

A year or so later, we decided to expand beyond the single store in the financial district. We found a property in New York on Fifth Avenue and began to negotiate a lease. Sam Osman and I were in on the negotiations. Sam asked the landlord how long it would take to have the store ready for occupancy, and the landlord told him a year. "For you, that's a short time," Sam said. "For me, it's probably half of my remaining life." So I decided to bring in our own development and construction firm, KM Development, and the store opened six months later. It was a beautiful store.

As it turned out, Sam Osman beat the cancer and went back to work. Isn't it amazing? He cut a deal because he thought he was dying, then went back to work when he found out he wasn't. Sam lived another 20 years or so, passing away in 2000 at the age of 88.

In a deal separate from Unicare, Phil Cohen also got me to buy a ton of merchandise in the bankruptcy of Robert Hall Clothes. In its heyday, Robert Hall was the king of discount clothing and a pioneer of the "big box" store. They started out before World War II and grew into a giant success, in part because of their creative advertising. The company had a reputation of coming up with very catchy radio and television jingles. Les Paul, the legendary guitar player and songwriter from Waukesha, Wisconsin, wrote and recorded a handful of jingles for Robert Hall Clothing with his wife, Mary Ford, including one with this memorable lyric:

> "When the values go up, up, up,
> And the prices go down, down, down
> Robert Hall this season
> Will show you the reason
> Low overhead, low overhead!"

One day in 1977, Phil Cohen found out that Robert Hall was auctioning off its entire inventory in New York's Madison Square Garden. The clothing chain had 14 stores in Detroit. Because we operated toy stores in Detroit and had a lot of business connections in the city, Phil thought he could sell the merchandise and make a profit, but he needed cash to make a bid at the auction. He hadn't seen any of the inventories, but came to me looking for a cash deposit. Phil remembers it like it was yesterday:

> I went in to see Joe and I said, "I want a check for a half a million dollars. I want to go to New York and bid on this stuff." Joe said, "You're out of your mind" He never said yes, but he did give me the check. So I went to New York, and the Detroit inventory was the first one that came up in the bidding. Somebody came in very low. We raised the bid to 12 cents on the dollar. It went up to 14 cents, and we raised it again and bought it for 16 cents on the dollar.
>
> I went back to the Robert Hall stores in Detroit to look at the stuff. We'd bought millions of men's suits. To sell them fast, we started advertising. Starting at 30 percent off, we ran big ads on the television and in the newspapers: "Everything goes. Bankrupt." In the very first week we had all our money out. We made over a million dollars.

After the sale, we decided to give some of the odds and ends to a charity, but there was a slight problem. The charity called us and said, "Hey, some of the suit coats don't match the pants!" During our big sale, customers had grabbed anything that looked like a good fit for them. If they didn't buy something, of course, they didn't bother to put things back on the hangers. When the suits were boxed up after the scramble of the sale, nothing was put back in order, and different pants were mixed with different coats.

So we said to the charity, "We'll give you everything we've got left. Whatever money you can make, keep it all." And they were satisfied with that. All of this we did in under 30 days.

Phil Cohen would bring in deals like this all the time. With Phil, most of them worked out very well. Companies would approach us, too, interested in becoming part of the Unicare family. Unicare by then was a huge conglomerate, with subsidiaries across the country — from retirement centers to fitness salons, toy stores to pharmacies, discount merchandisers to truck washes, video stores to restaurants.

We listened to a lot of offers, but we also passed on a lot of offers, for one reason or another. Sometime in the early 1970s, just before we bought the Fair Lady Figure Salons, we met with the bodybuilder and TV star Jack LaLanne to talk about partnering with him on his health clubs. Nothing ever came of the proposal, but meeting Jack was special. He was in his late 50s at the time and in the peak of health. He was quite an impressive guy, and I'm sorry we couldn't work out a partnership with him. It would've been interesting.

In the earlier years, around the late '60s, we were approached by another company. The people at McDonald's restaurants were entering the Milwaukee market and wanted to know if we would be interested in buying a franchise in the city, on South 27th Street. Danny Tishberg and I talked it over and decided to pass. We thought, "Who's gonna want to buy a quality hamburger for 15 cents?" Well, I guess we now know the answer to that one — everybody! That store on 27th Street became McDonald's top store in the city.

My mistake was that I had never eaten a McDonald's hamburger. Maybe if I had, my decision would've been different.

Sometime in early 1985, I got another interesting offer. Henry Maier, the mayor of Milwaukee, called me one day out of the blue and asked if I would like to buy the Milwaukee Bucks basketball team. The Bucks were playing in the smallest arena in the NBA at the time, and the city didn't have the funds or political support to build a new one. The owners were hot on selling, though, and the people of Milwaukee were afraid some investor from outside of Wisconsin would purchase the team and move it out of Milwaukee.

It was a Friday when Mayor Maier called, and I was at my home in Hawaii. I had planned on returning to Milwaukee the following Monday to put together an offer for the Bucks, but when I got to the office, I found out my friend Herb Kohl had already bought the team! Herb was an extremely successful businessman. He had turned his family's grocery store business into a very popular chain of supermarkets and then built a chain of department stores bearing the family name. I had done a few real estate deals with Herb and his brothers Sid and Allen, and, of course, I had known their father, Max Kohl, from way back.

A few days after Herb made his offer, I got a telephone call from him. "Do you want to go in with me as a part owner of the Bucks?" he asked me. I wasn't interested. "Not for what you paid, Herb," I told him. "You paid too much."

It just goes to show how wrong I was. Herb bought the Bucks in 1985 for $19 million. In 2008, *Forbes Magazine* estimated the team to be worth $278 million.

Herb Kohl, now a United States senator, still owns the team. In hindsight, I could kick myself for passing on the deal, but I guess you can't always be right.

❧   ❧   ❧

For 15 years, starting at the ground up, we went full speed ahead with Unicare Services Inc. — taking it public, buying existing companies, creating new ones, and expanding the company coast to coast. We thought we could do it all, and for a longtime we *did* do it all. It was a hell of a ride. By 1983, Unicare Services had total assets of more than $173 million.

After awhile, I saw that it had become difficult to manage so many different types of businesses at once. This was on top of the hundreds of real estate transactions that Towne Realty was doing every year. The complexity of running Unicare was taking its toll on my relatively small management team — and on the company's bottom line.

One day in January 1983, I got a phone call from a third party representing Extendicare Ltd., a nursing home company based in Toronto. This caller said the company was interested in buying Unicare, and he wanted to set up a meeting. I didn't think much of the call at the time. Just another deal, I thought, and I asked my guys to take a look at this Extendicare outfit. As always, I was more interested in being a buyer than a seller. That was my approach, to buy businesses and expand our company.

My management team came back to me with some very impressive information: Extendicare had been acquired by Crown Life Insurance Company, one of the largest companies in Canada, with a history dating back to the mid-1880s. Crown was a huge conglomerate, with holdings in the billions of dollars and businesses in Great Britain and the United States. Extendicare had nursing homes throughout Canada and was expanding into the U.S.

This was serious. It didn't look like I could be the buyer this time. I told my team to set up a meeting with Extendicare so we could listen to what they had to say. With a couple of my guys, I flew up to Toronto and met with Harold Livergant, the president and CEO of Extendicare, along with two of his senior officers. Livergant told me they were interested in buying Unicare's nursing homes, and *only* our nursing homes.

I had a problem. What about all our other divisions — the toys, the fitness salons? "You'd have to buy the whole company to make it work for us," I said to him, and that began several months of negotiations. We finally came to an agreement on how to structure the sale: Extendicare would acquire all of Unicare's businesses and then transfer the non-nursing home assets back to our company. Extendicare's acquisition ultimately would only be the nursing homes.

During one of my last meetings in Toronto with Extendicare, CEO Harold Livergant tried to sell me a racehorse farm that he owned. I thought, racehorses? What in the world would I do with racehorses? I told Harold no thanks on the horse farm — and sold him my nursing home company instead. It's funny the direction things can take sometimes.

As part of the transaction, I set several conditions that were important to me at the time and, in hindsight, made a huge difference to the city of Milwaukee and the people who worked for me. Number one, Extendicare would have to keep all of Unicare's employees on their payroll. Number two, they would have to base their headquarters in Unicare's current offices in downtown Milwaukee. Number three, Towne Realty's design and construction division, KM Development, would be Extendicare's contractor of choice for any new nursing homes they built.

Extendicare agreed, and all of the conditions played out over time. As it happened, Guy Smith was the chief operating officer of Unicare when the sale was finalized. When Extendicare bought us out, he was hired to become Extendicare's president.

As I mentioned previously, I had discovered Guy years earlier when he was single handedly running a House of Pancakes in Milwaukee. I could see his potential, so I brought him in to Towne Realty and then moved him to our nursing home division. He worked his way up from there, and went all the way to the top in his field. Here's someone who impressed me when I met him and who rose to the occasion when I gave him an opportunity to prove himself. He had some of the same characteristics that I had when I was first starting out — drive, ambition, perseverance — qualities that I had learned from my parents long ago.

Guy Smith eventually left Extendicare to start a chain of assisted living facilities for seniors. I invested in his company and became a silent partner. Years later, when Guy decided to sell the operation, my share in his company proved to be one of the most profitable investments I ever made. Today Guy and I are talking about starting up another business together. We've had a friendship that spans four decades, and it has come full circle. All from that day at the House of Pancakes.

Extendicare's acquisition of Unicare was completed in July 1983 as a transaction of cash and bank notes for the Unicare stock. The offering for Unicare was set at $5.89 per share for all shares of Unicare stock — a long way from the $200 per share price that it was worth at its peak. As part of the agreement, we bought all the non-nursing home assets. I knew the added capital would help our balance sheet.

With the transaction behind us, it was time to move on and make some tough decisions. We now had to deal with the non-nursing homes companies — Elaine Powers, Job Lot/Pushcart, car washes, and all the others. But what to do with them? I called my team together, and we unanimously agreed to get rid of them all.

I knew it was the right move. We had learned enough about these businesses to know they were not the businesses we wanted to be in long term. I strongly felt that we needed to take the company focus back to real estate. So we began work on divesting what remained of the Unicare subsidiaries.

Some of them went smoothly. For example, we sold the Union Prescription Centers back to Extendicare in a later transaction. It made sense for Extendicare to operate the drug stores with their nursing homes.

Other deals were more of a challenge and took a lot of time, effort, and legal expense. The Elaine Powers Figure Salons, for example, became tremendously complicated. We had come up with a plan and thought we had our problems solved when one day I got a phone call from Tom Fatjo Jr. and Roger Ramsey, founders of the Houstonian in Houston, Texas. The Houstonian was one of the finest hotels in America, a beautiful, 23-acre luxury hotel and spa with more than 2,700 members, including then-vice president George H. W. Bush, who made a suite in the Houstonian his permanent Texas address. Tom Fatjo Jr. knew the vice president well. He had served on the President's Council for Physical Fitness under the Reagan and Bush administrations.

Fatjo and Ramsey had started Browning-Ferris Industries, or BFI, and grew it into one of the country's largest waste management companies. They took individual waste management operators from around the United States and put them under one umbrella to create a huge company. They wanted to do the same thing with the Houstonian and a group of fitness salons they bought called Livingwell. They believed our 300 Elaine Powers Salons would make a great opportunity for their mega-chain, but what they didn't have was capital.

They wanted us to loan them $10 million to buy the Elaine Powers Salons. We agreed to the loan predicated on the fact that we would get the $10 million back from a public offering that would occur as soon as the acquisition of Elaine Powers was completed. We agreed to the merger, and in 1985, we closed on the sale of Elaine Powers to the Houstonian. A year later, the public offering was completed and we got our $10 million back.

The president of this new company was a guy named Ron Hemelgarn, the founder of Livingwell. Hemelgarn was a colorful character. He owned a jet plane and a team that raced cars in the Indianapolis 500. One of his cars won the Indy 500 in 1996. I was a board member of the Houstonian, and soon after I met Hemelgarn, he asked me to approve Elaine Powers Salons as a sponsor for one of his race cars. I don't know much about racing, but Ron convinced me to fly down to Indianapolis to watch time trials on the car.

We went straight to Hemelgarn's auto shop from the airport. He had a number of cars in the garage, just frames and engines mostly, and none of the bodies had been painted yet. Ron illustrated how the Elaine Powers car would be painted, he showed me where the name Elaine Powers would go. He asked me whether I wanted my name painted on the car. He was laying it on thick, pushing for a sponsorship.

From Hemelgarn's shop, we went to the track. Ron had reserved the Miller Brewing luxury suite. Meeting us there was another Houstonian board member, Ahmed Mannai, who had invested with Tom Fatjo in previous deals. Mannai's home was in the country of Qatar, and he had offices in Paris and London. He was a real jet setter. We sat down for a catered lunch, and the cars were brought out onto the track one by one for the time trials.

Ron's car was wheeled out to the oval track, and around and around it went, noisy as hell. As we watched, Hemelgarn started pitching Ahmed and me to commit a quarter of a million dollars to sponsor his car. He was pushing us hard, so Ahmad and I decided to have a little fun with him. "I think it's a great idea. I'd go along with it," I said.

And then Ahmad would take the opposing side, playing the Devil's advocate. "I'm not so sure, Ron. I can't get behind it," he would say, and then I'd agree. "Maybe investing a quarter million isn't such a good idea after all," I'd say, smiling at him. Then we'd trade positions, switching sides, going back and forth, just playing with Hemelgarn.

Meanwhile, another car was wheeled onto the track, and it went screaming by us at a speed twice as fast as Hemelgarn's car. I couldn't believe it.

"Who's driving that car?" I asked Ron.

"That was Mario Andretti," he said.

"Well why doesn't the board sponsor *that* car?" I asked.

Hemelgarn said, "Mario Andretti doesn't drive for us."

The board of directors later approved sponsorship of one of Hemelgarn's car — without my vote, I might add. Like owning a race-horse, I just couldn't see approving an Elaine Powers race car. Since that day, whenever I watch an auto race, I have always cheered for Mario Andretti if he was in the race.

After the merger, everything was going great for awhile for Elaine Powers and Livingwell, but soon the company got too big too fast, and the management team just was not capable of dealing with such fast growth. By the end of 1986, the salons were losing money by the millions. Livingwell filed for bankruptcy in 1989, and the whole affair turned into a drawn-out legal drama that went on for 10 years as the company and its lawyers fought with the bankruptcy trustee. In the end, matters went into mediation, with nobody being completely satisfied, concluding the saga of Elaine Powers Figure Salons.

❦ ❦ ❦

Selling our Job Lot stores ended up being just as tough. As I've said before, I'm a buyer and not a seller, but I had agreed to sell the companies in the Unicare deal. We found a company in Southern California that sold closeout merchandise, and we worked out a sale. It was a way out for us. The company, Pic 'N' Save, was one of the largest closeout retailers in the country. They bought our company.

A couple of years after the deal, Pic 'N' Save came back to us and said they were closing many of the stores. As we negotiated with them to avoid getting stuck with empty rental space, Phil Cohen put us in touch with a businessman in New York that he knew from the toy industry named Ike Perlmutter.

Perlmutter was known at the time for buying troubled companies. He went on to become CEO of Marvel Entertainment, the comic book company. We thought he might be interested in Job Lot, and he was. In 1990, we cut a deal with Perlmutter to buy our leases on the stores. Our next step was getting him together with the Pic 'N' Save people and ne-gotiating a deal for the merchandise. It was an all-day negotiation, with all the parties meeting in Milwaukee. We went back and forth between Perlmutter and the Californians, but we finally made it happen.

Ike Perlmutter wasn't any more successful than we had been with running Job Lot, and the business eventually folded. However, we were still the guarantor on the leases for one Job Lot store on Nassau Street in New York. The owners pursued us relentlessly for unpaid rentals. We went to New York to negotiate and tried to get them to agree to a sum of $780,000 payable over three years.

Well, they insisted on $800,000, and for a difference of $20,000 the whole deal began to unravel. They wouldn't budge and I wouldn't budge. Finally I suggested settling it the old fashioned way — with the flip of a coin. I let the owners call it, and they called heads. I flipped the coin into the air and nobody in the room breathed. It fell into my hand, and guess what? It came up tails. Score another one for the kid.

❧❧ ❧❧ ❧❧

We were then left with one non-nursing home asset, Wisconsin Toy and Novelty, but instead of selling off Wisconsin Toy, my partner Phil Cohen had the idea that he wanted to take the company public. The toy company had grown to 50 stores in some 30-plus states, and the stores were turning a profit. How could I say no? The public offering was finalized in March 1987.

Soon after the public offering, Phil saw an opportunity to purchase another retail company, Everything's A Dollar. Phil's son Jay was working with Job Lot at the time and had seen an Everything's A Dollar store in Virginia Beach, Virginia. It was one gigantic store, loaded with merchandise. The store sold everything — giftware, books, toys, cosmetics — and each item cost no more than one dollar. Jay persuaded his father to take a look at the place, and Phil liked what he saw.

Phil decided to wait and keep his eye on the business, thinking they might overextend themselves and get into trouble. That's exactly what happened. A year later, after expanding with a couple more stores on the East Coast, Everything's A Dollar was going down the tubes, headed for bankruptcy. So we went in and made a deal with the owners and the creditors. It was a win-win proposition. We offered to pay the creditors 50 cents on the dollar. The creditors went for it. They would have lost millions if the company had gone bankrupt. It was a winning offer for the two owners. They needed capital to keep their stores afloat and provide additional capital for expansion.

Everything's A Dollar became part of our public company, Wisconsin Toy. We changed the name to Value Merchants Inc., or VMI for short. We brought in a new person as a chief operating officer to run the company. He was a younger guy who came highly recommended, and soon he was made the CEO. He turned out to be overly ambitious and clashed with Phil and some of the other principals. He wanted a clean sweep of the company and didn't want to have to deal with the "old timers" like Phil Cohen. He was wrong. Phil quit and sold his stock, and others resigned from the board. VMI continued to grow but at a pace that was way too fast. By fall 1995, VMI was out of cash. It filed for bankruptcy the next year.

That was it for Unicare Health Services Inc., from its beginning as a public company in 1968 with 10 nursing homes to its culmination, the liquidation of its non-nursing home subsidiaries. We took the good with the bad. Today Extendicare, the buyer of our health care facilities, continues to successfully operate in its Milwaukee headquarters. My long-time partner Phil Cohen is happily retired he and his wife Mickey split their time between homes in Milwaukee and South Florida. But like me, Phil cannot completely stop working. You'll find him doing deals now and then, sometimes on his own, and sometimes for a California toy company that is run by his son.

Meanwhile, the pharmacy company that we sold to Extendicare proved to be successful and was eventually acquired by the Walgreens Company. Several of the Sveden House smorgasbords that we owned and eventually sold are still doing business (to the pleasure, no doubt, of many hungry truck drivers and Golden Agers). The Video Exchange stores, the car washes, and the truck washes are gone, and the Elaine Powers Salons are only a memory, though when we owned them, they were on the forefront of the fitness craze and very likely inspired hundreds of thousands of people to take better care of themselves.

We expanded into all kinds of business over the years, for many reasons. Some of these businesses were a stretch for us, but we looked at each of them seriously and weighed our decisions carefully when considering the opportunity. Was it the right business? Was it a business we wanted to be in?

In the end, we always came back to real estate. It's what we do best. Building and selling real estate, that was always our core business. And now, finally, after nearly 25 years of looking at other businesses, we're back at operating as a pure real estate company. The journey outside of real estate was interesting, but it was good to be back.

CHAPTER 10

GAS PAINS AND
250,000 BALL BEARINGS

In all my years of making deals, a few have gone bad. Actually, more than a few. Some have been outright disasters. We took on bad partners, or made bad decisions, or maybe we were just a little too eager to put together a deal. Sometimes people tried to take advantage of us, or cheat us, and we had to fight back. It wasn't always smooth sailing. You try to put the bad projects behind you and go on.

Sometimes, looking back, the mistakes can be entertaining. I remember shaking my head and laughing about one particular job: we had a contract to build a swimming pool at a country club. Workers built the pool and — don't ask me how — it didn't have a deep end. They dug the hole, lined it with concrete, put a diving board over the shallow end, and that was it. Obviously, the country club wasn't too happy about it. A construction crew had to tear out the pool and start over, this time with a deep end.

On another project, workers built a two-story house and put in a stairway, but for some reason, they neglected to raise the ceiling on the second floor above the stairway. So when you walked up the steps, you knocked your head into the ceiling before you'd even get upstairs. Mistakes happen.

One of the more frustrating projects we ever did was a church designed by Frank Lloyd Wright, the famous Annunciation Greek Orthodox Church in Milwaukee. A local developer had started the project, but he had some problems and came to Towne Realty for help. We put the

developer in touch with our commercial construction company, the
Woerfel Corporation, and Woerfel took over the job.

The Greek Orthodox Church was Frank Lloyd Wright's last church
design and one of his very last commissions. In the years that it took to
build, Wright certainly lived up to his reputation as being a cantanker-
ous SOB. It seemed like he'd come to the construction site every Friday,
look at the work the construction crews had done in the past week, and
say, "Rip it all apart and do it over." An interior wall, or a ceiling support
— whatever it was, the workers would have to rebuild it according to
Wright's new specs. It was a real learning curve for Woerfel, but that was
Frank Lloyd Wright.

The church was a circular structure with a concrete domed roof, 106
feet in diameter. It was just enormous. To top it off, the leaders of the
church wanted the roof to rotate, so Wright had come up with a design that called for the dome to rest on a circular track that contained
250,000 ball bearings. Two hundred fifty thousand ball bearings! It was
a unique design, Frank Lloyd Wright at his best, but it just was not possible to build. Workers would set the ball bearings into place, line them
up, and seal them into the dome, and they'd start falling down when the
roof turned. I thought we'd never get done with that job. It was extremely complicated, and no matter what we tried, we never could get that
roof to turn.

The building turned out to be beautiful, just stunning, a true landmark
— even though its rotating roof never rotated. I'd had enough of Frank
Lloyd Wright. If he had asked me to build another building for him, I
would have turned him down cold.

Wright was a pussycat compared to the Disney Corporation. In the
late 1980s, we became a subcontractor on the construction of the Grand
Floridian at Disney World in Orlando. This was Disney's premier property, a five-star restaurant and hotel on a lake. You can see it as you enter the park, a huge, white building. We were hired to do all the siding,
railings, and a number of windows, basically the exterior envelope of
this 900-unit hotel, and time was of the essence. Our people were working very long hours, putting in lots of overtime — all at the request of
Disney. We finished the job according to Disney's timetable.

A few weeks after completing the work, we noticed that Disney was
billing us for installing what they said was inferior cedar siding. They

claimed the fire retardant in the cedar wood was discoloring the white paint. We knew that wasn't true. We had been given a certain specification by the contractor, and we had met that specification. So we filed an application for final payment, but Disney refused to pay.

They claimed we did a defective installation, and they filed a claim against us for five million dollars. So we filed a countersuit for the two-and-a-half-million dollars that they owed us, plus attorneys' fees. We consulted a lot of experts about the fire treatment, and we felt we had produced the proper wood with the proper treatment. Disney was adamant, though; they didn't believe us and took a very hardnosed position against us.

Disney, as we later learned, had a reputation for breaking subcontractors. They were the 900-pound gorilla in the Orlando real estate market at the time. They played like a bully, and the more we worked with them, the more we realized that this would be very difficult to resolve.

Months and months later, after all kinds of depositions were taken, we were not any closer to settlement. Then one day, our construction manager Don Mantz made a business trip to Orlando. Don remembers:

> I decided to visit the job site before catching my plane home. I had a few hours to spare, and I needed to see for myself what Disney was saying as being a major problem. While I was walking around the buildings, I could hear a water compressor. So I walked around the hotel, and here is this gentleman spraying the white siding with a power washer. The sprayer was forcing the water upward and into the inside of the siding. In addition to that, I could smell ammonia.
>
> I asked the worker what he was doing, and he told me that since the building had become occupied, his job was to spray the siding with this water-and-ammonia solution to make it look nice and white. He basically was bleaching the siding, and the solution was leaching through the white paint and deteriorating the wood underneath. I called our attorney, and he said I had found the smoking gun.

Suddenly, Disney did an about face. They saw it was their own fault. Their own people had inadvertently caused the problem. We ended up in mediation with Disney and collected our two-and-a-half-million dollars plus attorneys' fees, which were costing us about $50,000 dollars a month.

In retrospect, some of the deals that bombed are pretty amusing. At the time, they were huge disappointments, but today I can only laugh. Here's an example. When we ran the Elaine Powers Figure Salons, members would keep track of their weight. Elaine Powers, after all, was a weight control program. We came up with an invention that we thought our customers would love. We designed an exercise machine that recorded a member's weight gain or loss and then, in a computerized voice, would tell the person the results every time she used the machine. It was a talking machine, literally. It could tell you whether you had gone up or down in pounds since the last workout.

All of our salon members were women, of course, and they didn't like it one bit. A woman did not want to hear her weight announced to every living soul in the salon every time she stepped onto the machine. Our idea was an absolute flop.

We had another brainstorm that was worse! With our partner in the salons, Dr. Richard Proctor, we developed a high-protein diet supplement called Shape, a powdered substance that you'd mix with water. You'd drink it and lose weight. Elaine Powers was a great brand name, and we thought we could compete with Slim Fast, which had come onto the market a few years earlier. We thought we were on to something. We'd sell it in the salons and make some money.

It didn't work out that way. It tasted great, just like a milkshake, but there were a few unpleasant side effects. Mike Mervis, our public relations and marketing director at the time, still remembers when we tested the stuff:

> We were just about to roll it out and Joe had been all excited about it. "Oh, it tastes great," he said. "It'll be a big hit. We'll be able to sell the hell out of it." So we had some samples delivered to the office. It came in three flavors — vanilla, chocolate, and strawberry — and all the office girls wanted to try it. They drank the samples for a few days and then all of a sudden stopped, but nobody wanted to say anything to Joe.

> Then, finally, one of the girls had the guts to go up to him and say, "You know, that diet drink really tastes good, Mr. Zilber, but I'm afraid it's giving people gas." Imagine what a mistake it would have been to have the drink in all our salons. Not a dozen women but *thousands* would have been stricken with terrible, terrible flatulence.

> The manufacturer tried to reformulate the ingredients, but whatever it was that gave people gas also gave it its good flavor, so it ended up tasting too chalky. This was going to be a big seller, the diet drink of all diet drinks — and it gave everybody gas.

That was the end of Shape. When we moved out of that office building, there were still cases and cases of the stuff in the basement storage room. Not our best idea, that's for sure.

Then there's the story of Ken Alles and the Fiats. Kenny had been a contractor for Towne Realty in Milwaukee. We provided land and financing to him, and he built houses. He moved to Florida after awhile, and in the early '70s got us started in Florida real estate. Kenny was a buddy of mine, a real character, footloose and fancy free. It seemed like he worked out of his car most of the time.

Once in awhile, Kenny flew over to Freeport in the Bahamas to gamble and do some business. One day he called me with a deal. "Joe," he said. "I've got a chance to buy 500 Fiat convertibles for $1,000 each. Little two-seater sports cars, Fiat Spiders. They're worth around $10,000 apiece."

"How can you get them so cheap?" I asked him.

"They were on a barge in Philadelphia," Kenny said. "There was some kind of accident and the cars fell into the harbor. They were salvaged, but because they got wet, the catalytic converters are shot and the EPA won't allow them to be sold in the United States. I figured I could sell them off shore, maybe in the Bahamas. So I told the owners I'd take them off their hands for a half a million dollars, and they agreed. Joe, you put up the money and I'll sell the cars."

I wasn't so sure I wanted to be a car dealer, but Kenny could be awfully persuasive. I thought to myself: for $1,000 a car, how can I go wrong? So I wrote out a check for a half a million dollars and sent it to Kenny.

A month went by with no word from Kenny on how the cars were selling. Finally I decided to investigate. Jerry Stein, my CEO, was planning on a business trip to the Bahamas to meet with Kenny about another deal. "I guess you better see what's going on with the Fiats," I said to Jerry.

When he got to the Bahamas, he asked Kenny about the cars. Looking a little sheepish, Kenny took him to a car lot somewhere in Freeport. There sat the Fiat Spiders, rusted out and ruined from the salt water they'd been submerged in. The deal was a bust. Kenny was out of the car business, and I was out a half million bucks.

⁂ ⁂ ⁂

We're in the development business and we put up buildings. That means we move around a lot of dirt, excavating sites for foundations, grading property, things like that. We never know what might be hidden underground. I can think of a time in Sparks, Nevada, a suburb of Reno, where we had built a Mini-Price Motor Inn. About a half a mile from our property, at a railhead, there were a number of fuel storage tanks owned by several oil companies, Texaco, Shell Oil, and a few others. The tanks contained petroleum and gasoline that was distributed to the residents of Reno.

Meanwhile, right next to our Mini-Price was a quarry owned by the city of Sparks. It was abandoned and filled with water. The city had planned to develop the quarry into a recreational lake. One day somebody noticed oil slicks on the water surface. Nevada's Division of Environmental Protection was called in and they found excess oil and gasoline from the "tank farm" contaminating the lake. The state was concerned that the slick would make its way into the nearby Truckee River, a pristine river that originates near Lake Tahoe and is the main source of drinking water for Reno.

Soil samples were taken and water tests were done. The state said oil and gasoline were traveling from the tank farm to the underground water table and into the quarry. Our Mini-Price was in a direct line between the oil tanks and the quarry. If the oil and gas contaminated the groundwater beneath our property, it would hurt our chances of selling the property someday. So we filed a lawsuit against the oil companies, the railroad, and nearly a dozen companies who used the tank farm. A dozen property owners in the area filed lawsuits separately.

In the course of our investigation, Jim Young, our in-house general counsel, talked to an individual who worked at the tank farm. This employee told Jim that the companies who used the tanks — basically all of the defendants in the case — were negligent in turning off the spigots. It was the evidence we needed — an eyewitness.

It turned into quite a case. For each of the depositions, there were over a dozen plaintiffs and a dozen defendants, along with their lawyers. So, over time, there must have been 25 or 30 lawyers on the defendants' side, charging up to $500 an hour. We had just one guy that we hired from a Reno law firm who was at $250 an hour. We entered into mediation, and at first, the oil companies laughed at us.

They soon realized, however, that this was a big problem. In fact, at one time, the state of Nevada said if it hadn't been discovered, the leakage could have been one of the worst environmental disasters in the state's history. Fortunately, the mess was cleaned up in time and the contamination was limited.

As it turned out, we ended up with a settlement of $5 million. Bottom line, it was a well-deserved but unexpected windfall. It was like striking oil and gas on our property without having to drill for it.

Towne Realty ran into yet another environmental problem right in our own backyard. As with the property in Nevada, we weren't at fault and it all worked out in the end, but it was a legal and ecological nightmare that dragged on for almost 40 years. In the early 1970s, we bought a large piece of land along Lake Michigan called Marina Cliffs in the city of South Milwaukee. It was a beautiful piece of property overlooking the lake that we planned to develop.

One day sometime in the 1980s, we got a notice from the U.S. Environmental Protection Agency. They had discovered abandoned barrels and 55-gallon drums that had been left behind by the former owner of the site. The EPA did some testing and found that quite a few of these barrels and drums had once been filled with oil, gasoline, paint, and other industrial wastes. From the barrels, potentially toxic chemicals like lead, chromium, and PCBs had leached into the soil.

The EPA believed portions of our property were contaminated and the agency was designating it a "Superfund" site. Superfund was a program in which the government identified and cleaned up some of the worst hazardous waste sites in the country, usually at the expense of the polluter. No developer in the country wanted to be near a Superfund site.

We had this big, thick report from the EPA, and we really didn't know how to handle it. I thought, "Well, we're eventually going to want to develop this property. We better figure out who's responsible." We went to the Wisconsin Department of Natural Resources and told them we wanted to get rid of these barrels, and they put us in touch with a firm that did this kind of environmental remediation. The firm estimated it would cost $50,000 to clean up the property. When they went in, they located more barrels and drums buried underground than they expected, hundreds and hundreds of containers.

The estimated cost of the cleanup jumped to $100,000 at that point. We had little choice. We told them we needed to get the site cleaned up so we could go back to the EPA and have Marina Cliffs removed from the Superfund list.

As the remediation company got deeper into the project, it found buried pits where chemicals and paint had been dumped. Three giant pits were discovered that had been covered up over the years by dirt and grass and trees. At that point, we thought, this is getting out of hand. We didn't pollute the site, all we did was buy it. Here we were, getting into expenses of maybe $200,000 or more. It would eventually run into the millions.

Towne Realty's in-house attorney, Jim Young, hired an investigator to look into the history of the site. Jim is a terrific attorney. He's dedicated and hardworking. Well, the investigator informed Jim that a company named Northwestern Barrel Company had owned the land from the early 1940s until 1964. The company's 14-acre site was the largest barrel recycling facility in the Midwest.

It turned out that there were probably 200 companies that trucked or shipped by rail thousands and thousands of barrels of hazardous waste to this plant. Jim, now a senior vice president and general counsel, worked on the Marina Cliffs case from the start and remembers it vividly:

> We got old aerial photographs of the site. There were barrels everywhere, all around the property — along dirt roads that crisscrossed the site, in the woods, down a ravine that led to the lake. In the aerial photos, you can see this recycling plant with a railroad spur running to it. Northwestern also had a fleet of trucks that went around the Midwest to factories like Chrysler, Pittsburgh Paint & Glass, and 3M, picking up chemical waste stored in barrels and 55-gallon drums. Northwestern would haul the barrels and drums back to their site, empty them out, clean them, and resell them. Whatever material was inside was dumped into one of the pits.

During the course of all this, Jim Young got a call from out of the blue from a guy who had once worked for Pittsburgh Paint & Glass. This former PPG employee told Jim that every week or so he would load up a truck with 55-gallon drums that contained paint that had been rejected because the colors weren't right, then deliver the drums to the Northwestern Barrel site and dump them into the open pits.

This was damning information, yet another smoking gun. As Jim and our investigator collected more evidence of this kind, we could see that Towne Realty had to take strong legal action to protect itself.

"We put these 200 companies on notice that we had a contaminated site and that they were culpable parties who had to help clean up this site," Jim continues. "The companies sent us letters back saying, 'You're crazy. We're not going to pay you a nickel.' This dragged on and on for years. Of course, our position was 'You guys are the ones who contaminated it, all we do is own it. We're innocent purchasers and we shouldn't be liable.' The Marina Cliffs Apartments that we had originally purchased claimed the apartment site was contaminated and they ended up suing us. So between what we ended up paying for the initial clean-up and the attorneys fees — fighting litigation by the homeowners, fighting with the liable companies, and then pushing the EPA to get this done — we ran up six, seven hundred thousand dollars worth of expenses."

A meeting was arranged at a Milwaukee hotel with Towne Realty, the EPA, the Wisconsin Department of Natural Resources, and the companies that were identified as potential polluters. The EPA basically said, "If you guys don't get together and clean up this site, we're going to sue you all." So the companies grudgingly came to the table and agreed to pay a figure that exceeded $20 million.

Today the clean-up at Marina Cliffs is completed. From the beginning, we had worked with the EPA and the State of Wisconsin to get our property restored to the condition it was in before it got contaminated, but the companies responsible wouldn't own up to it. Instead, they stonewalled for decades. As 2009 came to a close, it was finally time to finish the development we had started in the 1970s.

The Marina Cliffs saga certainly was discouraging. It took us by surprise and seemed to go on forever. However, the most painful moment of my professional life was the collapse of a high-rise we were building in Cocoa Beach, Florida. Even today, it's difficult for me to talk about.

Towne Realty was constructing a luxury condominium project called Harbour Cay on Highway A1A. It was a brand new building, one of two that would be built along the Banana River in Cocoa Beach. It was March 27, 1981, a Friday afternoon. Workers were topping out the building, pouring the concrete for the roof on this five-story condo. It should have been a day of celebration, but at around 3:00 p.m., without warning, the building collapsed. Tons of concrete came crashing down, taking down dozens of workers in the wreckage.

Within an hour, hundreds of rescue workers converged on the site, including Air Force personnel from nearby Patrick Air Force Base. Two heavy-duty cranes were brought in from the Kennedy Space Center to remove enormous concrete slabs from the lower floors, but the casualties were many. A total of 11 people lost their lives, nearly all of them construction workers. Another 27 people were injured.

At the time, it was the worst construction accident in Florida's history. Questions were raised about the quality of construction materials used on the project. What happened? How could a huge building just collapse? We had worked with the contractors before. They knew what they were doing. We knew they had followed the plans. Were the specs wrong?

The architect and engineer we had hired were questioned by the Occupational Safety and Health Administration, and eventually the engineer, who once worked as a NASA engineer, surrendered his license to the State of Florida, responding to charges by the state's Department of Professional Regulation. When the investigations were completed, Towne Realty was exonerated of any wrongdoing in the collapse. Still, it was devastating to all of us at Towne. It was the first time anyone had been killed on one of our construction projects.

Shortly after the collapse of Harbour Cay, we hired engineers to inspect three other condominium projects we had built that had been designed by the same engineer. People were living in these condos, and we wanted to make sure the buildings were safe. After a thorough inspection and some minor repairs, our consulting engineers reported that the buildings complied with the highest standards of construction.

The name of that Banana River condo was changed to Fountain Cove, and a new building eventually was put up at the same location, but that accident is a sad and haunting memory, and I'll always think of that site as Harbour Cay.

❁ ❁ ❁

Years ago we remodeled the old Blatz Brewery Brew House in downtown Milwaukee. Dating back to 1846, Blatz was the third largest brewery in Milwaukee at one time, and the first to sell its beer nationally. It closed down in 1959, the first of Milwaukee's breweries to go out of business. A company out of Minneapolis contacted us in the '80s. We cleaned the Cream City brick on the exterior of the building and converted it into apartments.

It was the oddest thing I ever built. Much of the space inside the Brew House had been used by Blatz for grain storage — huge empty spaces, with no floors. When we renovated, we put in full floors to create a 12-story apartment building. The windows, though, had been installed by Blatz when the building was originally constructed. Our floors, of course, had to meet very specific ceiling-height requirements, but the existing windows didn't always line up with the floors.

So you'd have windows at different heights, depending on what floor you were on. Some units had windows in the middle of the wall where they belonged, some were way up high near the ceiling, and some were at floor level. You'd have to see it to believe it. It was quite a job, but we built it up and rented out the units. Needless to say, we had to come up with a very creative marketing program.

Then there's the story of Al Hubbard. Al had been working for us as an independent contractor for years and years, doing small construction jobs, hauling away scrap lumber, things like that. Al was a good partner. He followed his contracts to a T. One of Al's jobs was the demolition of older, small buildings. One day Al came to the office with an invoice asking for $500, which was what he was supposed to get paid to tear down a garage on 22nd Street in Milwaukee. The people in the front office noticed that Al's bill was for tearing down a garage on 23rd Street, not 22nd.

"Al you wrote down the wrong address on the invoice," they told him.

"No, I didn't," he answered. "The garage I tore down was on 23rd Street."

The bookkeeper immediately came to my partner, Dan Tishberg, and me. I looked at the invoice and turned to Danny. "Now what?" I said to him. Without hesitating, Danny picked up the phone, found out who owned the 23rd Street property, called the owner, who lived in California, and bought the property over the telephone before the owner ever knew his garage was gone. Everybody was happy. Including Al Hubbard, who got paid a second $500 to tear down the right garage, on 22nd Street. All's well that ends well.

Over the years, for some reason, we've seemed to run into our share of problems with bulldozers.

Sometime in the 1990s, Towne Realty was working on a housing project in Hawaii near Mililani. There was an old farm road down in a valley, and up along the sides of the valley there were huge pineapple plantations. We had a Caterpillar moving around dirt on the side of a hill, punching in a road, and a small area of the hill started to slide. No one was hurt, but suddenly, at the base of the small landslide, somebody saw an arm or a leg of a skeleton.

Of course, the whole project came to a screeching halt. The Hawaiian workers refused to continue. The authorities had to be notified as well as the police, the medical examiner, and historical groups. Before you know it, our project was delayed for almost two weeks. As it turned out, the skeleton was not of historical nature. It was not a native Hawaiian. It could very well have been a World War II victim, because we were working not far from the harbor off Ford Island, which was one of the places hit at Pearl Harbor.

Before the Hawaiian construction crews returned to work, they held a ceremony to purify and bless the site. It's something their religion dictates. A kahuna, or priest, was summoned to deliver his prayer in native Hawaiian tongue, and a number of local dignitaries were invited. The engineers and the architects came, a gathering of maybe 50 people. After the blessing, it's customary to have kind of a luau, so there was a tent and refreshments and Hawaiian music. Then after an hour of celebration, everybody finally got back to work.

Another time, I went in on a deal with a well-known Milwaukee developer named Gene Posner. Gene was a contemporary of mine, just a couple of years older than me. We both went to the same high school and got our law degrees from Marquette Law School. Like me, he got his start in real estate after World War II. Gene died in 2005 at age 90. He was a wonderful guy. We played poker together once in awhile, and from time to time our paths would cross in the real estate business.

One day Gene approached me about developing some property for a Kmart store on the west side of town.

"You want to go in on this deal?" he asked me.

"Yeah, I'll go in," I said. "When do we start?"

"They have to do some soil testing. I'll let you know when it's done."

Gene hired a construction company to do the soil boring on the land, and they sent a bulldozer out to drill the cores. Gene never told me that much of the land was either marshland, or just swamp, and as the bulldozer drove onto the marshland, the land underneath suddenly gave way. The operator jumped off, ran to his pickup truck, drove to a gas station, and called his boss. His boss told him to hire a tow truck and have the 'dozer towed out of the swamp, but by the time the tow truck got to the property, the bulldozer was gone. It had disappeared into the ground.

A couple of weeks passed, and I hadn't heard from my friend Gene. So I gave him a call.

"Gene, how's the deal going?" I said.

"Well, there might be a problem with the land, Joe," he said. "I'll get back to you."

A couple more weeks passed and I called Gene again.

"What's going on with the land, Gene? One of my guys drove by and says there's nothing going on out there."

"Well, Joe, I'm not sure if this deal is right for me, to tell you the truth. Maybe you'd want to take the whole thing and do the project on your own."

"I don't know. It's possible, but I'd have to think about it. How did the soil tests go, by the way?"

There was a long silence on Gene's end of the phone.

"Gene, I said how did the soil tests go?"

Finally Gene answered: "Not well. Not well."

We never did that deal, and as far as I know, they never got that bulldozer out of that swamp.

We were ahead of the curve on many of the businesses we got into. Video rentals, for example. We started our Video Exchange stores just as renting videos was taking off. We were also one of the first to develop the pager. We called it the Pagette, and we marketed it to doctors; they could be paged while on the golf course, or wherever. At the time, doctors didn't want to use a pager, so we didn't pursue it. I have one of the first devices in a display case at my office. It was a forerunner to beepers and cell phones and all that.

If there was a business we thought we could run better than somebody else, we tried it. If there was ever a company for sale that looked like it could make money for us, we bought it. If it didn't work, we got out. You'd have a bad day and you'd move on. That's how we built up Unicare as a public company. If there was a good deal to make, we'd make it. That was always my philosophy.

Some things are more emotional, partnerships in particular. You find someone who you thought would be a good partner and a good person, but it ends up they're neither, and that can hurt.

I've taken on my share of bad partners, people who didn't live up to expectations. You don't always know where a partnership is heading, and you certainly don't know at the outset. In some cases, I got into partnerships with guys who were not completely reputable. In fact, some of them turned out to be con artists and crooks. They oversold themselves and, unfortunately, I believed what they told me. I've always liked the challenge of working with somebody that nobody else could. It's that appeal of helping out the little guy, helping out the underdog. I wanted to give them a chance. Like I've said before, I've been a risk taker, but on a few occasions, that philosophy cost me.

One of my most disappointing partnerships was with a Milwaukee music promoter named Joe Balestrieri. He operated Alpine Valley Music Theater, an outdoor amphitheater near Lake Geneva, Wisconsin. I was introduced to him by his father, Tony Balestrieri, a helluva nice guy. I had sold one of Unicare's mini nursing homes to Tony, and he converted it into a center for autistic children. It's a wonderful program that still exists today. At the time, the late, '80s, the Riverside Theatre that I owned in Milwaukee had gone dark. I was looking for someone new to promote shows, and Tony put me in touch with his son Joe, and I hired him to run the Riverside.

Joe Balestrieri and his wife, Leslie West, founded a company named Joseph Entertainment Group. They had expanded Alpine Valley from a capacity of 25,000 to nearly 40,000, making it one of the largest outdoor venues in the Midwest. They began booking big-name acts like The Rolling Stones, The Who, and the Grateful Dead. (My son and daughters informed me that these acts were the hottest acts on Earth, but I didn't know them from Adam.)

Joe Balestrieri was making the same mistake that many others had done before him — growing his company too big too fast. He was light on capital, something that happens, unfortunately, too often in businesses. He began having trouble paying his staff and those big name bands he kept booking. He asked me to help him out, and I agreed to invest in Alpine Valley as a part owner. I also brought in another investor, my friend Ahmed Mannai from Qatar. As I mentioned before, Ahmed and I were once courted as business partners for the Indy 500 car.

Ahmed and I weren't involved in day-to-day management of the company, and as Alpine Valley grew, the complications began to stack up for Joe Balestrieri. Attendance grew, and fans complained about ticket prices. The local sheriff's department had problems with traffic and sanitation.

In summer 1989, Balestrieri ran into a streak of bad luck when bad weather forced him to cancel several shows. The New Kids on the Block cancelled a show and were never rescheduled. Fans demanded refunds and refused to pay their credit card charges. The company was compelled to take out more and more loans to cover the costs. The bankers weren't happy with that arrangement, and they quickly told us so.

The partnership wasn't working; I could see that. We were losing money, and even worse, the relationships with our banks was suffering, something I never wanted to happen. So I decided to end my partnership with Joe Balestrieri. We found someone else to run the Riverside and approached a national management company to take over the operation of Alpine Valley Music Theater.

To force Balestrieri's hand, we filed for foreclosure on the Alpine Valley mortgage. He would have to come up with the money to stay in the game, or buy us out. He owed millions to creditors, employees, musicians, and ticketholders who had filed claims for refunds.

Balestrieri's company was headed for bankruptcy, and he blamed me. One day, his anger boiled over when he and his wife accused me in the press of "raping" their company. It was a foul and outrageous thing to say. I had bailed them out again and again. Where was their sense of loyalty, their sense of decency? I was angry and offended, and wasn't going to stand for their insults. I filed a lawsuit claiming they had slandered me and my company.

After talking to their lawyers, Joe Balestrieri and Leslie West issued a public apology as part of our settlement. "Having gone through the bankruptcy proceedings of the Joseph Entertainment Group," they said of their company, "we realize now that Mr. Zilber offered us sound financial and personal advice. Many of the losses and problems that occurred during our management could have been avoided had his advice been followed." I accepted their apology and dropped the defamation suit.

Eventually the bankruptcy of Joe Balestrieri's company was finalized. As part of the proceedings, Zilber Ltd. retained the title to Alpine Valley Music Theater. We leased it to a national concert promotion outfit, and still own the property to this day.

Joe Balestrieri's troubles continued long after he and I parted ways. He was convicted of income tax evasion and mail fraud, and sentenced to 15 months in prison. According to the federal prosecutor, Balestrieri had taken $234,000 for personal salaries, luxury car leases, and other expenses while cheating the government on his income taxes.

Joe Balestrieri was certainly likable enough. He was a gregarious, independent entrepreneur, the type of partner you should enjoy working with.

Looking back on all the partnerships I've put together, it's not hard to sort out the characteristics of the good partners from those of the bad partners. Part of it is personality, part of it is background. The good partners have experience in the field they're bringing us into. They usually invest their own capital. The good partners work the project themselves. They're honest, current in their income taxes, and have a solid reputation with banks and other investors. These are people you'd be happy to introduce to your wife and kids, people like Phil Cohen, Guy Smith, Duane Moen, Joanie Greggains, and any number of partners I've had. Many of them, in fact, became part of our company family. These are the ones with whom we made money.

On the other side of the ledger, the bad partners typically aren't inclined to invest. They don't like working with my managers. They're arrogant and blame somebody else for deals that go wrong. These are the people who, in the end, cost us money.

Hindsight is 20/20, of course. You live and learn. Even today I'm still learning.

CHAPTER 11

SAND DOLLARS, CIRCUS CIRCUS, AND A TEXAS GUSHER

Deals go wrong. Believe me, I've seen my share, but more often than not, things go right, sometimes very right. If they didn't, I never would have lasted in business as long as I have.

We had a good run with our public company, Unicare. We made money, we lost money, and we diversified the company significantly. Now that Unicare had been sold, and we no longer ran a public company, our attention shifted back to the real estate game. Not that we had ever left real estate. In fact, at the same time we were building up Unicare, Towne Realty had been working its way into the Sunbelt states. That proved to be a pretty good business strategy. In fact, it was one of the best we ever had.

Back before he took a wrong turn by selling me that fleet of water-logged Fiats, my occasional partner Kenny Alles had led me into real estate in Florida. Kenny was always up to something. He was the kind of guy who would walk down the street, see a building he wanted, and buy it. He wouldn't do any research, he wouldn't do any legal work. He didn't have any staff to speak of, and his bookkeeping was nonexistent, but he was a guy who could bring things to you. He was what I would call a "bird dog."

I hadn't heard from Kenny for a couple of years. Then, out of the blue, the phone rang and there he was. "Joe, I've found the fountain of youth," he declared. "I'm selling condos. Come on down and join me." I told him we were done with Florida, but somehow he convinced me to send my executive VP Jerry Stein to Florida to witness what Kenny said was "the wave of the future."

We bought Jerry a plane ticket, and he flew to Florida a day early to do a little research. He called every real estate broker in Cocoa Beach, and guess what? No one had any condominiums left to sell. There was a backlog of buyers and nothing for them to buy. Kenny Alles was right. Condos were taking off. The supply was low and the demand was extremely high.

Jerry Stein met with Kenny Alles the next day. Kenny had three projects going at the same time, and had started construction on all three. He had a first mortgage, a second mortgage, a third mortgage, a fourth mortgage — typical Kenny Alles financing. He held units for people who said they would buy, but they hadn't signed any contracts yet because he hadn't finished the buildings. It was a chicken-or-egg deal: the buyer wouldn't sign a contract unless the unit was finished, and Kenny couldn't finish the units unless he had some cash flow. So he pretty much had hocked the building with multiple mortgages.

As Jerry found out, the Florida market was wide open, and we thought there might be a way to work with Kenny again. So I had Kenny fly to Milwaukee to meet with me.

I could have predicted the first words out of his mouth: "Put up some money to finish the building, Joe, and I'll make you my partner," he said, sitting in my office. I had heard the line a thousand times before. This time, though, I thought Kenny was on to something.

"I'll work on the project, Kenny. I believe in it," I told him. "But because of the way you keep books and records, I'm not going to become your partner halfway through a project. So we'll do this on a fee basis. Towne Realty will finish the building, we'll pay off the bills that have to be paid, and when you sell the condos, we'll take back our investment plus X number of dollars per unit."

That was the start of a long and lucrative venture in Florida real estate.

Kenny had options on a few other pieces of beachfront property, and we went in with him on a few more condominium projects under the same kind of agreement: we put up the money, we finished the buildings, the units were sold, we got our money back, and we got a fee per unit. It was all great.

Towne Realty was at the very forefront of high-rise construction along Florida's "Space Coast." In the community of Cocoa Beach, located on a barrier island between the Atlantic Ocean and the Banana River Lagoon, we constructed the first buildings that were over seven stories tall. After awhile, we told Kenny to concentrate on the sales of the units only, and Towne worked on the purchase of the land and the construction of the buildings. That's when we brought in Jack Bennett, who had been building military housing units for us in Texas and all around the country. That was 1977. Jack's still in Cocoa Beach today.

Over time, we did a lot of land deals in Cocoa Beach. As Cocoa Beach built up, we looked into Cape Canaveral. It wasn't as well known, but we saw possibilities for development along beach property. We began to clean up the area and build condo units. While constructing a high-rise called the Shorewood Condominiums in Cape Canaveral, the local fire chief informed us that his department's hook and ladder wouldn't be able to reach the top floor of the building in the event of a fire. So we bought the department a fire truck with a longer reach.

Next we went into Cocoa, Florida, building condos on the mainland where the Indian River meets the Banana River. Then we looked south along the barrier to Satellite Beach, adding buildings right along the ocean. We became very strong on the Space Coast, and became one of the largest developers in the area. Things were moving along smoothly.

Meanwhile, Kenny Alles was starting to get a little restless. He was looking for more to do. He walked into my office one day and said, "Joe, there's a motel on A1A called Ocean Landings with 170 rooms. We could take those 170 rooms and timeshare them."

I stared at Kenny with a blank look. "What's a timeshare?" I said. I'd never heard the term before.

Kenny explained. "Instead of selling each unit in the building as a condo, we sell each unit for a week at a time for, say, $5,000 a week to 52 different buyers, 52 weeks out of the year. That's called a timeshare."

I was skeptical. "Well," I said, "that sounds like some sort of magic, Ken. That's just not ever going to happen." But I asked my guys to spend a little time looking into the timeshare concept and, lo and behold, there were a number of people doing it. Most of them were "blue suede shoes" salespeople — people who were not very reputable. I decided, "Let's try it, and let's make sure we do it the right way."

Here's what we did: we bought the Ocean Landings motel and sold a full year's timeshare on a few units to outside investors at a discount. That helped offset our costs of developing the project. Then we converted the motel units into timeshares. We combined two rooms, turned one bedroom into a kitchen, another bedroom into a living room area. They were very basic, but we ended up selling them all. With the success of that first project, we added buildings to the Ocean Landings site along the beach. That was our introduction to timeshare.

Beginning with those early days in the '70s, we built one building after the next, after the next. Construction boomed in Florida. All told, between the four timeshares and all the condominium projects, Towne Realty constructed 117 buildings up and down Florida's Atlantic coast.

The West Coast of Florida was a whole different story. It wasn't until the early '90s that we began developing on the west side, starting with single-family homes. We heard that a well-known Milwaukee family had plans to develop a big chunk of land just east of Sarasota. We submitted a proposal. The land, some 40,000 acres, was owned by the Uihlein family, heirs to Milwaukee's Schlitz Brewing dynasty. There's an interesting history behind how the Uihleins came by that property.

It was the late 1920s, and a boat-building company from northern Wisconsin called the Schroeder Corporation wanted to purchase the 40,000-acre property. Much of it was forested, and Schroeder wanted to grow and harvest timber using the lumber to build their boats.

The Schroeder Corporation took out a loan from the First Wisconsin National Bank in Milwaukee, whose principal shareholders were members of the Uihlein family. As the country fell into the Great Depression, Schroeder ran into financial trouble. Rather than taking a loss, the Uihlein family purchased the property. Over the years, the Uihleins sold timber and raised cattle on the land because, in Florida, property that's used to raise cattle pays virtually no real estate taxes.

By the 1980s, the Uihleins were divided on how they wanted to use the land. Eventually, it was decided that real estate development would generate more cash. They changed the zoning on a 5,000-acre parcel, named it Lakewood Ranch, and started taking bids from developers.

Meanwhile, back in Milwaukee, we were introduced to a stockbroker named Robert "Brownie" Trainer, a member of the Uihlein family. We told Trainer we would be very interested in becoming one of the builders that the Uihleins were hiring to develop Lakewood Ranch. The Uihleins couldn't see how a relatively small company from Milwaukee would be competent enough to take on the project, when all the other developers bidding for the work were national or regional builders that already had a strong presence on Florida's West Coast.

Towne Realty was the outsider. The odds were against us, but we kept pushing. We sent our senior managers to meet with their board members and attorneys. Finally, after months of steady persuasion, we convinced the Uihleins to give us a chance. They hired Towne as one of six builders for the project. We signed a contract to build their first mid-level housing units, single-family homes priced for "move-up buyers." We bought 100 lots and started building. By the end of that first year, we were rated by customers as the number one builder at Lakewood Ranch in sales, architectural design, and finish work. From zero, we fought our way to the top — and worked our way into the market on Florida's West Coast.

⁂ ⁂ ⁂

Nevada was another big market for us. Like so many other opportunities that came my way, it came through a partnership. We had first started in Las Vegas when we opened that nursing home that we could never fill. When we ended up selling it to a group of doctors, who converted it to a hospital, the doctors hired a Las Vegas developer named Bob Rishling to do the conversion.

When I was introduced to Bob, we hit it off right away. I decided we should go in with him as partners. After the hospital deal, Bob took a look at a Mini-Price Hotel we had built in Milwaukee. "Let's build one of those in Las Vegas," he said to me, and so we did. Bob owned the land and we put up the building. It was very lucrative, and so we put up another Mini-Price in Reno.

Over the years, Bob became one of my best partners, and a good friend. Before I met him, he had run into a string of bad breaks and lost a lot of money. So when he started working with me, he turned over part of his salary to me to keep for his wife in case he died or couldn't work for some reason. I held onto it for him, put it into an investment fund. Eventually Bob began asking me for his fund, but I wouldn't give it to him. I had promised to keep it safe, and I stood by my promise. I held Bob's money for nearly 20 years, and finally I gave it to him. By then the fund was worth quite a lot of money, in the millions. Today, Bob Rishling is in very good financial shape.

Working with Bob was another one of those relationships that began with one deal and then led to another and then another — from the failed nursing home to the Mini-Price Hotel and on and on, like links in a chain. Over the next 35 years, I built and owned many buildings with Bob, some very big projects. We remodeled the Aladdin Hotel, built an addition to the Las Vegas Hilton, and built an enormous, high-rise addition to the Circus Circus Hotel. We did very well together.

The Circus Circus was an unusual project. It was a union job, and it was bankrolled by people who had alleged connections to the Las Vegas mob. One week the owners didn't pay us for our work. I called the union boss to give him a heads up.

"We haven't gotten paid yet," I told him, "so next week, we won't have any money to pay the workers. On Monday, you won't have any men on the job because we can't pay them."

"Don't kid me," said the union guy.

"I'm not kidding. I'm telling you, we can't pay the men," I said. Monday arrived, and sure enough, work at the site came to a dead stop.

Next thing I know, the phone rings. It's Frank Balistrieri, my old classmate from Marquette University Law School. Frank had investments in a couple of Vegas hotels, and he had certain, well, *connections*. He had also spent time in federal prison for tax evasion.

"Joe, what did you do?" Frank said to me.

"What do you mean what did I do?" I said.

"You have no men on the job."

"I know, Frank. I haven't gotten paid. So how am I going to pay the men? They won't report to the job site until I can pay them."

Frank paused for a second. "They'll be on the job tomorrow, Joe," he said, "and this'll never happen again."

We got our money in a matter of hours. And the next day, the men were back at work. We never had an ounce of trouble after that.

❦ ❦ ❦

In 1979, we opened an office in Scottsdale, Arizona. I had sent my construction guy, Don Mantz, there to supervise a senior housing project we were building, the kind of place snowbirds from the North flock to in the winter months. This facility had a couple hundred units.

At the time Don was running our construction company, KM Development. He still is. After the senior housing project was finished, we put up some attached condos. This was a third-party deal, and we developed a great relationship with the Arizona contractor. They liked what we had done and offered us more work. From there, we built projects in Phoenix and Tempe, Arizona.

The person who was in charge of sales had friends who were involved in a major land acquisition in Scottsdale. They were about to lose their option on a parcel that was approved for 1,200 units in a two-story condo. He asked Don Mantz to take a look at it with the idea that we might be interested in buying out the option. Time was of the essence. The option was going to run out in a week. So Don took a look and gave me a call.

"This one feels good, Joe," he told me. "It's a condominium, and a good sized project — it's what we do best." So I jumped on a plane to Arizona the next day.

The land was owned by Ron Boeddeker, who ran the California-based Transcontinental Properties, a major developer in the West. Boeddeker had put together a venture to develop the land with the Bass Brothers of Fort Worth, Texas. The Bass Brothers' organization was started by four brothers who had turned the millions they inherited from their father's oil and real estate holdings into billions as venture capitalists.

I met with Ron Boeddeker and the partners who held the option on the land. We got together in the afternoon, and by that evening, we shook hands on a deal in which Towne would develop the property. As happened so many times before, this one deal led to several more. We would later work with both Boeddeker and the Bass Brothers on real estate projects in Hawaii and in Texas.

The Scottsdale project was called The Villages at McCormick Ranch. It was a large condominium project that we worked on for the next 10 years. That was our first big project in Arizona, and out of that, we took on other developments. Eventually we set up a real estate team to sell property, and today our Arizona division builds and sells single-family residential housing. We've been successful in the Arizona market more than 30 years.

Around the time we were starting out in Arizona, we were also expanding our real estate operations in the Hawaiian Islands. We had first started in Hawaii during the 1960s and '70s with military contracts. We put up the cable for the U.S. Navy's radio navigation system in the mountains of Haiku Valley, built barracks at Hickam Air Force Base at Pearl Harbor, and handled a few other government projects. As I got to know Hawaii, Vera and I began vacationing there in the winters. We loved the climate, the people, and the laid-back attitude of the Islands.

Even early on, I knew there were business opportunities in Hawaii. In 1979, I heard about a development project in central Oahu. It was a 12-story condominium called Waikalani Woodlands, with 144 units in two buildings. The developer, who was based in Honolulu, had gone into bankruptcy. So we came in to pick up the pieces and finish the job.

Before the agreement could be signed, though, I had to deal with the creditors of the bankrupt company. A young attorney named Chris Lau was representing one of the secured creditors — an insurance company. Although Chris didn't represent us, it was to his client's benefit that Towne Realty took over the project, so he was watching out for our interests.

I remember sitting in Chris Lau's office in Honolulu. In one conference room were the secured creditors and their lawyers, and in the other room were my Hawaii managers, my general counsel, Jim Young, and me. Chris was shuffling back and forth from room to room, negotiating the deal. I was getting impatient just sitting around, and when Chris came into my conference room, I told him so.

"You know Chris, I don't need this," I said. "I have other things to do. I don't need this deal," and I stood up to leave.

Chris gave me a look that could stop traffic. "Mr. Zilber," he said, quietly, "sit down and shut up, and I'll get you your deal." That's just how he put it. He was just three years out of law school, but he had *chutzpah*.

Well, I did what he said and I sat down. Chris went back into the conference room and put our deal together. When it was done, we all walked over to bankruptcy court with Chris and got a bankruptcy judge to bless the transaction. As we were walking back to Chris' office, I turned to Jim Young and said, "Jim, Chris can talk for me anytime. Why don't you hire him?" From that moment on, Chris Lau began working for Towne Realty as outside general counsel in Hawaii.

Towne Realty eventually opened an office in Honolulu, and I put my longtime friend Joe Belin in charge of running it. Not only had Joe been one of the original employees at Towne, I had known him since we were kids, and I had an enormous amount of trust and confidence in him. He was also familiar with Hawaii, having served there in the Navy when Pearl Harbor was hit.

It's always been important to me to have one of my most trusted guys at my right hand. First it was my partner Danny Tishberg. Then it was Jerry Stein, who eventually became president of the company. I followed the same thinking when opening new division offices, state by state: Jack Bennett in Florida, followed by his son, Kohn Bennett. Don Mantz in Arizona, followed by Kevin Kiesl. Ray Brown in Texas. Jeff Pemstein in California. In each place we went, I had one of my best people running the show.

In 1987, my dear friend Joe Belin passed away. It was a huge loss for Vera and me. Joe's wife Shirley had become good friends with Vera, and his death was a blow to all of us. After Joe's death, Chris Lau came on board full time to run our Hawaii development office. He has stayed with me ever since, and he has done a terrific job.

From the start, Hawaii was a crap shoot. We started out small, taking on a project that a bankrupt company couldn't handle, and we went on from there, unsure where things would lead. I just didn't know, but I was a risk taker. I was determined to find out, just as I had in Florida, Nevada, Arizona, and everywhere else we did business.

After coming in on that first condo project at Waikalani Woodlands, we got several option rights on other properties. We bought out a few creditors and, as a result, ended up with the entire Waikalani Woodlands development project, which was huge. Through the years we built nearly 1,000 units.

A few years after we got Waikalani Woodlands, we found ourselves back in business with the Bass Brothers. They were building a Hyatt Hotel on the Big Island of Hawaii, and they wanted condominiums constructed adjacent to the hotel. We proposed a joint venture and ultimately built the condos, called The Shores.

I remember, as we were negotiating the deal with the Bass Brothers, I flew over to the Big Island near the city of Kona to take a look at the hotel as it was going up. I wanted to make sure the Grand Hyatt Waikoloa, as it was named, broke ground before I actually signed on and made a commitment to build The Shores condos. The hotel was coming along nicely, and I felt confident it would work well for us. There was nothing to worry about, I told myself.

On my flight back to Honolulu, the plane I was in suddenly caught fire, and we nearly were forced to ditch it in the ocean. "We blew out an engine," the pilot yelled, and in the next instant, the second engine was on fire. He notified Kona Airport, and they had all of their emergency equipment on the runway when we landed. The fire was extinguished, and miraculously no one was injured.

When we finally made it home, Vera was scared half to death — and furious. I had taken along our grandson, Shane, and for some reason she blamed *me* for the plane catching fire.

Vera grew more and more fond of the Islands, and eventually we bought a condominium near Honolulu and divided our time equally each year between Milwaukee and Hawaii. I remember on one of our very first trips to the Islands, I told Vera I would buy a hotel in Hawaii someday. A few years later, I did just that. We purchased the Waikiki Gateway Hotel in Honolulu, with the famous Nick's Fish Market on the ground floor and the Kuhio Mall nearby. Both were very popular tourist attractions.

The owner needed cash, and I bought both properties. In the contract, I gave the seller the right to buy them back. This was in the late 1980s, just as the Japanese bubble started taking off. Japanese investors were buying properties left and right at greatly inflated prices, so the original seller bought the Waikiki Gateway Hotel and the Kuhio Mall back from us and flipped it to a Japanese buyer for a big profit.

What goes around comes around, though, and we did all right with Japanese investors on another deal soon after selling back the Gateway. In Wailuku Village, we built a 260-unit apartment project called The 216. A year after the project was completed, a Japanese buyer approached us, and we sold the project. It was a big score for us. It could have been more, and Chris Lau remembers why:

> The sales contract was for $27 million. Joe and Vera were on a cruise, but Joe called me at every port just to ask me how the sale was going. During one of the legs of the cruise, I told the buyer we would settle for $26 million. So when Joe called from his next port of call, I had to tell him I gave away a million bucks. Did I get the earful from him!

Over the years, one deal led to the next and the next and the next. To date, we've now built a total of 5,000 residential units to date on three of the Hawaiian Islands — Oahu, Maui, and the Big Island of Hawaii — nearly all of them mid-market units geared for second home buyers. It has been a very successful market for us, as Chris Lau explains:

> In Hawaii there's really a scarcity of zoned land that has already been approved for construction. Through the years, Joe was able to take advantage of a lot of opportunities where the company was able to purchase zoned land, or land that was determined to be zoneable. Then we would hold on to it until there was enough demand for us to start building.

❧❧❧

After divesting ourselves of all our various Unicare companies, we were finally back to pure real estate, always my first love. Over time, that's where we experienced the most growth. As we shifted back to real estate, I also reorganized my company, creating Zilber Ltd. in 1980. The restructuring created a corporation that would not require my signature or guarantee on every single business transaction. My senior management team could negotiate loans with our bankers, for example.

Zilber Ltd. was formed with me named as chairman of the board and chief executive officer, Jerry Stein as president, and Jim Janz as senior vice president. I tapped our longtime chief financial officer and treasurer, Art Wigchers, to become president of Towne Realty.

This was now the third generation of leaders that would be running the business. It was a strong, competent lineup. Looking to the future, I knew that under this new structure, my company would survive without me. It was a wonderfully comforting thought.

In its earliest days, Towne Realty built single-family homes throughout Milwaukee. That, in turn, led to the business of apartment construction. When those two markets slowed down in the '60s, that's when we got into nursing homes and began to diversify, creating the many companies within Unicare.

Diversification was good — it ultimately made us a stronger company — but to me, it was never as good as building homes. When we decided to open up offices in the Sunbelt, we found that there was a future for home building in those states like nowhere else, including Wisconsin. By 1990, it became clear that this could be a greater opportunity than we even had back in the 1950s, when we were first starting out. That realization was our motivation for expanding our operations in the Sunbelt regions.

By the late '80s, we had divisions in Florida, Nevada, Arizona, California, and Hawaii. We had single-family homes in Arizona and California, hotels in California and Nevada, and hotels, condos, and a golf course in Hawaii. The Sunbelt projects became very good for us.

We always had to keep an eye out for the next recession, though. Recessions in the real estate business are just a fact of life. The recessions in the '70s, the '80s and the '90s were what we saw as regional recessions. One area would be down and another area would be up. We had a recession in Arizona, but Hawaii was doing well, and we had a recession in Florida, but California was doing well. It would go back and forth. We always used to joke, "If we could get all the areas up at the same time, it would be like Nirvana." It never happened — until 2000, when all of a sudden, *all* of the areas were good at the same time.

We entered the 21st century and we simply couldn't do anything wrong. The real estate markets were booming, and sales were going through the roof. There had been a shift in the way people were thinking. They no longer looked at real estate as merely a place to live. People saw real estate as an investment vehicle, a way to make money.

To keep up with the demand, our teams in each division kept ratcheting it up. The deals were ambitious and bold, the building designs were more and more creative, and the sales just kept coming. In Arizona, for example, we bought a parcel of land for condos in Scottsdale, and built our first "five-plexes," as we called them — two large units on the first floor, two large units directly above them, and a fifth unit above the parking garage. The design was unique. A finished five-plex resembled an estate home and became very appealing to buyers.

Florida was still a land of opportunity. Our projects there went in a number of different directions. We completed our third timeshare, the Resort at Cocoa Beach, in 2001 and had the best year ever from timeshare sales. We constructed and sold 210 condominium units in Titusville along the Space Coast. That project turned out to be one of the highest profit margin projects the company ever saw. And, in a very creative partnership, we teamed up with Ron Jon Surf Shops, a famously popular surfwear company with shops up and down Florida's coastline. We used the Ron Jon name to build a beautiful timeshare resort called the Ron Jon Cape Caribe Resort, next to Port Canaveral on the ocean. It's a magnificent, 525-unit development geared for families, with a water park, tennis courts, restaurants, mini-golf, and a movie house — all sorts of attractions and amenities.

As Zilber Ltd. charged into the 21st century, we had a string of banner years, with record sales in nearly each of our divisions. All of our careful planning and hard work really was paying off.

As it goes, sometimes things line up in just the right way. Sometimes you just get lucky. I think about a deal we did in Texas. In 1996, I bought a large piece of property in Burleson, Texas, from the Bass Brothers, the billionaires from Fort Worth. We paid a million dollars for a thousand acres, a tremendous buy, and we started to subdivide that land. We called it Mountain Valley Lake and started building single-family homes. We had a trouble selling the homes because there just weren't enough people in Burleson at the time to justify a housing project of this size. It seemed the Bass Brothers had proved smarter than us.

Then, years later, we found out that natural gas deposits had been discovered under the property. We owned the mineral rights underneath that land, and in 2009 had two wells drilled into the deposits by Chesapeake Energy. Our lemon had turned into lemonade. Our luck had changed, and we really did get the best of the deal after all.

The years 2005 and 2006 were the most profitable years in my company's history. From Florida to Texas, Arizona to Nevada, California to the Hawaiian Islands, all of our divisions were making money at the same time. It was a company first. In 2006, we sold and closed the most units in the history of Zilber Ltd. It was quite an achievement, and I was extremely proud.

Like I say, markets go up and markets go down. I can't tell you how many charts I've drawn over the years showing the booms and busts of real estate. The latest boom was very good for the company, and for me personally. Vera and I had been spending more and more time in Hawaii, wintering in Honolulu and returning to Milwaukee for the warmer months. We had everything we wanted, and had set up an estate plan to ensure the security of our family and of Zilber Ltd. These banner years also allowed us to place more investments into a family foundation we had started in 1962. After Vera and I were gone, this foundation would have the capacity to do even bigger and better things than we ever imagined it would do back in the 1960s.

Sometimes life's circumstances take hold and lead you in unexpected directions. Before long, I would be faced with a world of changes.

CHAPTER 12

BEST OF TIMES, WORST OF TIMES, BEST OF TIMES

When you live as long as I have, you really do see life as "the best of times and the worst of times," as Dickens put it. If you're lucky, you see the best of times return again. I was very lucky. I had Vera at my side for a long time. We were married for 61 years. She was my life mate, my first true partner — wife and mother to our children, my confidante and companion throughout life's journey. We celebrated life, and we suffered some disappointments, enduring a family tragedy that shook us to the core.

In our later years together, the good times came around again, and a whole new chapter in our lives began. Because of Vera, I started down an uncharted path, trying to improve my community from the ground up, a direction I'm still following today.

Life can lead you to places you never expected to go, though. Vera and I went through a terrible struggle with our son, Jim. It was a family crisis that lasted for years. Jimmy was a bright, sensitive, and funny guy. He had a magnetic personality that rubbed off on everyone. He was very smart, so much smarter than me, in every way. He was generous — he'd give you the shirt off his back — that's how he was.

That was Jimmy, but Jimmy also had a drug problem. Somewhere along the line, he became addicted to drugs and was never able to defeat his addiction. It's not clear how my son became addicted to drugs. We talked about it many times, but I don't think we ever came to a conclusion as to what caused his addiction and what his mom and I could, or should have done to help him beat it.

He started with marijuana in high school; in college he tried heroin and was hooked. He suffered from this addiction off and on for the rest of his life. Sometimes you never knew which Jimmy you were getting, Jimmy the smart, sensitive son, or Jimmy the struggling, desperate son who was abusing drugs.

Vera and I tried everything to help him. He went into all kinds of rehabilitation programs. He entered a center in Massachusetts, supposedly one of the best in the country, but we later found out that Jimmy was able to get drugs at the center the second day he was there. He violated the conditions of rehab and they threw him out.

Jimmy moved around a lot in his life. He lived in Milwaukee, Boston, and then Hawaii. He went through many drug treatment programs, but the pattern was always the same, and so was the result. He'd stay for a couple of weeks, or a month, and Vera and I would think, "It'll be different this time."

Everybody wanted to believe that, but he always got back into drugs, disappearing for days, or weeks, at a time without telling us where he was. It was a nightmare, and very hard on Vera. We just didn't know what to do. Jimmy knew he had a serious problem. We talked about it often. He would agree to change his life, to go into rehab, to assume more responsibility, the list went on and on. He would sign a piece of paper that I would keep in my wallet, and before too long the deal was broken. He was my son. I loved him very much, and I always hoped that one of our deals would stick, but they never did.

Looking back, I wondered if I should have been tougher, more harsh, taken the "tough love" approach that some of my friends used with their children. The fact of the matter is that with some of them, "tough love" didn't work either. I know this for sure: drugs and drug addiction are very bad things. They hurt all those who come in contact with them, and they cost me my son.

In 1997, Jimmy heard of a treatment started in Israel. As part of the treatment method, doctors forced addicts into withdrawal by filtering their blood and cleansing it. Jimmy decided to give the program a try and heard it was available in Tijuana, Mexico. Once again, we were hopeful that this would be the treatment that would take, that would finally cure Jimmy of his powerful addiction, but once again we were disappointed.

After a week at the clinic in Mexico, Jimmy got his hands on some drugs, and was tossed out of the program before he completed it. He left Tijuana and went to San Diego, where he rented a hotel room, went to a drug house, took a "speed ball"(heroin and cocaine), and went into a coma.

My assistant, Mike Mervis, was very close to Jimmy. Like all of us, he tried to straighten Jimmy out over the years, but in the end, no one could. "Because of his addiction, Jimmy lived a very, very bumpy life," Mike says. "All the hope that Joe had for him, and all the hope that Jimmy had for himself, was wiped out because he could not find a way to deal with his addiction. From time to time, he tried mightily. At other times, he was incapable of generating the massive mental and physical strength that it takes to overcome addiction."

Not long after Jimmy returned to San Diego from Mexico, Vera and I got a phone call. Jimmy was in the hospital in intensive care. I sent Mervis to find out what needed to be done. He called to tell me the situation was not good. I flew out to California immediately to meet with the doctors. Vera remained at home. It was just too hard for her. She couldn't bear it all. I was in constant contact with her by telephone.

Jimmy was at the University of California San Diego Medical Center. When I got to his room, he was comatose and attached to a ventilator. The doctors didn't give him much hope. A neurologist told us Jimmy would never recover, that he was in a "persistent vegetative state." I wanted to get a second opinion. I tracked down two experts in Berkeley, California. They came to the same conclusion: Jimmy was gone.

After consulting with our daughter Marcy, who had flown down from her home in Vancouver, we decided to place Jimmy in hospice care. It was the right thing to do. His years of addiction had finally taken its toll, and there was nothing else that could be done. We wanted to make him as comfortable as possible in the little time that he had left in this world.

Hospital staff recommended the San Diego Hospice. It was a wonderful place, a state-of-the-art facility. Joan Kroc, the wife of the McDonald's restaurant founder Ray Kroc, had contributed millions of dollars to the facility to make it one of the finest in the country. Located high on a hill, with lush landscaping all around, you could see the ocean from the hospice windows. Patients could be wheeled outside onto a patio in their beds to enjoy the sea breeze and the sunset.

Jimmy survived at the hospice for five days, living out the end of his life in a peaceful environment, calm and untroubled, never regaining consciousness. He died on October 13, 1997. He was just 50 years old.

Vera and I were devastated. Like any mother and father, we asked ourselves whether there was something else we could have tried to help him, whether there was something we should have done differently. He was not a pampered child. He worked for my company for years, and he worked hard. When he was just 16, I gave him the responsibility of final cleaning in all the new houses we built. When we built an apartment building, he was the one who cleaned up after the construction was finished. Jimmy didn't live a privileged life. None of our kids did. He was my only son, and I would have given him anything to help him out.

My son loved real estate, and he was smart about it. I'm sure he would be running my company today if he had lived. He would have been my successor, no question. His death was my greatest sorrow. My legacy was erased.

My longtime secretary, Kim Treis, saw how Jimmy's death tore me up:

> I would see Mr. Zilber sitting at his desk with tears running down his cheeks. Then he'd have a meeting scheduled and people would be coming down the hall to his office, and he would go from being devastated to putting on a big smile. "Oh, hi. How are you?" he would say, going into his business mode. It would break your heart knowing what was going on inside of him.
>
> Maybe the hardest thing for him was that he used to talk to Jimmy every day. We had Jim on speed dial and this was a nightly, or an afternoon, ritual. After Jimmy died, I'm sure there were times when Mr. Zilber would reach for that phone to call him. It was so sad.

Jimmy's death is a painful thing to write about. I look back now and think to myself, "Maybe I should have sent Jimmy with one of my guys to an island someplace where there was nobody around and no place to get any drugs." I feel like I failed Jimmy. My daughter Marcy tells me we did all we could, but Jimmy could not break out of his self-destructive behavior. His habit was too strong. It was a sickness that was overpowering.

No one has a hundred percent happiness, and no one has a hundred percent misery. We learn to accept the bad with the good and move forward through life's hardships. To this day, Jimmy is always on my mind. Yet out of his tragedy eventually came hope and happiness.

❦❦ ❦❦ ❦❦

A few years after Jimmy died, Vera's sister Joan developed a terminal illness and was placed in a small hospice in Arizona. Marcy, Vera and I went to visit Joanie and we were impressed with the care she was given in the last days of her life. Joanie had run into some tough times with one of her sons. He also had problems with drug abuse. So Vera and I helped out with his education costs. He finally went through rehab and got squared away.

Around the same time as our visit to Arizona, Aurora Health Care in Milwaukee called the head of our commercial division, John Kersey. I didn't know it then, but Aurora was raising money to open a hospice near Milwaukee, their second hospice in the area. The Aurora people knew Towne Realty had built and operated dozens of nursing homes years ago through its Unicare subsidiary, and they asked Kersey if I might be interested in contributing to their capital campaign for the new hospice.

Kersey mentioned the hospice project to me, and I talked to Vera. As we found out, the project was being led by Aurora's branch of the Visiting Nurse Association. The VNA of America was a pioneer organization nationally in the area of hospice care. They go back more than 100 years, caring for the disabled, the elderly, and the terminally ill. Both Vera and I were excited about the possibilities of helping out, having seen first hand how both Jimmy and Vera's sister Joanie had benefited from hospice care.

I asked Mike Mervis to set up a meeting in early November of 2002 with a group of people from Aurora. We sat around my conference room, and they laid out their plans for the hospice center. Sue Ela, who was at that time president of the Aurora Visiting Nurse Association, was at the meeting and remembers what happened next:

> We had presented our overview of the concept and all of our plans, and then everybody left to get lunch. We were going to discuss dollar amounts after lunch. As I was leaving the room, Joe asked me to stay behind. I sat back down and he said to me, "So how much are you going to ask me for?" I told him, "Well, our intent was to ask you for $1 million." That was the largest gift we had ever asked for at that point in this campaign. He said, "We can do that, but you have to learn to think bigger than that."

He then excused himself to make a phone call, and when he came back he said, "Vera thinks this is a very good idea, too. She's really pleased." Everyone returned from lunch, and with a big smile, Joe said, "Vera and I decided we're going to do this." And that was it. The meeting was over. Even his advisors were a little surprised. The Zilbers were just so enthusiastic. A gift like that lends great credibility and legitimacy to any campaign. Once Joe and Vera committed to their gift, we were then able to raise $3.5 million in just six months, record time.

Sue Ela and her people later agreed that our gift would be for naming rights. The facility would be called the Aurora VNA Zilber Family Hospice. It was a special project for Vera and me, and it energized us both. Vera's keen awareness of health care stemmed from her own interest in medicine. When she was young, Vera had considered becoming a doctor. The hospice took on a personal importance for her.

Soon Marcy also became involved in the effort, and in a way, Jimmy contributed to the creation of that hospice, too. Although there was no way he could have known it, the fact that he lived his final days in the San Diego Hospice inspired Vera and me to contribute to the Aurora VNA.

Out of the hospice project would come my decision to get actively involved in a number of philanthropic projects around the city of Milwaukee. When everything is measured, indirectly, Jimmy played a role in helping who knows how many people.

A groundbreaking ceremony for the Zilber Family Hospice was held in February 2004. I was at my home in Hawaii; however, Marcy spoke eloquently on behalf of the Zilber family, standing beneath a white tent amid snow-covered trees at the construction site:

> Over the last few years, our family became experienced with hospice care in two different hospices in two different parts of the country. One was state of the art, the other was a small, simple home converted into six rooms — two different places, but both of the same feeling. The compassion, the caring, and the dedication of the staff turned these structures into homes and allowed our loved ones to pass from this life's journey surrounded by friends and family.
>
> The first thing we do when we're born is we take a breath in and then we cry. And the last act of life before we leave is we let a breath out and everybody else cries. In between are all the joys and the sorrows, but

we will all pass from this earth one day. The young die, the old die. The sick die, the healthy die. The rich die, the poor die. The doctor dies, the patient dies. This is something that no one is exempt from. It's part of the circle.... It's important to ensure that those who are near and dear to us leave with the same love that they were born to when entering this world.

Marcy then presented the first installment of our gift to the Aurora VNA. "This is one way that we as a family have chosen of giving back to a community that has given so much to us over the years. I thank you all," she concluded.

Construction began that spring, and by midsummer the building began to take shape. This would be the first hospice in the state of Wisconsin to provide end-of-life care for children as well as adults. It also would be a clinical training site for Marquette University's College of Nursing. I was sure it would be on the cutting edge of hospice care.

According to the architect's plans, the facility would have living quarters for 18 patients in three wings, with a courtyard at the center. The building was situated on nine acres on Honey Creek Parkway, a green space just west of Milwaukee's city limits in the community of Wauwatosa. It would be set back from the road and at the base of a thickly wooded hill.

At first, some neighbors opposed having the hospice built on that site. They thought it would disrupt the quiet of the parkway. Aurora Health Care did a good job of assuring the neighbors and local officials that traffic would be limited, and the building would fit the character of the neighborhood. In my opinion, the property really couldn't have been more perfect for a hospice. The site is tranquil and remote, completely surrounded by nature.

By the end of summer 2004, the exterior of the building was almost finished. A stone chimney rose at the middle of the wood-and-brick structure, and the roof near the entrance was topped off with a two-story, eight-sided cupola, the crown of what would become a meditation space inside.

Sadly, Vera never got to see the completion of the hospice. In early October 2003, she was admitted to a Milwaukee hospital. She wasn't feeling well, and her doctors said she should have a blood transfusion, a routine procedure. I consulted with Vera and her doctors. The transfusion was performed and she was scheduled to spend the night in the hospital. I went home for the night and was going to pick her up the following day.

At 7:00 a.m., the next morning, I got a call from a nurse at the hospital. "We're very sorry to tell you that Vera passed away," she said. I didn't believe it. "That can't be. You're making a mistake," I said. "I was just leaving for the hospital to pick her up and bring her home."

Vera died on October 2, 2003. She was 81 years old. The doctors said it was an aneurism that killed her.

My daughter Marilyn was at home in Milwaukee with me, and Marcy came from Vancouver with my grandchildren, Melissa and Shane. Vera's funeral was held at Congregation Emanu-El B'ne Jeshurun, our temple. Hundreds of people came to say goodbye.

Her death was a shock to me. In all my years, I never, ever dreamed that she would pass away before I would. I wasn't sure what I would do without her.

I knew I had to keep busy. After she was gone, I felt compelled to keep working. That was my thinking: I had to be busy all the time. Without Vera, work became my closest companion. Those were dark days for me, some of the darkest days of my life.

⁂ ⁂ ⁂

Nearly one year after Vera's death, in August 2004, workers were finishing off the interior of the Zilber Family Hospice. The rooms were laid out and walls were going up. At my request, hospice administrators put together a private "hard hat" tour of the site for some of the donors, and my family, friends, and employees. It was an opportunity for us to get a progress report. Around 50 of us came out — my daughters and my grandchildren, and people on my senior management team, all of whom had made donations to the hospice — and all of whom had known Vera very well.

The smell of sawdust filled the air as we walked through the building. Toward the end of the tour, we were led to what would become a family sunroom, a gift to the hospice from Sue Ela and her husband Tom Ela. Sue handed each of us a carpenter's pencil. The walls in the sunroom were still roughed out, just unfinished drywall. Each person on the tour was asked to write a message to Vera with the pencil on the walls before they were sealed.

One of the messages was written by the then-president of Zilber Ltd., my friend Art Wigchers, and his wife Mary Ann. "Vera," they wrote. "What a tribute to your family in this beautiful setting! May the patients who come here feel your welcome and the eternal blessings of God!"

There were dozens more like this, prayers, wishes, and notes to Vera and to the future occupants of the building. The written messages would be preserved for years and years within the hospice walls. In a way, those messages gave the hospice a soul.

The Zilber Family Hospice opened in March 2005. It turned out to be a superb facility, absolutely state of the art. The hospice occupies 31,200 square feet, but looking at it from the outside, the structure — with its wood siding and brick walls — blends in beautifully with the surrounding parkway. Bordered by walking trails and ponds, the low-slung building looks more like a country inn than a medical facility.

Inside, the hospice has a welcoming feeling to it. There's a solarium, a library, a meditation room, a therapeutic spa, a hair salon, a family lounge with a full kitchen, and a dining room where they will make everything from a milk shake to a steak sandwich. It's very accommodating to both patients and their loved ones.

Each patient has a private patio. A bed can be rolled outside through a sliding glass door. Patients can decorate their rooms any way they choose. I heard about one woman who was a Harley-Davidson fan and had traveled in her lifetime 150,000 miles on the back of a motorcycle. She put up a Harley display in her room, with miniature model motorcycles and photographs of her road trips.

This hospice is one of the few in the country that accepts children who are terminally ill. There's a playroom with toys and videogames, plenty of things for them to do. Pets are even allowed to visit. People from all over the world come to visit to see how the hospice is run. It's a model program, one of the best anywhere.

Not only do the patients get excellent care, but they're treated with dignity. Whenever a patient passes away, someone on the staff rings a bell and everybody stops to pay respect, in memory of that special person. For me, that person has always been Vera.

❧❧❧ ❧❧❧ ❧❧❧

Learning how to cope without Vera in my life was not easy. I had known Vera since I was 20 years old. She brought out the best in me. She was generous and clever. I think back on all the trips we took together and that radio show she hosted so long ago. Vera was so very smart. The knowledge that lady had was unbelievable. We would sit and watch *Jeopardy!* together, and she knew the answers before they finished the question. Over and over, friends use the words "down to earth" to describe her. She was practical, never pretentious, and never smug. She didn't like to be wasteful. One of her favorite puns was referring to Neiman Marcus as "Needless Mark-up." What a great sense of humor.

I pushed on without Vera, remembering the happy times she and I had enjoyed together. I looked at all the good that had come out of our work on the hospice, and I was pleased to know Vera had a hand in it. It was really her idea to donate the gift for the hospice construction. I think it was one of her finest moments.

After Vera's death, my work began to take on a new purpose. I was at a turning point. I had new ideas about what I wanted to do in my remaining years. I set out on a different path, inspired by Vera, doing exactly what she would have wanted me to do.

Joe and Vera Zilber at Israel Bonds fundraising dinner.

Polished copper kettles and the stained glass window of King Gambrinus
in the old Pabst Brew House, now the Brewhouse Inn and Suites
in Joe Zilber's Brewery development in Milwaukee.

Joe Zilber stands in front of one of his condominium
projects on the Space Coast of Florida.

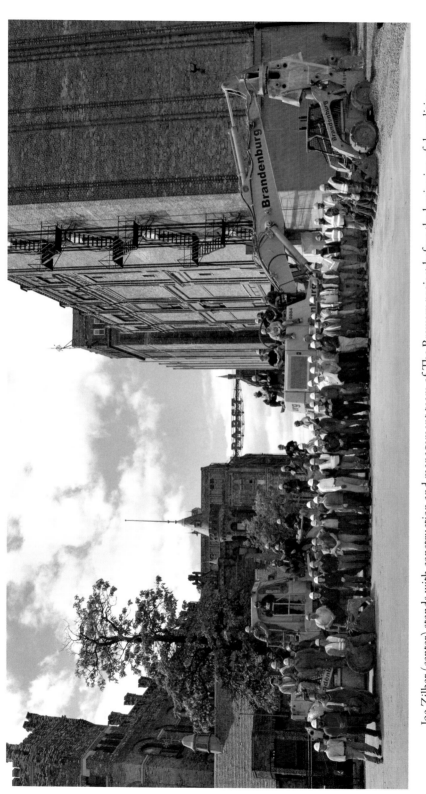

Joe Zilber (center) stands with construction and management team of The Brewery project before the beginning of demolition, construction and renovation. Captain Pabst's office is directly under the flagpole to the upper left of the picture.

Joe Zilber meets with members of the Joseph J. Zilber Boys & Girls Club
just prior to its opening in Joe's old neighborhood.

VENTURES

ENTERPRISING IDEAS FOR THE V   SEPTE   TOBER 2005

COOL BRAND. IDEAL LOCATION.
A TIGHT, WELL-HONED STRATEGY.
JIM BORRIS &
JOE ZILBER HAVE **BIG PLANS**

FOR GETTING BIGGER AT
RON JON CAPE CARIBE RESORT.

Joe Zilber (right) and Jim Borris pictured on the front of Ventures magazine.
Zilber would go on to select Borris as the President and Chief Executive Officer of Zilber Ltd.

This ad, which ran in Milwaukee and other major communities with Zilber operations around the country, was Joe Zilber's statement against the terrorists and ran within days of 9-11.

Statue of Joe and Vera Zilber in Zilber Park at The Brewery.
The gabion wall, with its trickle fountain in the summer turns into a
constantly changing ice sculpture in the winter, is in the background.

Joe Zilber with his wife Vera (front), and daughters
Marcy (right) and Marilyn (left) taken at his 90th Birthday Party.

Joe Zilber (left), Joe's son Jim (center) and Joe's long-time assistant, Mike Mervis (right).

At the groundbreaking for Congregation Emanu-El B'ne Jeshurun – left to right, Steve Marcus, Bud Selig, Joe Zilber, Marilyn Zilber, Sue Selig, Doris Chortek and Michael Green.

Joe Zilber (left) talks with Mayor Tom Barrett after making a $50 million commitment to establish the Zilber Neighborhood Initiative in Milwaukee.

A new home comes off the rails at Zilber's Towne Manufacturing Corporation and awaits transportation to its new home on the south side of Milwaukee. The homes were originally priced at $19,999.

Jim Zilber, Marilyn Zilber and Marcy Zilber (front row); Vera Zilber, former First Lady Eleanor Roosevelt and Joe Zilber (back row) at the Zilber's home.

One of the first Towne Realty offices in Milwaukee.

Joe and Vera Zilber in one of their favorite pictures taken
at the Captain's Table on one of their many ocean cruises.

CHAPTER 13

BURYING EVIDENCE, AND THE MORAL CODE THAT DEMANDED IT

We all have guiding principles that we follow, values that we've learned from our parents and friends, teachers and faiths. Often it's simply living according to the rules of fairness — making decisions that are just, and trying to correct things that are wrong. It's doing what you believe is right. I've tried to live a life that's based on the set of principles that I learned long ago and that still hold true. Let me give you a few examples.

In all the projects Towne Realty did in Nevada, I never wanted to get into the casino business. It wasn't the type of business that I viewed as reputable. Nevada was an important segment of our commercial division, and Towne was building hotels in Las Vegas and Reno. We put up the buildings and leased the properties to hotel operators, many of whom opened casinos in their hotels. We built the first phase of hotel rooms for Circus Circus, for example, which grew into a huge Vegas attraction, but we never got involved in its casino business.

I had been to Las Vegas dozens of times, of course, and I liked to gamble once in awhile, but when I gambled, I had a rule: If I lost a hundred dollars, that was it, I'd quit. So be it. If I made a hundred dollars, I'd take the money and buy myself a couple of new shirts. Sure, playing blackjack could be a lot of fun from time to time, but operating a casino was a different story. I didn't feel it was quite right to make money from the habits of people who really couldn't afford to lose.

We had plenty of opportunities to get into the gambling game. I remember one time in Las Vegas: we built our first Mini-Price Motor Inn, and a man named Carl Thomas, who ran a casino on the strip called Slots of Fun, wanted to go into business with us. He said, "Why don't you open a casino in your motel and I'll run it?" No dice, we told him. "Well, why don't you lease me a building adjacent to your motel," he said, "and I'll run the casino." We leased him the property, and independent of us he opened a place called Bingo Palace.

A year later, Thomas came to us again, wanting to expand and offering us a partnership interest. "You guys are crazy not to be in the casino business. We make so much money," he told us. Again we told him no thanks.

The next issue with "connected" people came from Frank Balistrieri. Frank had been a law school student with me at Marquette University. Frank also became a tenant of mine. We owned a building in downtown Milwaukee that housed a night club that he rented called The Ad Lib. I remember one day he arrived at his club to find the doors padlocked shut.

Frank called me immediately. "What the hell are you doing?" he said. "One of your guys locked me out." I said, "What are you talking about, Frank? Why would anybody lock you out?" He paused for a second, and said, "Well, maybe I didn't pay the rent or something." I said to him, "Well, that would be good reason for one of my guys to lock you out." A half hour later, Frank was there with cash for the rent.

Frank ended up going to federal prison for income tax evasion in the late 1960s. He was convicted and sentenced to prison again in 1985 following the investigation of a skimming operation at the Stardust and the Fremont casinos in Vegas. Carl Thomas received immunity in exchange for testifying against Balistrieri and organized crime figures from Kansas, Chicago, and Cleveland.

Frank Fertitta bought out Thomas' interest in the Bingo Palace and changed the name to the Palace Station. He came to Milwaukee to visit me once, trying again to get me to become an investor in his expansion. Fertitta had started out as a bellhop and a blackjack dealer and eventually became somewhat of a Las Vegas legend. His son and grandson got into the business and founded Station Casinos Inc., a chain of casinos in Nevada, which filed for bankruptcy in 2009.

When Fertitta met with me, he was building a 1,000-room hotel tower and huge casino. Again I decided to pass. The gaming business was just not for me. While I got to know quite a few people in the casino industry, including my old college classmate, I never believed it was a good business. I never really thought it was right.

❧ ❧ ❧

Living by your principles doesn't always mean making a big statement. One day someone had discovered what looked like Nazi swastikas etched in the wall tiles of a school in a Milwaukee suburb. There were a couple dozen of them above a staircase in the entrance to the swimming pool at Shorewood High School. The swastika design has been traced back 3,000 years and has been found over the centuries in Chinese, Indian, and European cultures. However, in modern times it's mostly known as a symbol used by Hitler's regime. It's offensive to people, Jews especially, who know it as a mark of anti-Semitism.

The school's swimming pool building was old, built in 1930 or so, and no one knew why the swastika design was there. The Milwaukee Jewish Council talked to the school superintendent about what to do, and I wanted to help out. I made an anonymous donation to the Jewish Council, and the swastika tiles were removed and replaced with a different design. It was the right thing to do, and the entire operation was carried out without unnecessary attention.

Then there was the time I went to bat for Bank of Boston. My company had a long history with the bank and had established a very good relationship over the years. We had a great partnership. I was both a depositor and a borrower, and I knew the chairman, Chad Gifford, very well. At the time, Bank of Boston had gotten some bad press.

I believed the bank got a raw deal. The people I knew who ran Bank of Boston were top notch, and I said so publicly. I placed an ad in the Boston Globe newspaper, saying I had been a customer for 10 years and could count on their superior financial services. "I have the highest regard for Bank of Boston, its management team, and its staff," I said in the ad. "Good and loyal banks are hard to find in America's hectic and constantly changing financial system. When you find a good bank, I firmly believe you should stick with it. I'm sticking with Bank of Boston — a good bank — that's done a good job for me."

From the chairman on down, the morale of everybody at the bank had been in the gutter. So on the morning that the ad ran, I had someone place copies of the newspaper ad on the desk of every bank employee. They were very grateful that someone had defended their reputation, and I was happy to do it.

As the son of immigrant parents and a veteran of World War II, I'm proud of my country and thankful for the opportunities I've been given. When terrorists attacked the World Trade Center and the Pentagon on September 11, 2001, it hit me pretty hard. Like everyone else in the country, I was saddened and outraged by the loss of so many American lives on our nation's soil. I live half the year in Honolulu, and I'm reminded every time I drive past the Pearl Harbor Memorial of that fateful tragedy on December 7, 1941.

The attacks on 9/11 got my hackles up. I wanted to make a statement to my employees, to my customers, and to the country, urging people not to alter their lives because of the terrorists. I placed an ad in several newspapers around the country, saying Zilber Ltd. would continue to do business as usual.

"The terrorists win if we don't have the courage to live our lives," said the ad. "We at Zilber Ltd. are determined to do our share to keep America strong. We will continue to buy land, construct and purchase buildings, and develop corporate parks. The terrorists will not win." I thought it was important to send this message — loud and clear.

One of the things that I have learned from Jewish tradition is that it is our given task to make the world a better place. That means we cannot disengage from what is going on in the world around us. We need to stay deeply involved.

❧ ❧ ❧

As I look back, one of the more uplifting projects that I was involved in was the remodeling of the historic Riverside Theatre. The Riverside had been a part of my life since I was a kid. It was built in 1929 during the "Golden Age of movie Palaces". Wonderful theaters like the Riverside, the Oriental, the Modjeska, and the Avalon were built in Milwaukee. The Riverside was high class, an opulent theater with opera seats, a huge balcony, and a deep, wide stage. A beautiful place. When I was a boy, I would take a street car to the Riverside to see vaudeville shows and movies. Hollywood had just started making "talkies," and for a dime I could spend an entire Saturday afternoon there.

The Riverside Theatre was the centerpiece of the Empire Building, an office building in the heart of Milwaukee's downtown on the Milwaukee River. As I've mentioned previously, I purchased the Empire Building and the Riverside years later, after buying and then selling 27 theaters in Milwaukee and around Wisconsin. We showed all the big blockbuster movies. For years, United Artists Theaters operated the Riverside for us, but eventually they let the grand theater get run down.

The original Wurlitzer pipe organ, a "one-man orchestra" that at one time filled the theater with magnificent music, no longer worked, and many of the lights in the auditorium's chandeliers were out. United Artists began playing horror pictures, Kung Fu films, and all kinds of B movies. When they started showing sex movies, I'd had enough. Sex flicks would destroy the reputation of the theater and were not at all good for downtown business. We let our lease with United Artists expire and the theater went dark.

The empty theater was a cash drain and an eyesore. We talked about tearing the Riverside down and replacing it with retail shops or a parking garage, but I love old buildings, and if there's a feasible and economical way to preserve them, I'm for it. So I put up the money for restoration — new lighting, new drapes, the whole thing. Patrons once again would hear the organist play "Down by the Riverside" on the Wurlitzer. New seats were put in, the movie projectors were removed, and the Riverside Theatre from then on became a show house for live performances.

Soon after the remodeling, Tony Bennett was booked into the theater. Bennett is a great singer, a living legend. He has a voice of velvet. Vera and I attended the opening night show, and the house was filled. After Bennett sang a few of his songs, he spoke to the audience: "Do you mind if I turn off the microphone?" He put down the mike and sang without any amplification — I think he probably did "I Left My Heart in San Francisco" — and the people up in the top rows of the balcony still could hear his marvelous voice. "These are the best acoustics I've ever seen in any theater I've been in," he said.

Years later, we decided to try another management company, which wanted to turn the Riverside into a dinner theater. That didn't work out, and the theater again went dark for several months. We decided to put together a deal with Michael Cudahy, a Milwaukee entrepreneur and grandson of Patrick Cudahy, the meat packing magnate. In the 1960s, Michael Cudahy had founded Marquette Electronics, a medical equipment manufacturer that he eventually sold to General Electric for a good amount of cash.

He had acquired Milwaukee's landmark Pabst Theatre and, with his experienced manager, Gary Witt, had done a good job of revitalizing the downtown showplace. I met with Cudahy at a local restaurant for a drink. I think it was the first time we had met face to face. Cudahy was in his early 80s at the time, a few years younger than me, and, like me, he was accustomed to making a deal with just a handshake.

We talked a little about our lives, about living in Milwaukee, and then we got down to business. Cudahy agreed to have his team take care of the bookings and management. I agreed to put new money into the theater to upgrade the sound system and the seats. "We don't need any goddamn lawyers to do this," he said to me, and we shook hands on the deal. Soon the doors to the Riverside swung open again. Today, in the lobby, you can see two portraits hanging across from each other on opposite walls, two partners, Cudahy and me.

To top it off, weeks after the renovation was completed, Tony Bennett came back to the Riverside to perform. Standing at center stage, looking out into the packed house, he called Cudahy and me to join him on stage. Bennett remembered playing the Riverside before. He remembered what outstanding acoustics it has. Once again, he asked that the sound system be switched off. "Turn off the mike, I want to do this again," he said, and then put down the microphone and sang solo, a cappella.

After the performance, he got on a coach bus and headed down the road for his next show. He was 79 then and still going strong. I couldn't believe he did what he did at his age. But I couldn't imagine Tony Bennett sounding any better than he did that night at the Riverside.

❧ ❧ ❧

As the president of a large company, I don't really look for the spotlight, but occasionally things come up that push me into the public eye. Back in 1996, I was able to close one of the most terrible chapters in Milwaukee's history, one that became an international news story.

I was at my home in Hawaii. Vera and I were having breakfast and I was reading the newspaper. An article caught my eye: the families of the victims of infamous serial killer Jeffrey Dahmer were going to auction off all of his remaining possessions. The victims' family members wanted to sell everything that had been confiscated from Dahmer's apartment, including the materials he used to commit his gruesome crimes.

Vera and I were sick to our stomachs. "They can't let that happen," Vera said to me. "It would harm Milwaukee's reputation so much. Can you do anything about it?" Five years earlier, the Dahmer case had left a smirch on Milwaukee's image. Vera and I couldn't bear to see the city get dragged down again.

Jeffrey Dahmer had been arrested in his Milwaukee apartment in the summer of 1991. He later confessed to murdering 17 young men, dismembering them and cannibalizing some of their bodies over a period of 13 years. I don't want to get into all the gory details, but it was a horrible case. His two-week trial was on the news every day, all around the world. A jury found him guilty, and he was sentenced to 15 consecutive life terms in prison. He only lasted a couple of years. He was beaten to death in a prison bathroom by another inmate.

Now it's over, I thought at the time. It was some kind of prison justice, but for years after, whenever people thought of Milwaukee, they thought of Jeffrey Dahmer, one of the most notorious serial killers who ever lived.

Before Dahmer was killed, the families of the victims had filed several lawsuits against him. Dahmer didn't have any assets, but the families wanted to prevent him from profiting in case he got paid for any books, movies, or personal appearances. After his death, a judge appointed an attorney to represent his estate. The attorney was given permission to collect and sell Dahmer's belongings in order to settle the claims by the families of his victims.

The families believed they were entitled to the value of his estate for the grievances he had caused them. That's when I heard that the families' lawyer wanted to hold a public auction to sell the possessions. I had no problem with the families receiving some kind of compensation for their pain and suffering, but I just couldn't see the Dahmer materials becoming worldwide souvenirs. It wasn't right.

The police had been holding the stuff as evidence, but with the trial over, they released a long list of Dahmer's possessions: handcuffs, a hypodermic needle, a power drill, a hand saw, a claw hammer, a hatchet. Instruments of torture and weapons of murder. I knew that these things should never again see the light of day. I wanted to do something about it, for the good of the city. So I called the lawyer who represented the families, an attorney named Tom Jacobson, thinking maybe he would sell me the possessions at a reasonable price and I could get rid of them.

Jacobson had big plans and an ego to match. He had contacted an auctioneer in New York City who had sold crime memorabilia in the past — macabre things like the gun used by Jack Ruby to shoot Lee Harvey Oswald and the toe tag worn in the morgue by Oswald after he was killed. Jacobson said his asking price was $1 million: non-negotiable. Just a week or two earlier, at an auction in New York, the possessions of the late Jacqueline Kennedy Onassis had brought in $34.5 million.

"We have two sides to our psyche, the Camelot side and the Dahmer side," Jacobson said to the press. "You can only imagine what people would pay for some of this stuff . . . and the sicker the connotation, the bigger the bucks."

Jacobson's price was way out of line. I knew I could convince him to come down — everything is negotiable — but I needed a little time to see how much money I could raise. "Give me a couple of months," I said to him. We set Memorial Day as a deadline, and I got on the phone to a few of my friends. I kicked things off by contributing $100,000, and sizable donations were made by three good friends of mine, Steve Marcus, chairman of the Marcus Corporation, John Burke, owner and founder of Burke Properties in Milwaukee, and U.S. Senator Herb Kohl, owner of the Milwaukee Bucks.

It didn't stop there. People everywhere were outraged. They wanted to help put an end to this insane idea. I formed a group to raise money called the Milwaukee Civic Pride Fund. Before I knew it, donations from all across the country and around the world were pouring in. Mostly small amounts, $10, $20. It was amazing.

My office was contacted by media outlets from around the world: German TV, British TV, *The Times* of London, *The New York Times*. The local newspapers got on the bandwagon, too, backing our plan to buy the material and dispose of it. I still remember the reporters at *The Milwaukee Journal* were betting on whether or not we would be able to pull it off.

Our deadline arrived, Memorial Day. We had come up with $407,225. I got attorney Jacobson on the phone. "This is what we've got. It's all we're going to raise," I told him. "It's a fair price. Take it to your clients. Do it for your city." Jacobson did the right thing. He took the offer to the families and they accepted it. Eleven families in all would get about $32,000 each after paying the attorney fees. It was a very satisfying day.

We held a press conference with several of the families and announced that the citizens group, the Milwaukee Civic Pride Fund, would buy the legal rights to all of Dahmer's possessions. "This will allow us, once and for all, to close the book on Jeffrey Dahmer," I said.

What would we do with this awful stuff?

We talked to a couple of foundries to see if they would take the belongings and incinerate them, but they said no, they didn't want anything to do with it. We contacted an industrial recycling plant that compacted and sold scrap iron, but they were also worried people would get their hands on pieces of the scrap and say, "This is part of Dahmer's refrigerator," or something like that.

So I called Bill Katzman, the head of Waste Management of Wisconsin, and told him we were looking to dispose of Dahmer's stuff. Katzman agreed to take it and to donate the equipment and labor to have the items removed. I sent my right-hand man, Mike Mervis, down to the police department to document the transfer of the items.

At 5:00 a.m. on June 26, 1996, Mervis walked into the evidence room in the basement of Milwaukee's Third District police station. He was met by three police officers — the captain of the district, a sergeant, and another officer. I remember Mike telling me the police had set up a large table adjacent to the police evidence room. On the table was a master inventory list of all the evidence, almost 250 items.

Officers began bringing out the evidence, piece by piece — most of it in paper evidence bags. Each piece was matched against the items on the list — the 57 gallon drum that had been filled with acid, the big pot that Dahmer boiled the body parts in, the spoons, the knives, the freezer he stored the heads in, the porno tapes, his hairbrush, his toothbrush, his lava lamp. Every item was recorded on video by a crew hired by Waste Management.

Mervis signed off on each piece, then the entire load was hauled up the back stairs and into the alley, where Waste Management had a huge dumpster on the trailer of a semi-truck. They loaded everything into the dumpster and drove 100 miles south of Milwaukee to a Waste Management landfill near Elgin, Illinois. Workers had dug a huge hole into the base of the landfill, 40 feet deep.

The material was dumped into the hole and crushed by a 30-ton Caterpillar compacting machine. Garbage was piled into the hole until it was completely filled, and over the next month, another 40 to 50 feet of garbage went on top of that. In the next year or two, the site was capped with soil and planted with grass.

Mervis called me at my home in Hawaii from the landfill and told me the items were gone, buried. I thanked him and walked into the kitchen to tell Vera. "It's done. No one will ever see any of it again." She gave me a kiss and said, "Good." And that was the end of it.

From time to time, someone tries to sell something on eBay, or auction something off in some bizarre catalog, claiming it's an item that belonged to Jeffrey Dahmer. People will see it advertised and call my office, and we tell them it's not possible. All the material has been buried and destroyed. I have the video documentation to prove it.

For years, we kept the location of the landfill a secret. It was never disclosed — until now. There's no chance that the possessions will ever be unearthed. Today that landfill is closed and the Dahmer stuff lies under a mountain of trash. I don't want to get too high minded about it, but I like to believe this was one of the best things I did for the city of Milwaukee. It was a gesture of good will. To think that those things might have been scattered around the world would have been terrible.

CHAPTER 14

LAVERNE & SHIRLEY AND THE PABST MAKEOVER

I f you've ever watched the TV show *Laverne & Shirley*, you probably remember the opening credits. The two friends are standing on the bottling line at "Shotz Brewery," where they work, and they're goofing around, dousing each other with beer foam and fitting rubber gloves to beer bottles. It's a funny scene. Shotz, of course, was fictitious, a made-for-TV brewery. That opening scene was actually shot at Milwaukee's famous Pabst Brewery, once the largest brewery in America, dating back to 1844.

Some Milwaukeeans cringe whenever somebody uses the *Laverne & Shirley* show to characterize Milwaukee's image. I think it's all in good fun. In fact, just a few years ago, on Milwaukee's RiverWalk, the city installed a bronze statue of "The Fonz" from the *Happy Days* show, which was also set in Milwaukee.

The real story of the Pabst Brewery isn't as amusing as *Laverne & Shirley*, however. The Pabst Brewing Company pulled out of Milwaukee abruptly in 1996. The owners just turned off the lights, locked the doors, and walked away, putting thousands of people out of work. They left all of the brewing equipment, all of the offices, file cabinets full of paperwork, and employee lockers stuffed with personal items. Every calendar stood at the same date. It was like the people had vanished and everything else stayed in place.

Just two employees remained on the site, a security guard and a part-time maintenance worker, but no repairs were done, and for years, the historic buildings sat empty. The Brew House, the Mill House, the

Keg House, the Bottling House — they all were left to crumble. It was shameful what happened there.

Starting in 2001, a group of developers called the Wispark Company started putting together proposals to turn the Pabst Brewery into an entertainment and retail center. Funded in part with a $41 million, city-backed financing package, the plan was ambitious. The developers believed the project would be a great addition to the city, but a lot of people didn't agree. The plan failed to win the backing of the Milwaukee Common Council, and in 2005, the Pabst Brewery site was still a ghost town.

At that point, I decided to step in. I have always wanted to do good for my hometown, so I put together a deal. It wouldn't be just another real estate transaction, remodeling a building here, putting up a new building there. Not at all. I bought the entire brewery, all 21 acres — lock, stock and (beer) barrel. When we're finished with the redevelopment, The Brewery, as it's now called, will be a milestone for Milwaukee, a one-of-a-kind project.

We will have created a neighborhood that's both historic and "green," with apartments, condos, hotels, retail shops, restaurants, office buildings, a manufacturing plant, and college classrooms. Sitting on a hill overlooking Milwaukee's skyline, the whole area is going to change. That one-time blighted 21 acres will be transformed into a vital, new neighborhood.

The Brewery won't be much of a money maker. In fact, plenty of people advised me not to buy it, including most of my own management team, as I wrote about in Chapter 1. It's costing me an awful lot of money, much more than I ever would have expected, but to me it's worth it. I'm determined to make it work. As I've said, I want to give back to Milwaukee. The city has given so much to me. I'm pleased at what I'll be able to do for the city. That was my purpose, to make The Brewery something of a legacy. Milwaukee has a chance to improve itself. It's on the brink. The Brewery may very well play a role in the city's revival.

The story of how The Brewery came together is worth telling. It's an interesting "anatomy" of a real estate deal, but it also shows just why I'm so passionate about this project.

Go back to September 2001. A Milwaukee accountant named Jim Haertel had put a $50,000 nonrefundable deposit on a contract to purchase the Pabst Brewery for $11 million. Under the agreement, he had one year to raise $500,000 and close on the deal. Haertel, who had worked for Towne Realty in the '80s, was something of a beer historian and quite a character. He had a dream. He would buy the Pabst Brewery and sell it off to third parties, who would then redevelop the site.

As fate would have it, Jim signed the agreement on September 11, 2001. Following the terrorist attacks on that day, economic development slowed to a halt, and Haertel had a difficult time finding developers to go in with him. He scrambled to change course.

A year later, just days before his deadline, Haertel sold his contract for $13 million to Wispark Company, the development arm of the giant utility Wisconsin Energy Corporation. Wispark brought in a Cleveland developer who had renovated the Heinz food factory into housing in Pittsburgh. Haertel retained title to the visitors' center, the gift shop, and Blue Ribbon Hall.

The Wispark people put forth a plan to turn the brewery into a retail and entertainment center. They would call it Pabst City. They got letters of intent from the House of Blues, Sega Game Works, and the Marcus Corporation for a movie theater, and a handful of retailers. At the same time, they went to the city of Milwaukee for $41 million in financial assistance in the form of a tax increment financing district, known as a TIF.

The plan was backed strongly by Mayor Tom Barrett, but in my opinion, Wispark overplayed its hand. The hospitality businesses in town saw Pabst City as a huge competitive threat and rallied against it. After a number of public meetings, in July 2005, Milwaukee's Common Council voted 9-5 to reject Wispark's request for TIF money, and the proposal died.

I thought I could do better. A day or two after the vote, I called up the head of Wisconsin Energy, Gale Klappa, who had been made chairman, president, and CEO just a year earlier. Klappa had not been part of the original development team, and Wispark's defeat on Pabst City put him in a jam. His company, a public company, was stuck with a deteriorating property that he would now have to sell — and probably at a loss, something his shareholders certainly weren't going to like. I'd had some real estate dealings with Wispark, so I knew Gale. He was very smart, and an honorable guy. I thought we could do a deal.

"Gale, this Pabst Brewery project really isn't for you," I told him. "You're in the electric business, not the real estate business. Why do you want to do this kind of stuff? Maybe I'll buy you out." From there, we began to have serious discussions about how I could acquire Pabst.

Mayor Tom Barrett also had come out on the short end of a stick with the defeat of Pabst City. With the abandoned Pabst site being such a potential city problem, he had been confident he'd get the support of the Common Council for the Wispark Plan, so confident that he felt comfortable enough to be out of town when they called Pabst City to a vote. Now he was faced with the politician's dilemma: now what?

I had spoken with the mayor before the vote. At a meeting at Mike Mervis' house, I had told the mayor I was interested in doing something for Milwaukee. He asked me if I would help fund a study of public safety issues and the operation of the city's Department of Public Works, which I agreed to do. We didn't talk about Pabst Brewery at that point, and, frankly, the Mayor's expectations were lower than what I had been considering.

After the Pabst City plan went down, I telephoned Mayor Barrett from my winter home in Hawaii and laid out my idea in black and white. I told him I had been talking to Gale Klappa and that I wanted to buy the Pabst. I told him that I needed his support on the public financing piece, and that I wanted to request a TIF, although not as large as Wispark's. Barrett welcomed my idea and gave me his backing. Since the Pabst City vote, no one else had come forward with an alternative. As he remembers, my proposal was music to his ears. Barrett recalls:

> Pabst looked like Beirut after a bombing. Although the buildings themselves are beautiful, there just was nothing there. I was still obsessed with moving forward on that site because I had put so much energy into it. So it was manna from the heavens to get that phone call from Joe Zilber. He talked about how he wanted to give back to the community that he loved. "I want this to be my legacy," he said. As the mayor, you get phone calls like that once every career. Not once every year, not once every term, once every *career*.

After talking to Mayor Barrett, back I went to Gale Klappa at Wisconsin Energy. I knew I held a strong hand. Klappa was in a bind. As the new

CEO, he had a whole new management team that was looking to succeed. No one would be happy about the potential impact Pabst would have on their earnings, including Wisconsin Energy's board of directors.

In addition, Wisconsin Energy needed to cultivate community support in order to develop a positive regulatory climate. The public utility had a couple billion dollars worth of major projects on the drawing board, one of them an expansion of a coal-burning energy plant right in Milwaukee's backyard.

So when it became known that I was interested in buying out Wispark's interest in the Pabst, they faced a potential public relations nightmare. The brewery buildings were leaking water, and walls were caving in. As the Mayor said, it looked like Beirut. Klappa couldn't just fold the deal and walk away from the Pabst if there was a viable Plan B on the table, and there I was — Plan B.

"What'll you take? We'll buy it at your cost," I said to Klappa. I knew the utility had bought it a few years ago for $13 million; maybe it was worth a little more.

"I've got $25 million in it, so I'll say $25 million," Klappa said.

His price seemed on the high side, so I took it to my senior management team to kick around.

From the start, my management guys didn't see the wisdom of my plan. When I first began talking about buying the brewery, we arranged a tour of the site for all of my senior managers. They wanted to see firsthand what we might be getting into. Dan McCarthy was working for Wispark at the time. We later hired Dan over to our side after we made our pitch for the Pabst. When the managers' tour was put together, I was in Hawaii. But I've heard Dan, now vice president of The Brewery Project LLC, describe the tour:

> I started by handing out hardhats and flashlights to everybody. Now, I hadn't shown the property much, but I knew my way around a little bit. I wanted to show them the Brew House, which is one of the most spectacular buildings, and the only way I knew how to get there was by going down a very narrow stairway through this pitch-black basement and then up another staircase. We literally had these high-powered executives from Zilber Ltd. hand to shoulder in the dark, each holding a flashlight. Pools of water were on the floor, and green moss was growing on the walls. It was like we were miners.

Mike Mervis, my assistant and vice president of The Brewery Project, went on the tour, too. "We come back to the office and everyone was shell shocked . . . and filthy." Mervis remembers. "We're sitting around the executive conference room, and Joe calls in from Hawaii on the tele-conference system. 'Hey, fellas,' he says in a cheerful voice. 'What do you think? Let's go around the table and get a vote.' And so we took a vote.

"Joe always says the vote was 12 to 1 *against* buying the brewery, but he wanted the property badly. It was his goal. So we told him, Joe, if you want to do it, we'll get it done. It's good to be king, you know."

Ever the risk taker in real estate, mine was the only vote for purchasing the Pabst. Knowing that my senior management team was not in favor, I took it upon myself to buy the Pabst on my own rather than have the company do it. My managers probably were right. It was not anything a profitable company should have undertaken. There were a lot of risks, a lot of downsides and not many upsides. Sure, there were easier ways to make money, but I had made up my mind. I viewed it as a civic project.

I decided I would take the purchase of the Pabst out of Zilber Ltd. so the company's banks wouldn't be involved and our credit wouldn't be at stake, and I decided I would pay for it myself. I would form a company, Brewery Project LLC, and hire the management team of Zilber Ltd. to run the project.

I continued negotiating with Gale Klappa, going back and forth, offering him cash and a note at first, then just cash. He came down, I went up, and finally, after all was said and done, on the day before Thanksgiving 2005, we signed a contract on a cash sale of $13 million.

The next step was putting together a strategy for our public financing request. We wanted the city to approve tax increment financing to pay for infrastructure work. The mayor already was with us, so I got busy talking to members of the Common Council. I sat down with nearly every alderman, face to face, asking for support.

It was a good strategy. Our plan was fundamentally different than the Wispark plan. They were going to build nearly everything new. All but five or six of the historic buildings would have been razed and replaced. Wispark was going to own everything, and the entire project would come online at one time. John Kersey is the president of The Brewery Project. He's smart and trustworthy, and I can rely on whatever he says and does. John is good at explaining why our plan was an improvement over the first proposed project:

> We took a less aggressive approach. We decided that we would act as the master developer — do all the dances, do all the heavy lifting, install the new utilities, install the streets, remove the equipment in the buildings. We would tear down certain buildings that couldn't be saved, but save most of them. Once that was done, we would put entire blocks of the brewery up for sale, so developers would come in and do whatever it is they do best. The fundamental difference between the Wispark plan and our plan was they had specific uses for each piece of the property. We were just going to prepare it and see what happened.

It made sense for us, and it was a good political strategy as we looked for the city's support. To sweeten the deal, I told the aldermen that I would split any profits with the city. "God forbid, if this makes a profit we'll give you half," I told them. That kind of disarmed them. Not surprisingly, they liked the idea.

Our request was for tax increment financing of $28.7 million, which we would use to pay for new streets, sewers, water mains, demolition, and environmental cleanup. Interest charges would cost us $12.5 million over about 20 years. The Common Council approved our request in December 2006. The vote was 14 to 0 with one abstention.

❧❧❧ ❧❧❧ ❧❧❧

We closed on the property in August 2006, and in the first three years, we made incredible progress creating a new neighborhood. Developers came to us with creative, first-rate ideas. We did everything we could to help, and then watched as they turned their ideas into realities.

The former Keg House — once a soot-covered brick building where half barrels and quarter barrels were filled with Pabst Blue Ribbon beer — was converted into an apartment complex. It's a spectacular development. It has 95 units — the exterior Cream City brick restored to its original color — with a movie theater, fitness center, and small recording studio. The complex, called Blue Ribbon Lofts, was designed with an industrial feel: acid-washed cement floors, lots of interior ironwork, and huge wooden beams, all part of the original building.

The apartments are geared for the "creative class," people who love the urban environment and who seek unique areas for their living space. Some units include space that tenants use as art studios, with wide, overhead sliding doors that open up to inside common areas and corridors. Musicians perform and artists hold "gallery nights" in the building to display their artwork. It's truly an exceptional place.

Meanwhile, several other buildings sold and the developers have turned them into a good mix of uses. The original Boiler House is now an office complex, occupied by an architectural firm, a medical business, and a real estate management company. It's very high class.

A building known simply as Building 13 once was the brewery's research labs, where different types of brews were concocted and tested. Today it's the College of Education and Leadership for Cardinal Stritch University. Every day hundreds of students and faculty file in and out of classrooms in old Building 13.

Building 7, the manufacturing and cold storage building, is scheduled to become the University of Wisconsin-Milwaukee Graduate School of Public Health. I made a pledge to UWM of $10 million to get that school off the ground. The field of public health was extremely important to my wife Vera. Before we were married, Vera was studying medicine. She was the kindest, most caring woman I knew, and the thought of anyone being unable to access essential health facilities was not acceptable to her.

Across the street from Building 7 is the Brew House, and what an amazing structure it is. Built in 1892, the building is rich with the history of Milwaukee's Golden Age of Brewing. A winding grand staircase, trimmed by a brass railing, leads to what once were Pabst's corporate offices. Arched doorways and lath-and-plaster walls reflect the quality of the century-old construction — it's no wonder the building is still intact.

The real show stopper, however, is the brewing room. Standing in a rectangular atrium are six huge copper kettles and their flues, reaching three stories high from the ceramic tile floor to stained glass windows at the top. One story up, you look down on the tanks from an open mezzanine, which was once a small mechanical penthouse. It's a sight to behold.

These buildings, like the Keg House, are being developed by Gorman and Company of Madison, Wisconsin. They plan to create an extended-stay hotel featuring 90 suites, and on the ground floor they are working on plans for a beer hall and restaurant franchised by Hofbrauhaus, the same name as the famous beer hall in Munich, Germany. It will also have an outdoor beer garden. It will be a spectacular facility and should be a regional draw.

As some kind of accidental dividend, we apparently have God on our side, too. If you stand on the corner of 10th Street and Juneau Avenue, at the very center of The Brewery site, and look to the west, you will see a beautiful church, its narrow steeple reaching toward the sky. If you turn 90 degrees to the left and look straight to the south, you will see another beautiful church with another towering steeple, and if you turn around and look north, you'll see another beautiful church. You might say that the new neighborhood is at the crossroads of heaven.

Just down the street from the Brew House, we built an eight-level parking structure on the site that holds 880 vehicles. We put it up in just four months, using 700 precast pieces of concrete, some of them weighing as much as 20 tons. It's a remarkable construction. In any city neighborhood, parking is key. That parking structure was a great addition for people living or working at the west end of downtown.

With the TIF financing, we also rebuilt the infrastructure. We connected the roadways inside the brewery to the surrounding city streets, extending 9th Street and 10th Street and opening up Juneau Avenue to traffic again. For the first time in almost 10 years, the brewery is integrated with the rest of downtown. The Milwaukee Area Technical College and the Bradley Center basketball arena are within walking distance.

The famous red Pabst neon sign still hangs five stories above Juneau Avenue, on a narrow, bridge-like structure that stretches somewhat precariously from the Mill House across the street to the Malting House. That sign is a Milwaukee icon, a tribute to the city's long beer brewing history. We hope to save it for generations to come.

Behind the Brew House is another historic marker — the brewery's grain silos. The silos themselves have no real practical value anymore, but topping the silos are four stories of office and operational space, which would make a terrific space for a destination restaurant or nightclub. You can see all of Milwaukee and 20 miles beyond from up there.

The silos overlook an interstate freeway, I-43, which cuts through the center of Milwaukee and offers great exposure of The Brewery to tens of thousands of vehicles that pass every day. There's a freeway ramp at the southwest corner of the site, which provides easy access to the site. In fact, The Brewery stands as a gateway to downtown's west end. We'll certainly find a way to dress up the silos with a design, or a mural that highlights the new neighborhood.

We paid great attention to the history of the Pabst Brewery. We've gone out of our way to keep as many historic buildings intact as possible, razing only buildings that could not be salvaged. Preserving the past is essential, but we've also looked to the future. I take great pride in the fact that we've incorporated "sustainability guidelines" into The Brewery Project. Many of the buildings have been renovated using "green" design techniques and construction methods. Certified sustainability guidelines were incorporated into the site's infrastructure as well.

Here's one example: To recapture storm water runoff that ends up in the city's sewers — and sometimes Lake Michigan — we added porous paving materials and runoff systems that absorb, or recapture, storm water. Storm water runoff is collected from a section of Juneau Avenue, which has been paved with a porous material. That water is then filtered and stored in a 100,000-gallon underground reservoir. In addition to that, "bioswales," which are like small, vegetated ditches, have been installed along the streets to catch and store up to 225,000 gallons of rainwater.

I credit our decision to use many of these green building standards, including the bioswales, to my grandson, Shane Jackson. Shane is director of environmental projects for Towne Development of Hawaii and has developed a real expertise in this field. In fact, because of Shane, Towne was part of a pilot program in the Hawaiian Islands for Leadership in Energy and Environmental Design (LEED) certification, an important distinction in the green building movement.

⁂

As it turned out, our decision to sell parcels of the site to other developers was a smart move. Constructing everything on our own all at once would have been enormously expensive, $200 million or more. In hindsight, I can see now that the buildings would have been finished and ready to lease just as the lending crisis and the 2008-09 recession hit. It could have been disastrous. It's one of those odd quirks of history, but with luck, our timing turned out to be pretty good. We teamed up with some fine developers who put together high-quality projects. We put in the utilities and redid the streets, so all the major obstacles were eliminated for them. They were able to come in and go right to work developing their own successful projects.

As the recession eased and the economy recovered, The Brewery was about as shovel ready as you could get. On the 21-acre site, we had raw land for new construction ranging from 18,000-square-foot sites to 2.8-acre sites. We had buildings ranging from 6,000 square feet to a quarter of a million square feet. With the economy coming out of the recession, we were in good shape.

For me, personally, my decision to buy the Pabst Brewery was a call I made from the gut. It was the right thing to do. I make decisions for all kinds of reasons, and a lot of them are gut calls. Some of them are purely business decisions, some are social, and some are personal. With the decision to buy the Dahmer possessions, Vera and I were outraged, so I made the call.

When I ran the ad for the Bank of Boston, I thought it was wrong that the bankers were being pushed around, so I stood up for them. I saw the Pabst Brewery property as a blight that was bad for Milwaukee, so I decided to buy it myself. My guys know how I come to my decisions. They don't always agree, but they understand how I think. John Kersey, president of The Brewery Project and executive vice president of Zilber Ltd. has been with me for more than 30 years. He says:

> Ten years earlier, there's no way that Joe would have undertaken this project. Clearly when he was first building the company, there was no room for this kind of financial risk, but I think he reached a point in his life where he was certainly financially stable and looking to give back. As always, Joe wouldn't give in to the naysayers. People would say "Joe, you are nuts to do this. There's no way this is going to be successful."
>
> Which, of course, is like pouring gasoline on a fire. "I'll show you" — that's his way of thinking. So now he's bound and determined to be successful. He is *willing* this to be successful. There's no detail too small for him. If a prospect contacts us, I'll say to Joe, "Would you mind giving him a call?" Then I find out Joe's already talked to the guy.

Joe's our best salesperson, he's our best closer, because this is something that he wants very badly — whether he's here to see this thing to completion or not.

I admit that I can be pretty damn good at rallying support for a project that I'm sold on. I remember telling my plans for the Pabst to Don Mantz, who heads our construction company, KM Development. I was in Hawaii at the time, and it was a weekend. I called him at home.

"Don, I want to buy the Pabst Brewery." I told him.

"Okay, what do you want to do with it?" he said.

"I want to create a neighborhood where people can live, where there are homes, stores, and offices," I said to him.

"That's great, Joe. That's sounds just great."

"And I need to rely on you to see that it gets done. That means I have to be sure that you aren't going to retire."

Don paused for a second. "Joe, are you serious?"

"Of course I'm serious. What do you mean?"

"Well, Joe, I'm 65 years old, and you have just described the opportunity of a lifetime to a person who loves to build, but why did you wait so long to do it?"

I chuckled into the phone. "I'm 89, Don. What the hell is your problem?"

Don Mantz is still on the job today.

❧ ❧ ❧

My favorite thing about The Brewery is a small piece of land called Zilber Park. The park is environmentally sustainable, built over an underground water retention basin and using porous materials on the walkways. It's just a wonderful space, an urban "pocket park" tucked between the Boiler House and the Brew House, with a dozen maple trees, flower beds, stone benches, and a long wall, 12 feet high and nearly 100 feet long, made of chunks of granite that are held in place by recycled steel netting. In the summer, water spills over the wall; in the winter, ice sculptures form.

Off to the side of the park — and not too showy — is a statue of Vera and me, standing together overlooking the site, her hand in mine. It's a lovely likeness of the two of us. I can't think of a better place for it.

PART THREE

RESTORING THE AMERICAN DREAM

CHAPTER 15

THE DINNER THAT
CHANGED MY LIFE

Two years after the opening of the Zilber Family Hospice, the administrators held a dinner at a Milwaukee restaurant. I was invited to meet eight families whose loved ones had lived at the hospice. On a July evening, I walked with my daughter Marilyn and my assistant Mike Mervis over to the restaurant from my condominium just blocks away. Marilyn and I expected to have a nice dinner with friendly conversation, and that's just how it went. Everyone sat around a big table, enjoying wine, cocktails, and hors d'oeuvres, making small talk over our meal.

After dinner something happened that changed my life. Going around the table, one by one, the families took turns telling me about their hospice experiences, story after story about the things they had done at the hospice in the final days of a dying family member.

Their stories knocked me off my feet. There was one story from the family of a man who was Irish, so they had a St. Patrick's Day parade for him right there at the hospice. They all dressed in green and brought in bagpipers, then rolled his hospital bed out the door and down a walkway around the building. It was a great memory for the family, their own personal St. Paddy's Day parade, a memory that I'm sure they will cherish forever.

The children of another hospice patient told of how their father wanted guests to visit him only during the cocktail hour. So four or five of his good friends would stop by for drinks every day between 5:00 and 6:00 p.m.. They had a ball, living it up together right until the end. Another family held a wedding at the hospice. They brought the entire wedding party into the family lounge — bridesmaids, flowers, and everything — so the bride's mother could watch the ceremony from her bed. She passed away just a few days later, but the wedding was a great memory for the family. From the grandparents of a terminally ill child I heard how their disabled teenage daughter, the mother of the child, spent hours and hours alone with the baby, saying goodbye.

A former employee of mine also was at the dinner. Her name was Carole Pyter, and she told of putting her mother in the hospice:

> As the saying goes, "What goes around comes around." A rather mundane saying, but true. When I was pregnant with my firstborn in 1964, Mr. Zilber, you took good care of my needs. In fact, you held our daughter in your arms, and she laughed as you raised her in the air. Now, 41 years later, I needed to place my mother in a hospice. That hospice was the Zilber Hospice. The care she received was exceptional, and I just wanted you to know. Thank you for this hospice.

Working in real estate for as long as I have, I've seen how a piece of property can transform people's lives, whether it's someone's first home, a vacation condo, or the neighborhood churches we built in the early days of Towne Realty. I've dealt with people who were just starting out in life, or couples who needed bigger houses because their families were growing. Those stories were important and uplifting, but the hospice stories were different because they were about the *end* of life, not beginnings, about some of the final memories these people had of someone very special to them who was about to leave this world.

They played games in the sunroom with the kids and went for walks in the woods. They held parties in the courtyard and cooked dinners in the family kitchen. They laughed and cried, they celebrated and mourned. It was a home away from home for these families. It was a place where they could come to terms with the inevitable and experience the lives of a dying relative in positive ways.

The stories moved me, and I thought of my own family and our decision years earlier to place my son Jimmy in a hospice in San Diego. I thought of the hundreds of untold stories of people who had lived at the Zilber Family Hospice — nearly 1,200 patients, from newborn babies to people over 100, in the first four years of its operation.

What an impact the hospice was making, and what a great feeling to be a part of that. It was a real eye-opener for me. I realized, maybe for the first time, just how much of a difference a financial gift could mean to an organization. I knew that I wanted to do more. "I've got to figure out what else I can do for people who need help," I said to Mike and Marilyn on our way home from the dinner. "And I want to get started right away."

It would be my newfound ambition.

For years, I had figured I'd make charitable donations through the Zilber Family Foundation. I planned on letting the foundation's trustees give money away after I died. I figured it would be Vera who would handle all the gifting, but with Vera gone, that was not meant to be.

Vera and I had given to charities for years, groups like the Red Cross and United Way. We gave to the Jewish Federation every year. In her later years, Vera funded a studio at the University of Wisconsin-Milwaukee's School of Architecture and Urban Planning. We also had an annual tradition: we held parties on my birthday and asked each couple who came to give a donation to a charity of their choice. Vera and I then matched the contributions. That way we were able to spread the donations around, thousands of dollars to hundreds of worthwhile causes.

We had always tried to help out, but we had done it modestly and quietly. Frankly, I never wanted to advertise my wealth. What is wealth anyway? It's here today and gone tomorrow.

As a kid, I had lived through the Great Depression, and I saw my father and mother scrimp and save, only to lose the family grocery store. It could happen again. So I had put our money into the family foundation, invested it, built it up, and held on to it.

Maybe people thought I was miserly, but that wasn't it. I figured I would let my foundation handle the business of dispersing the funds one day after I was gone. The trustees who were planning my estate would harp at me. They'd say, "Look, you've got all this money in the foundation and you're going to have all this money in your estate. It makes sense that you tell us where you want it to go." I didn't want to make those decisions. For some reason, I just never set my mind to it.

All of that changed with that dinner in July. Listening to the hospice stories of those families made me feel appreciated. I had made a difference. For years, it had been against my better judgment to loosen the purse strings, but now I had enough tucked away to take care of my family and my company if another cold winter came along. The time was right. I was ready to let it go. That cliché "You can't take it with you" is absolutely true. Why leave it to the trustees to give it away? I'll give it away myself while I'm still alive, I decided.

Over the years, Vera made most of the decisions about how the family foundation would contribute to community charities. She worked with Steve Chevalier, a director and treasurer of the foundation, on the planning. Steve is also director of fiscal planning for Zilber Ltd. He's been with me since 1978. He was hired as the tax manager of our public company, Unicare, and stayed with the company after we sold it.

He planned to stay with the company for five years and then move on, but the professional challenges and opportunities kept him around for more than 30 years. "I grew to consider the people here as part of my family, and Joe and his wife and children always treated me as part of their extended family," he says. Steve is one of the smartest accountants I've ever known. He's very steady, and completely reliable. I trust him with everything I've got. Looking back, Steve says:

> The hospice was a big thing for Joe. He had been so busy doing business all of these years, he probably didn't spend as much time looking at the actual operations, or talking to people. On Vera's passing, he had time to think about philanthropy, maybe for the first time. Vera was very philanthropic. She had many discussions about what the Zilber Family Foundation should be doing.
>
> For example, she never was a big believer in giving money to only one cause, say the arts, as opposed to caring for the ill, the needy, feeding the poor, that kind of thing. She didn't want to just pay for the first violinist at the symphony; she also wanted to be sure that hungry kids were fed. She was very high on Milwaukee. Like Joe, she was a native and felt very passionate about this community.

It didn't take long for me to make the next move. Not long after the July dinner, I was presented with an award from the Aurora Visiting Nurse Association. The event was held outside at the hospice. It was a lovely summer day. The sun was shining, flowers were blooming. As I stood at the podium, I said:

> A building is only a building. But the staff of a hospice is so important, and here, I believe, is the best staff in the country, and I want to congratulate them. I'm not here to make a speech, but I am here to tell you how pleased I am at how the hospice turned out. The need is so great, and it is my belief that we should do whatever we can to create

wonderful hospice care in the city of Milwaukee. With that in mind, I am today pledging a million-and-a-half dollars to add another wing to this hospice for an additional six beds.

This was my new goal — to put my energy and resources into projects like creating hospice care in my community.

But how to do it? How do you come up with a plan to give away all your money? Where do you start?

❧ ❧ ❧

I've always had a warm spot in my heart for Marquette University. Marquette did an awful lot for me. Not only did I get my undergraduate and law degrees there, but it's where I met Vera on that fall day long, long ago. Years later, in 1983, Vera and I established annual scholarships for Marquette business and law students. The cost of college is astronomical compared to the days when we were students. So over the years, our fund has helped pay tuition costs for hundreds of these merit scholars.

In return, we got many letters of appreciation from the students, mostly from law students after they graduated and went into the legal profession. One became a public interest attorney in Maryland, another is a guardian ad litem with the Legal Aid Society in Milwaukee, and another is a real estate lawyer in California. From an appeals lawyer in Florida to a tax attorney in Texas, they went into all areas of law all across the country.

In a picture frame on my office wall is a letter from a special Zilber scholar. Dated August 5, 2001, here's what Rosalie wrote to Vera and me:

> I returned to school at age 70 when my husband had entered the more severe stages of Alzheimer's disease. The study of the law had always been a longed for venture. Although I realized that I would probably never earn professionally the cost of the tuition, my motive was more academic than professional. When I was informed of this scholarship, my confidence surged. It made me feel that Marquette not only admitted me, but believed in me. I am now entering my third year.
>
> I want to thank you for your role in encouraging me to engage this challenge. Rest assured that upon graduation, I will follow your example. This summer I interned with an immigration lawyer for Catholic

Charities. I see this now as a possibility for a career, or pro bono path after graduation. Whatever the future brings, I will always remember with gratitude the Zilber scholarship.

Handing out those scholarships had been gratifying, but I wanted to do more for my alma mater. One of my guys, Jim Janz, a senior vice president of Zilber Ltd., was also a graduate of Marquette Law School and a Marquette University trustee. He had been working on an estate plan for me with other senior managers.

As it happened, Jim also was sitting on a committee at Marquette when discussions began about constructing a new building for the law school. Jim and I kicked around the idea of making a major contribution to the Marquette scholarship fund. Jim recalls:

> For years, Joe had said that he didn't want us naming buildings after him, or putting up statues after he died. He clung to that. It was still his intent to be "the quiet man," but when we talked with Joe about the concept of having the law school building named after him, I guess it was just the right time in his life. Instead of saying "You're out of your mind!" — which he would say fairly often — he was curious about it, and one thing led to another.

> Joe has been giving scholarships all these years because he couldn't afford to go to school and he wanted to help other people who couldn't afford to go to school. It's that simple. He's not really much into bricks and mortar, frankly, even though he obviously has done a lot of construction over the years. He would rather have the money go to solve a problem, or to help a person.

I told Jim I wanted to make a significant donation, an amount that would benefit Marquette students for generations to come, so I came up with the figure of $30 million. I was in Hawaii at the time, and I told Janz that I would meet with the president of Marquette University, the Reverend Robert Wild, when I got back to Milwaukee in a few weeks. I wanted to finalize the deal myself, but before I got back to town, I got a phone call from Father Wild. I had known him for years, since he had become president of the university, and we got along very well. On this particular day, he sounded a little nervous on the phone.

"Joe," Wild said, "I don't know how to tell you this, but we got another offer from somebody who wants us to name the law school building after him. His name is Ray Eckstein, and he's also a Marquette alum. He sold his business and wants to give us $51 million. Joe, what should I do?"

"What do you mean, what should you do?" I said. "You should take it."

"You won't be upset?"

"Absolutely not," I told him. "You'll be getting $51 million for the law school." Up until then, the largest single gift to a Wisconsin university was $50 million, and Ray Eckstein wanted to top the record. Good for him, I thought.

What would I do now? This had come out of the blue. I had agreed to give $30 million, and I still wanted to contribute, but we had to renegotiate the details of the deal. When I got back to Milwaukee, I had lunch with Father Wild to try to come up with a new plan. As we sat and talked, Wild laid out on the dining table a rendering of the new law school building. It would be a magnificent addition to the campus.

Then Father Wild pointed to the drawing: the center of the building would be a four-story atrium, he said, with balconies and glass windows facing into the open space. It would be a spectacular area, the crossroads of activity in the law school building, sort of an indoor public square.

"We want to name the atrium the Joseph and Vera Zilber Forum," he said.

I liked the idea. The atrium would look great. It was a beautiful design, and I was very pleased, but I wanted to contribute the lion's share of my gift to the scholarship fund. So I proposed that $25 million would go for law school scholarships and $5 million would go toward building the new law school.

Father Wild had another idea. "You know, we're also building a new administration building on campus," he said. "It isn't named at this point, but we could call it Zilber Hall." The new building would be in the heart of the campus and would become the University's "corporate headquarters," housing the executive offices, the scholarship fund, admissions office, student services, things like that.

It was settled. The scholarship fund would be greatly expanded, and the Zilber name would go on a key campus building.

Like so many deals, the timing was right for everyone involved, and Father Wild understands that today:

> There's a point in people's lives when they realize they're not immortal, and they begin thinking about the giving of money. For some those

thoughts come earlier, and for some they come later. Joe had often thought about more financial gifts, but he had come from poor circumstances and really could not imagine himself giving away large sums of money. It didn't make sense to him. Then there came a moment when he realized, "Well, wait a minute, I'm alive. I could do this now." So he did.

My meeting with Father Wild turned out well for everyone. It was very satisfying to know that I would play a part in all the exciting changes that were in the works for Marquette. Then, leaving Father Wild's office, I felt a little uncomfortable. I thought, what have I gotten myself into? I can't announce that I'm giving all this money to Marquette University and then not give anything to the other groups around town who have asked for help.

I began planning my next move. I gathered people on my management team and met with leaders in the community — CEOs, heads of non-profit organizations, university presidents, the chief of police, the district attorney — asking them to identify problems in our community. I started making a list of issues that reflected my own values, principles that were important to me that I could use to shape the criteria of a wide-reaching philanthropic initiative.

First on the list was drug abuse, an obvious choice. My son's addiction was heartbreaking to me and to my family. I wanted to lend a hand to others who had similar problems. We added job training to the list. As an employer, qualified workers are critical to the successful operation of a business, and employment is vital to the success of a community. Domestic violence and public safety were also issues that concerned me. I believe we need to do a much better job of helping citizens who are destitute and vulnerable, therefore, help for the homeless and hunger relief were two more key issues. Finally, Milwaukee's schools were in trouble — the graduation rate of our public school system had plummeted to an alarming 50 percent. We added education to the mix.

I'm a realist. I knew these were enormous challenges and they wouldn't be solved with the wave of a magic wand, but I had a blueprint for a plan of action. These seven core principles — drug abuse, job training, domestic violence, public safety, homelessness, hunger, education — became the themes of what I would call the New Potential Initiative for Milwaukee.

I had a new-found mission. My goal was to use all I had to improve the lives of others.

⁂ ⁂ ⁂

On a muggy day in late August 2007, I sat on an outdoor stage on the Marquette University campus. It was the site of the future law school building, a green and grassy knoll called Tory Hill. Sitting beside me was Father Wild and the dean of the Law School, Joseph Kearney. Milwaukee Mayor Tom Barrett was there, and a bunch of other local dignitaries, and out in the audience, almost 200 first-year law students. There were also teams of reporters from the newspapers and television stations. Just a few weeks away from my 90th birthday, I was on hand to announce my gift to Marquette, and it was shaping up to be quite an event.

The dignitaries took turns at the microphone, praising Marquette University and eventually turning the attention to me. Dean Kearney took the microphone.

"Joe Zilber would have been entitled during this, his 90th year, to focus on the past, on a job well done," Kearney said. "But that is not his style." He went on with some very kind and flattering words about me and my gift to the school, about the mission of the law school itself and how fortunate it was that I had attended Marquette and that my parents settled in Milwaukee, bringing up in his speech the name of Emma Lazarus and her wonderful poem about the Statue of Liberty. It was a good speech, but I have to say, lawyers sure do like to talk.

Then it was Father Wild's turn to address the crowd. He spoke about the expectations that Marquette has for its graduates — "to make the world a better place by what they accomplish in their personal and professional lives," is how he put it, and then he worked up to an introduction of me. "I am proud and grateful that Joe Zilber continues to see Marquette University so closely tied to the future success of our city. I'll now let him tell you more about his vision for Milwaukee's future."

My time had come to speak. I talked about Milwaukee's history, how it was once a booming industrial city filled with opportunities, and how I was able to take advantage of those opportunities when I started building homes back in 1949. The city had changed in recent decades, though, due to the impact of a global economy, and we had lost our industrial muscle. We've fallen behind other cities, I said to the crowd, and we've lost our way. Today Milwaukee is no longer the city it once was.

"It's time for us to rebuild," I said. "We must not be afraid to take on the difficult challenge of fixing what is wrong. With the time I have left, with all the energy and resources that I possess, I will do what I can."

Then I dropped a bombshell.

"Today I am announcing an initial commitment of $50 million to charities, organizations, and institutions in our city who I believe can lead us on the path to achieving a New Potential for Milwaukee."

The wheels were in motion. Three weeks earlier, I had quietly made an additional contribution to the Zilber Family Hospice for more beds and services, inspired by the stories I'd heard at the family dinner. Now, under the tent on Tory Hill, I raised the bar for others to meet. I used my gift to Marquette as part of a more sweeping package of projects, which would be called the "New Potential for Milwaukee." My goal was to spark improvements through a number of organizations and institutions — from health and education to the social well-being of the community.

The next morning, *The Milwaukee Journal Sentinel* gave its stamp of approval on its editorial page, saying this: "The $50 million, to Zilber's credit, is as much a vote of confidence and an investment in the city's future as it is a gesture of Zilber's appreciation to his hometown."

I was invigorated, but this was only the beginning. I was ready for the next act.

❦ ❦ ❦

Lloyd Street Elementary School is five or six blocks from where I grew up in the Lindsay Heights neighborhood on Milwaukee's North Side. Like many other public schools in the inner city, most of the students at Lloyd Street come from low-income families. Two weeks after my "New Potential" speech at Marquette, I announced a gift to the Boys & Girls Club to expand its center at Lloyd Street School.

The Boys & Girls Club of Greater Milwaukee does a fantastic job providing after-school activities for these students by running clubs at the kids' schools. The clubs partner up with the public schools, hiring mentors to work with these young students. There's a long list of things to do — music lessons and acting classes, tutoring and computer classes, basketball, football, and baseball leagues. It's well needed. With my gift, the club would add more staff and more hours for kids, along with more activities in the summertime. The gift was the next piece in my New Potential Initiative, and I was happy I could help out a great organization.

Now I was on a roll. Next on the list was the University of Wisconsin in Milwaukee. Vera had been a student for a time at UW-Milwaukee, known then as the State Teachers College, before she transferred to Marquette. Like Marquette, UWM is an outstanding university, second only in size to the University of Wisconsin in Madison. It's a lively campus on the East Side of Milwaukee with around 30,000 students.

I had heard from one of my senior managers that UWM was working on some kind of plan to start a graduate-level School of Public Health in Milwaukee. UWM Chancellor Carlos Santiago and Milwaukee Mayor Barrett had been pushing the University of Wisconsin Board of Regents to approve a Graduate School of Public Health for the Milwaukee campus. The regents had been on track to change the name of the medical school in Madison to include a public health component, and that didn't sit well with the mayor of the state's largest city. Mayor Barrett made a strong pitch that the school should be in Milwaukee, which, after all, has the largest population of poor people in the state and a dire shortage of public health workers.

The mayor and the chancellor had marshaled a lot of local support for the school, but they would have a hard time selling the plan in Madison to the state legislature, which ultimately would decide whether or not the state would fund it. So I decided to see if I could add some leverage.

I had been in touch with Chancellor Santiago a couple of times by phone to discuss my interest in getting the school started, and he arranged to meet with me at my condo in downtown Milwaukee to talk about it. It was a good meeting. I mentioned to him that Vera had once been a student at UWM, and that she had a strong interest in public health. Because Vera wanted to be a public health doctor at one time, I knew for certain that she would have wanted to support a public health school. To make that happen, I told the Chancellor I would give $10 million toward the Graduate School of Public Health. I wanted to make an impact and give the proposal some serious momentum.

The amount of my commitment was unexpected, I could tell by the chancellor's reaction. Until then, my involvement with UWM had been limited, as Santiago now admits:

> Joe wasn't on any of our targeted lists of donors. We knew he was a Marquette graduate and had given significant amounts to Marquette. So when Joe and his staff came to us, it pleasantly surprised us. When I first talked to Joe, the amount had been kind of nebulous. It was going to be a naming opportunity, so we knew it was going to be more than a million, but I also got the sense that timing was an issue.
>
> Joe's good friend Shel Lubar had given $10 million to create the Sheldon B. Lubar School of Business about a year earlier. I remember Joe talking to me about Shel. Joe had just announced the $30 million gift to Marquette, and he told me, "You know I would have liked to do more for UWM, and maybe down the road I *will* do more. But I think this amount is appropriate, given what Shel gave." I don't think Joe wanted to upstage his friend.

My donation to UWM got a lot of people talking. "That a gift of this magnitude is coming from someone who isn't even an alum of UWM sends a very strong message that Milwaukee supports this idea," Mayor Barrett told the news media. "And that support runs very deep."

My gift helped push the project forward. Milwaukee is one of the few urban centers in the United States without a graduate school of public health. Usually they're based at major urban universities, like UWM, where educators train public health workers to go out into the community and researchers can study problems like infant mortality, teen pregnancy, lead paint poisoning, and the racial disparities in health care treatment.

Along with Vera's concern with health care issues, I myself had once sat on the board of directors of a Milwaukee hospital that cared for the bulk of the city's indigent patients. So I was aware of health care costs and the great numbers of uninsured residents in the city. The public health school would have a wide-reaching effect in the community — and it was another good fit for the New Potential Initiative.

My commitment got the attention of the UW regents. Several months later, after announcing my commitment, I was invited to speak before the regents with Mayor Barrett and Chancellor Santiago at a regents board meeting that was held in Milwaukee. I pushed pretty hard for their backing, asking for their thumbs up:

> We are not adequately dealing with public health problems of every shape and scope that are destroying our communities large and small throughout Wisconsin. I am here today to ask you to do what is right. Create a school of public health, make it the responsibility of the University of Wisconsin-Milwaukee, and locate it in Milwaukee — the seventh poorest, I repeat the seventh poorest, city in the United States — and support it as if lives depend upon it, because they do.

The Regents approved the idea unanimously.

UWM will acquire a building on The Brewery site for the school. Meanwhile, the city's Department of Health decided to have facilities at the school as well. So when all the pieces are put into place, this could develop into a great center for dealing with public health issues.

That was something Chancellor Santiago understood. "Joe is someone who wants to leave a mark, who has the resources to do it, and who really is committed to doing it in Milwaukee," he said. "When you think of the legacy that Joe will have left, one is the state's first accredited schools of public health. That's great, that's really important, but if you think of what the possibilities beyond that are, he will have left a legacy of health care in Milwaukee like nobody else has done."

I was excited to see this come together. My help in creating the Graduate School of Public Health will rank as one of my proudest accomplishments. It might take 10 years or so to really show an impact, but it will be great for the community. I should have been doing this a long time ago. "What took you so long?" I said to myself.

The New Potential Initiative was still not complete. For years, I had made contributions to groups within Milwaukee's Jewish community. I'd given to my temple, Congregation Emanu-El B'ne Jeshurun, and I had given to the Milwaukee Jewish Federation. Now there were also other projects that needed a boost. Two weeks after announcing the UWM gift, I provided $3 million to the Federation, of which $2 million was committed to its capital campaign. Renovations were being made to the Federation's community service building and its Milwaukee-area campus, and a new Hillel Student Center was going up at UW-Milwaukee. My donation would stretch into the future, hopefully guaranteeing some security to the Federation for many years to come.

Again, seeing the difference I could make was inspiring. "I've never had so much fun in my life as I have these last couple of months," I said to the Federation's board of directors as I announced the pledge. "I'll be back here at my 95th and my 100th birthdays, and I promise you we'll have a real party."

Finally, to cap it off, I turned to the United Way of Greater Milwaukee. United Way had started a project called "Breaking the Cycle of Poverty." It focused on job training, early childhood education, preventing teen pregnancy and sexual violence against girls, and helping low income people get a leg up in the world by buying their first homes and going to college. The campaign was right in line with my own goals to improve the city. I set up a 10-year community fund of $1.5 million in the name of Vera and me.

❧ ❧ ❧

Launching the New Potential Initiative was energizing. I felt like I was a young man again. In something like two-and-a-half months, I had given away nearly $50 million. For most of my life, I had been involved to some degree in giving. My gifts prior were relatively modest amounts and made under the radar. With the New Potential gifts, I was being called a "philanthropist," not "Joe Zilber, real estate developer" or "Joe Zilber, Milwaukee businessman." Joe Zilber, "philanthropist." I felt proud to hear those words.

Being considered a philanthropist was different. It suited me at that point in my life. I was the same Joe Zilber as always, looking for the best deal and the biggest challenge, and still not afraid to take a risk. Now I had a new calling, and a new mission in life. Inspired by Vera's vision, and because of the dinner I'd had with those hospice families, I had made a conscious decision to take action in a particular way with a particular result in mind: to spend my life's investments on worthy causes in my hometown.

Why not? I was almost 90. I figured we come into the world with nothing and go out with nothing. Giving it all away was the right decision.

There was still more I wanted to do.

CHAPTER 16

CAN I REALLY
CHANGE THE WORLD?

When I first started out, I never dreamed I would find myself in the position where I could give away a fortune — certainly not $50 million. It was a great feeling, knowing my family foundation could really make a difference. The philanthropic commitments represented a lifetime of hard work and a devotion to the city that had given me so many opportunities. Like most things I've done in my life, I couldn't just sit back and watch things unfold. I wanted to be involved.

As a businessman, I could spend weeks working on a deal, and as soon as I had an agreement, I was on to the next one. Movie theaters, nursing homes, fitness centers, Dawn Dolls — after I signed the bottom line, I didn't sit still for very long. I looked for what was next. I was never one to sit back and watch the world go by. After I bought the Pabst Brewery site, I became personally committed to finding a buyer to develop each parcel.

I guess that goes back to when I was a kid, watching my parents play penny poker. I couldn't just sit there and watch. I wanted to play. I wanted to get in the game. I wanted to deal the cards.

Our New Potential Initiative would go a long way toward improving and sustaining Marquette University, the University of Wisconsin-Milwaukee, the Boys & Girls Club, the Jewish Federation, and many others. Even as I reveled in the satisfaction of my contributions, I looked around and I realized something: it wasn't enough. I wanted to take it even further. I wanted to make a lasting effect on the very neighborhoods where I had grown up, on neighborhoods that had been crippled by poverty, violence, and crime. I wanted to do something that would better the lives of the people in these communities.

"We've got to think of the neighborhoods," I said to myself. "You've done okay, but you haven't done enough to really help the poor."

Living through the days of the Great Depression, I knew what it was like to be poor. I was raised on these same city streets, and I care about the quality of life throughout Milwaukee. There are people in every neighborhood who want to make their communities good places to work and raise families. I want to help these people, young and old, do whatever they can to enjoy happy and productive lives.

The groundwork had been laid with the New Potential Initiative. It was time to take the next step.

On a Monday morning in the middle of May 2008, I stood in the rotunda of Milwaukee's historic City Hall. At my side was Mayor Tom Barrett and Common Council President Willie Hines. Before me was a crowd of community leaders, politicians, and reporters. With the TV cameras rolling, I introduced what I called the Zilber Neighborhood Initiative — pledging $50 million over 10 years to revitalize Milwaukee's inner city neighborhoods.

"I love this city. I love its people, and I'm optimistic about its future," I said to the crowd. "It's going to take a lot of money, a lot of hard work, and a lot of heart from each of you — from *all* the citizens of Milwaukee — to get the job done."

The idea of the Zilber Neighborhood Initiative was to target 10 central city neighborhoods that are in trouble, beginning with my own childhood neighborhood. I don't like to waste money, and I didn't want to just give money to outside organizations to solve the problems. Instead, the lead partnerships in the Initiative and I would go to the people within those neighborhoods and ask them to tell us what they needed, what kind of programs they wanted.

It's got to come from the bottom up, I told the city leaders. It can't come from the top down. Most people don't want somebody telling them what to do. They want the means to be able to help themselves. The people in these neighborhoods must want the help. If they don't, there's no use in continuing, but if they say, "We want to get lead paint out of our houses.

We want to paint our places and keep up the neighborhood," then the Initiative will be there to help make it happen.

"In 10 years I will be 100 years old — I hope," I said to the city leaders and the media on that morning in May. "The Zilber Neighborhood Initiative at that time will be 10 years old. I hope to be with you again at that time, to mark its first decade and to celebrate our common achievement. You all know that there is no future without hope. Our hope is for a brighter future for Milwaukee, and it starts right here, right now. We've all got to roll up our sleeves and get to work."

I might have sounded overly optimistic, maybe even idealistic, but I was confident we could make it work. I was determined to at least try. To make it a reality, I asked for others to pitch in. I challenged individuals, institutions, and other foundations to contribute. I even set a price: come up with an additional $150 million through grants and donations. I wanted to leverage an additional $3 for every dollar I put in.

"If everything comes together in the Initiative I have the hope that everybody will benefit," I said. "To have everything, one must give everything. That's what I'm doing, and I hope others will join me."

With my latest commitment — my *second* $50 million donation — I had come full circle. I was back in the business of Milwaukee neighborhoods, rebuilding neighborhoods, entire communities, really, in the hope of contributing to a brighter future.

As with the New Potential Initiative, the response to the Neighborhood Initiative was extremely positive. For days after I made my announcement, my phone rang off the hook. The Common Council and the Mayor were on board. "You have clearly made a decision to leave a legacy to this city that is going to last for decades, if not centuries," said Mayor Barrett.

The press was supportive as well. All of the television stations aired reports of my announcement, and *The Milwaukee Journal Sentinel* and *The Business Journal* published editorials encouraging others in town to step up. "Zilber's gift presents a rare opportunity to dramatically improve the city. It cannot be wasted," said *The Business Journal*.

Members of the business community backed me up, too. Before I made my announcement, I wanted to sell the idea to leaders in the community. I wanted to put together an advisory board, so I called on Dennis Kuester, chairman of the board and CEO of Marshall and Ilsley Bank, the biggest bank in Wisconsin. Kuester, who grew up in the same neighborhood I did, chairs a lot of civic organizations. He's a very busy guy, but I thought he would make a great partner.

"What I didn't need at the time is another task," Dennis says. "But I like Joe a lot. He's got a real passion for helping, and he's so generous that I wanted to play whatever part he wanted me to play."

Dennis Kuester's commitment was a good start. With his help, we put together a list of people who we thought might help, and I started making calls. Everybody I asked said yes. Not one person said no.

I ended up with an impressive line up of movers and shakers: Daniel Bader, president of the Helen Bader Foundation; Michael Bolger, president and CEO of the Medical College of Wisconsin; John Daniels Jr., chair of Quarles & Brady law firm; Ricardo Diaz, executive director of the United Community Center; Jim Janz, executive vice president of administration at Zilber Ltd.; Gale Klappa, chairman, president, and CEO of Wisconsin Energy, whom I had negotiated with for the Pabst Brewery site; Shel Lubar, founder and chairman of the Lubar & Co. investment firm; Deloris Sims, president and CEO of Legacy Bank; Ed Zore, CEO of Northwestern Mutual; we later added Robert Arzbaecker, CEO of Actuant Corporation.

These people would make up the advisory board for the Zilber Neighborhood Initiative, providing me with strategic planning and looking at the investments and the outcomes of the program.

❧❧ ❧❧ ❧❧

I needed someone to design and run the Neighborhood Initiative, someone who had done this kind of thing before. I wanted to hit the ground running. I got in touch with Leo Ries, program director of the Milwaukee chapter of LISC, the Local Initiatives Support Corporation. In Milwaukee and a lot of other cities around the country, LISC helps turn failing neighborhoods around. They bring together investors, government agencies, local employers, and community organizers to turn declining neighborhoods into places where residents want to live and work and raise children.

The Milwaukee chapter of LISC seemed like a good fit, so I got a couple of my senior managers together for a meeting with Leo. I was in Hawaii at the time, so we arranged a teleconference at my Milwaukee office. Leo brought along a consultant from Chicago named Susan Lloyd. She had worked with the John D. and Catherine T. MacArthur Foundation, one of the largest private foundations in the country. One of its missions is the support of programs that make cities better places.

Leo Ries invited Susan Lloyd to the meeting so she could talk about her Chicago experience. Maybe there was something we could duplicate from the MacArthur-backed projects. We tossed around ideas and did some brainstorming. I began asking questions of Susan, and was struck with how informed and articulate she was. Suddenly, in the middle of the meeting, I asked everyone to clear the room except for Susan. I wanted to speak to her alone. I do this all the time. It's my M.O. It's how I get to know someone by talking one on one.

Everyone left the room, and I asked Susan some specific questions about the programs she had worked on. What was her vision? What was the most challenging part of her job? Then I looked at her and I asked straight out: If given the opportunity, could she run my Neighborhood Initiative? Could she pull it off? She could do it, she said, and, with barely a pause, she explained at great length how she would structure the Initiative and how she would make it successful.

I decided on the spot that Susan was the one who would head the Initiative. When I see someone who I think can perform, someone with the drive, the desire, and the brains, I don't hesitate to bring them in. I've done it again and again. It's how I operate.

Two weeks later, at the end of May, 2008, Susan and I had an agreement. She would direct the Zilber Neighborhood Initiative, with input from me, my foundation board and the newly created advisory board. Susan had the credentials. She had worked on a LISC-supported initiative called the New Communities Program, which focused on improving the quality of life in 16 low-income neighborhoods in Chicago.

The New Communities Program seemed like a good model for the Zilber Neighborhood Initiative. In its first five-year phase, the program had received $21 million from the MacArthur Foundation. New Communities had also leveraged another $274 million from other private and public sources. These funds were used to support community-based organizations that carried out very specific plans that had been devised and written by each of 16 neighborhoods to improve the quality of life in those neighborhoods. The plans reached across all sectors

— from social, economic, and educational projects to the physical development of a neighborhood, the bricks and mortar.

I liked that concept. I've seen many urban revitalization projects come and go, burning up money with no tangible outcome. I wanted our Initiative to translate into real, on-the-ground progress, projects that were new and different.

Of course, I also want to see it happen sooner rather than later. I was 90 years old when I launched the Initiative, and I hoped to see the results. I was the same way with The Brewery project, the family hospice, the Marquette University Law School, and UWM's Graduate School of Public Health. I want to see each one succeed.

Susan Lloyd knows how passionate I am about the Neighborhood Initiative:

> I've had many different bosses over the course of my lifetime, and not one has ever said, "I'm counting on you personally to do this." And Joe means it. There is something about Joe that is so engaging. There are people who are into philanthropy, the science of it, and others who are into it for the leadership opportunities that it presents. Then there is a person like Joe. He's in it because when he drives through the inner city neighborhoods, he is distressed. That is the basis for his motivation to help.

❧ ❧ ❧

My plan to revive the neighborhoods really seemed to strike a chord. Suddenly everybody had an idea. Talk-radio shows were swamped with calls. Local bloggers posted commentaries on their websites. *The Journal Sentinel* printed a wish list from over a dozen community activists, politicians, and union leaders, suggesting improvements to public transit, public libraries, and the city's recreation programs. *Journal Sentinel* columnist Eugene Kane also offered his thoughts in an article titled "Here's How I Would Spend $50 Million." He came up with some pretty good suggestions, too, things like: launch a homeownership plan that would help low income people buy homes, set up a network of homework centers in the neighborhoods and have tutors work with students in the evenings.

Eugene Kane is a well-respected, popular newspaper columnist in Milwaukee. Because he's an African American, he's particularly influential within the Black community. I appreciated his outlook, and I thought I'd give him a call. "I read your column, and I liked what you wrote," I told him. "Let me make a suggestion to you. Why don't you ask your readers what they would do with the money? Let's get the people to weigh in," I told him. If I got just one good idea on how to improve the neighborhoods, it would be worth it.

Mr. Kane took my advice. In his next column, he invited people to send me their feedback. He called his journalistic exercise "How to Spend Zilber's Money."

We were flooded with ideas. In less than a week, Kane forwarded more than 300 emails and letters to me. It was unbelievable. I had copies arranged in a spiral notebook, and I read every one. There were letters from teachers, principals, nurses, social workers, real estate agents, attorneys, college professors, daycare operators, and veterans of the Iraq war. I got a letter from a Milwaukee County Children's Court judge, another from a chaplain at the Milwaukee County Jail, and another from a single mother of an eight-year-old disabled child who had gotten off welfare and was now helping out single moms like herself.

I was amazed at how thoughtful people were. Their suggestions touched nearly every aspect of life. One person suggested putting more money into helping teenage parents become better moms and dads. Another suggested giving out fix-up grants to improve rundown homes. Another thought I should buy vacant lots and turn them into community gardens. Create more literacy programs in the neighborhoods, someone said. Others suggested that we form an outreach project for gang members, put more money into college scholarship programs for inner city high school students, and fund a job corps to improve the park system.

The ideas came from people as far away as New York. One gentleman recommended starting a rehabilitation housing center for people returning from prison to society. "The center would not only house the returning individual, but would also have required courses in plumbing, sheet metal work, carpentry, and other contractor-type professions," said his letter. "Not only would the individual have learned a skill, but that skill could be used to gain fulfilling employment, as opposed to flipping French fries."

I was blown away by all the responses. The ideas were encouraging, just the kind of ground-up thinking that would bring a fresh approach to the Initiative. I was confident we could make this thing fly.

❀ ❀ ❀

The ideas came rolling in all summer. By fall 2008, we were well underway in designing the Initiative. We borrowed from the Chicago model, and identified two nonprofit organizations in Milwaukee that we believed were strong in community development — LISC and the United Neighborhood Centers of Milwaukee. They would act as intermediaries between the Neighborhood Initiative and the lead agencies in the neighborhoods themselves. We gave LISC a grant over four years to handle all the marketing, communications, and technical issues.

Meanwhile, United Neighborhood Centers — eight social service agencies with deep roots in the city — got a grant over four years to develop other programs. It was a good partnership — LISC had expertise in real estate, financing, and the actual physical development of projects and properties. United Neighborhood Centers is good at delivering services to the people, whatever it takes — food pantries, job assistance, preschools, or neighborhood watches.

Next we identified the first two neighborhoods that would become our target areas. The first was the North Side neighborhood of Lindsay Heights, my old stomping grounds. When I was a kid, the neighborhood was a bustling place where people had jobs and raised families. Across the street from our home was my grade school, Lee School, the same school Oprah Winfrey would attend years later when she lived in Milwaukee.

I don't remember what the classrooms were like (I guess I wasn't paying enough attention to my schoolwork), but I do remember the playground behind the school. It was a huge playground where kids from all around congregated to play ball, jump rope, whatever. Safety was never a question. In recent years, though, that neighborhood has had some of the highest rates of crime, unemployment, and poverty in the city. Lee School is still there, but too many houses are vacant, or run down. Windows are boarded up, lots are empty, and newspapers blow down the streets.

It's a sad sight. I've driven down those streets many times lately, and it breaks my heart to see the living conditions of some of those residents. Naturally I wanted my old neighborhood to be ground zero in our Neighborhood Initiative.

The second neighborhood was Clarke Square on the city's South Side. While Lindsay Heights is largely an African-American neighborhood, Clarke Square has a large Hispanic and Hmong population. It's very diverse. Many residents are young, in their 20s, and many don't have a high school diploma. There's a lot of poverty, unemployment, and crime. Youth gangs are a big problem. Both neighborhoods were two of Milwaukee's oldest, and both have problems that overshadow most other neighborhoods in Milwaukee. It isn't that unusual to see prostitutes and drug dealers or to hear the sound of gunfire on some of these streets.

Now there could be hope. In Clarke Square, there's a high percentage of people who own homes, higher than the city average. In five years, Lindsay Heights has seen the construction of 100 new homes and the rehabilitation of 100 more existing homes. Both of these neighborhoods have the potential to one day become great neighborhoods again.

Narrowing it down even further, we next chose the two lead agencies that would put the action plans into place. These would be the groups that would be responsible for encouraging the residents, social service organizations, school principals, and the police department to become involved. They would then follow through and make sure that things got done. We gave a large grant to the Walnut Way Conservation Corporation. Walnut Way is a resident-led group in Lindsay Heights.

Over the past 10 years, it has been doing great work to rebuild the neighborhood. By collaborating with city agencies, the University of Wisconsin-Milwaukee, and other community organizations, its members have done things like build a beautiful neighborhood center in a house built in 1910 that was about to be demolished. They've helped turn vacant lots into gardens and orchards, and installed rain gardens to manage storm water. They've provided job training for residents and recreational programs to neighborhood kids.

We gave Walnut Way an additional seed grant to expand the Fondy Mall fresh produce market, and to develop other retail ventures along North Avenue, a major street that runs along the border of Lindsay Heights. Plans like these fit perfectly with the aim of my Initiative.

Sharon Adams is the Program Director of Walnut Way Redevelopment Agency in Lindsey Heights. She started volunteering for the agency 10 years ago as a resident of the neighborhood. I met Sharon when we were still in the process of designing the Initiative. I visited Walnut Way with Susan Lloyd, Dennis Kuester, and Mike Mervis. Sharon recalls:

> We sat and we talked. I listened to Joe Zilber's view of changing the neighborhoods of Milwaukee. I laid out a map of Lindsay Heights on the table and located things that he and I had in common. We both went to Lee Street School, and we both went to the same North Avenue theater when we were young. We shared these same physical moments, though they were decades apart.
>
> When he was getting ready to leave, I reached over to say goodbye and he said, "Young lady, we'll be back." I had no context at the time for the Zilber Neighborhood Initiative. Then, in late September 2008, Mr. Zilber made the announcement that we had been selected as a lead agency, and we've been rolling ever since. We were challenged by Joe Zilber's Initiative and, like I tell people, "Never pass up a good challenge."

On the South Side, we gave a grant to an organization called Journey House. They have an outstanding record that dates back to 1969. At its first location, Journey House had just a couple of ping pong and pool tables, a soda machine, and space in a rented storefront. Volunteers kept city kids on the straight and narrow by teaching them artwork and photography. Now Journey House has 11 locations and runs all sorts of programs for kids and families — from drug prevention programs to daycare centers. They help people get their GEDs, teach immigrants how to speak and read English, and partner with three local public schools to run after-school programs.

One of their biggest success stories is their Youth Leadership Program. High school students can get involved in sports, cheerleading, recreational activities, and academic teams. All of the high school seniors who have participated have graduated and gone on to college or full-time employment. All of them, each and every one. What an amazing achievement.

With a seed grant of $250,000, Journey House will raise contributions, dollar for dollar, to build a Center for Family Learning and Youth Athletics in the heart of Clarke Square at Longfellow Elementary School.

In less than a year, Journey House made good progress. Under a new division called "Team Zilber," Journey House organized a neighborhood kickoff, which drew ideas from more than 400 residents and nearly 30 community agencies. Out of those ideas, action plans were formed in four areas: public safety, community services, neighborhood beautification, and parks, recreation, and youth activities.

"It is true community change," says Michele Bria, Executive Director of Journey House. "Mr. Zilber really walks the walk. He is genuinely concerned about the children in Milwaukee, specifically children who don't have the opportunities that some of us may have had. He wants kids to get access to those opportunities and move out of poverty."

To round off our first $5 million commitment under the Initiative, we gave $250,000 to Habitat for Humanity's "A Brush with Kindness" project. Their program is to paint and repair homes in the two target neighborhoods.

Word about the Initiative spread. In October 2009, Neighbor Works, a national organization that supports the revitalization of urban neighborhoods, hosted its annual conference in Milwaukee. More than 900 neighborhood activists from around the country attended, sharing their views on programs and projects in their own communities that succeeded, or fell short. The Zilber Initiative used the occasion to present the quality-of-life plans from the Lindsey Heights and Clarke Square neighborhoods. These plans were seen as a model at the conference, as something that could be replicated by neighborhoods in other cities.

At this conference, Milwaukee Mayor Tom Barrett and Common Council President Willie Hines pledged their support and promised to commit city resources to each of the targeted neighborhoods identified within the Initiative. As we move forward, I'm fully confident the Zilber Neighborhood Initiative, in the next 10 years, will have a major impact on the city of Milwaukee and beyond.

❦ ❦ ❦

The first grants were out of the gate, the first of the $5 million pledged to the Zilber Neighborhood Initiative. I liked the way it was shaping up. The lead organizations had long-standing connections to the community. They had respected track records and had made progress previously in rebuilding these neighborhoods. So many times you see revitalization programs run by outsiders. They parachute in with big ideas and inevitably they fail. We wanted to begin with groups that were made up of people who had a stake in these communities, who have seen the neighborhoods at their very worst, and who have the vision, the drive, and the courage to return them to their very best.

Originally when I began making substantial charitable gifts, my goals were to take care of the homeless and the hungry, to make sure people had good job skills, to help people with drug abuse, and to help kids get a decent education. The Neighborhood Initiative has gone way beyond that. We will also try to tackle some of the social problems that so many people face. I want to make sure that the children in these neighborhoods get a chance, and that their parents get a chance, too.

At the start, I thought we could give the houses in the inner city a good facelift and that would solve things, but as I drove around the streets and talked to the neighbors, I found out that it's going to take more than a new coat of paint to fix these neighborhoods. It's not just about repairing broken-down real estate, it's about repairing broken lives. We've got to teach people how to find jobs, how to raise their children, how to live safely and responsibly. People learn by doing. We've got to give people the tools so they can help themselves.

It's a mammoth undertaking, I know, but it's a challenge I accept, and one I enjoy. It has given me a new lease on life. I never expected it could be this gratifying to put a lifetime of savings and investments toward so many good causes. Between the Zilber Neighborhood Initiative and the New Potential Initiative — two major initiatives that stack up on a national level to what few other private foundations have attempted — I'm in for $100 million, all told. In the time and with all the energy I've got left, I plan to do whatever I can, and spend whatever it takes, to turn each of those good causes into realities.

People wonder if I've bitten off more than I can chew. I tell them, no, I don't think so. I'm a pretty determined guy with a pretty good track record myself. Throughout my life, I've always felt that you have to surround yourself with good people who share your values and concerns and give them the means to use their talents to build something better than you could on your own. In business and in life, you can make a difference if you're willing to take risks. As I enter the closing chapter of my life, I have decided to take that risk on a simple project — to help others and improve the quality of their lives. Now that's a risk worth taking.

EPILOGUE

People ask me all the time, What is the secret to living a long and happy life? My answer really isn't too complicated. The key is to keep yourself in good shape, surround yourself with people you love and want to work with, and find a way to keep doing what you love to do.

Building a company, hiring great people, rebuilding neighborhoods, putting together partnerships, chasing the deal — my work has always sustained me. It's what has kept me going. I couldn't live without it. I started with a small real estate company in 1949, built it into a successful operation, launched a public company halfway through my career, and returned to pure real estate, with new building projects across the country. It has been one hell of a ride. After more than 60 years in business, I'm still in the game, now focusing my attention on philanthropy — giving back to the city of my birth with gifts to its schools and civic institutions, and an innovative plan to rebuild its most challenged neighborhoods.

As I turn the corner once again in my long life, I've handed over the reins of my company to the fourth generation of leaders. I know they will do an excellent job. Each of them has been with the company for a couple of decades at least, and each of them is still in their 50s. They know where the company has been, and know where we should go from here. They'll be able to build on our tradition of success, and take the company to great heights.

I would like to give each member of the new leadership credit here. They deserve the recognition. The president and chief executive officer of Zilber Ltd. is Jim Borris. Jim joined the company in 1986. He's a straight shooter, a level-headed guy, and a very good thinker.

John Kersey was made executive vice president in 1979. He's also president of The Brewery Project LLC. John doesn't get unnerved very easily, and that's one of the best things about him. He takes things as they are and makes them work.

Bob Braun is executive vice president and chief financial officer. Twenty years ago, we moved Bob to Hawaii to gain field experience. He spent a couple of years there and was seasoned to become a first-rate manager. To me, Bob is the best there is in accounting. I depend on him especially for dealing with the banks. As I've said again and again, maintaining a good working relationship with our lenders is absolutely critical.

Each of these guys is a family man with strong ties to the community. They're hard workers, dedicated to the company, and to me. Not by accident, they're the same type of guys as all the other managers, partners, and team leaders that I've brought on since the very beginning of Towne Realty. That has been a conscious effort, not as much a strategy as a philosophy that I've followed over the years. I've found people from all walks of life: a cook at a Pancake House, a salesman at a furniture store, a fix-it man at a summer resort, a manager of a chain of movie theaters, an owner of a toy company, a construction foreman for military barracks.

I could go on and on. I've seen certain characteristics within each of them that made me confident they had what it takes to work with my company. It's how I've always operated. It's how I built my company, how I chose my partners, and how I groomed each generation of leaders.

And here's another important point: each of these new leaders has a family member who has worked with my company, a son, daughter, or close relative who's been part of the Zilber company family. From the beginning, I've tried to involve employees' sons and daughters in my company. You see family connections like this throughout the company. I've never looked at nepotism as a negative. It's not a free ride, though. These sons and daughters have a responsibility to show what they're worth if they come and work for us. I think if a kid sees value in what his father or mother does for this company, that kid will strive for quality, too. They've grown up in the Zilber company family and have a great understanding of who we are and what we do as a business.

As an example, I would say our guy Kevin Mantz is a great architect for us because he learned about construction from his dad, Don Mantz. For years, Don has done a great job running our construction outfit, KM Development. He passed something along to his son. It's all about family. Making my company a family has been my goal from the start. I have a personal stake in the lives of this family, and I trust them with the future of my company.

This changing of the guard doesn't mean I'll be retiring, though. I tried retirement when I was about 50. It didn't last. It wasn't for me. So I continue to stay in touch with my management team on a daily basis, looking for the next opportunity, planning the next move. I'll be involved in my company's major decisions until I can't take another breath.

Time brings change. In my biological family, I now have two great-grandchildren. What a wonderful gift they are. The Zilber household keeps expanding. I miss my lovely wife Vera terribly, and will always grieve the loss of my son Jimmy. Yet my family is thriving, and that gives me a feeling of purpose every day.

I have found a certain balance in life. Family brings contentment, my work keeps me motivated, and I've got another role these days: to do what I can to help the people of my hometown, Milwaukee. I'm inspired, driven by a sense of responsibility and urgency. Through my philanthropic projects, I see that I can play a part in making some real changes.

As I look back over the entire landscape of my life, I feel good about what I'm doing — watching a new generation of leaders take my company to the next level, and seeing the fruits of my labor ripen through my philanthropy. It's a proud feeling and a satisfying role, my last chapter.

At least, for now.

POSTSCRIPT

On March 19, 2010, Joe Zilber passed away. He was staying at the Zilber Family Hospice in Milwaukee. His daughter Marcy was at his side. His daughter Marilyn, who had been with him constantly for many, many years, was at Joe's condo in Honolulu waiting to come to Milwaukee. Services were held in the student union of Joe's beloved Marquette University. Over 1,000 people were on hand.

Marquette University's president, the Reverend Robert Wild, was one of several who eulogized Joe. "Joe Zilber's a great man, a great alumnus of this university," said Father Wild. "All of us really loved the fact that Joe could be such a force for good in this Milwaukee community. We are grateful for his life."

Joe's rabbi, Marc Berkson of Emanu-El B'ne Jeshurun, spoke of "the blessings" of Joe's life:

> The blessing of love and the sense of protection he bestowed upon his family, the can-do spirit he imbued in the family he built at work with Towne Realty and Zilber Ltd., the joy of creativity he bestowed upon so many institutions here in Milwaukee, and the blessing of love and the sense of hope he bestowed upon so many of us, his Milwaukee family, in his generous and far-sighted philanthropy.... We thank God for all that was good and true in Joe's life and for the precious memories which shall endure.

Milwaukee's Mayor, Tom Barrett, praised Joe for the influence he had on him:

> Whenever I would meet with Joe, I would see the part of the person that really made that twinkle in his eye glow, and that was the deal. There was always a deal involved, and I say that in a very positive sense, because I could see what he was doing. He was challenging me, and he was challenging us. He was challenging us to build a greater community. *That* was the deal: he would give back to the city that he

loved, but it was not a no-strings-attached deal. He wanted *everyone* — everyone in this room, everyone in this community — to give back as well.

Joe often met with Sharon Adams, program director of the Walnut Way Conservation Corporation in Lindsay Heights, one of the first of two target neighborhoods in the Zilber Neighborhood Initiative. She remembered:

> The final time I met him was on a videoconference. There he was in his home in Hawaii, his eyes as zesty as ever and his questions just as piercing. . . . He looked at a plan I had sent him, and he said, "I like it." Then he said, "Now, can you make it better?" The lesson that I took away goes back to a favorite writing that I have from Thoreau, and it says: "Live the life you imagine." How blessed are our neighborhoods to have Joe Zilber encouraging that, and showing it. I think Joe himself would say: "Live the life you imagine — in service, in urgency, and in love."

I also spoke at the eulogy:

> We gather here to fulfill Joe Zilber's final wish. We have a solemn obligation here to finish his work, to rebuild our city, to give hope to those who have little, to help those who need our help, to do what is right and just.
>
> I recalled a meeting I had with Joe at his home on the day after his last birthday. As always, Joe had a list of instructions for me — instructions that I was to carry out after his death:
>
> As one of his last requests to me he said "Thank the people who speak at my funeral." So, thank you. Then he added, "I hope they'll say nice things." Well, they did, Joe, they did. And then he added, with that Zilber twinkle in his eye: "Remind everybody to get back to work as soon as they can. There's much to do." So, consider yourselves reminded.

Joe's daughter Marcy gave the final eulogy. She remembered her father for his lasting deeds:

> A wise man said, "What we have done for ourselves alone dies with us. What we have done for others in the world remains. It is immortal." You, father, have left this earthly plane, but you are eternal. You will

remain in our hearts. You lived your life with purpose, you lived your life with action, you lived your life with a lot of love in your heart.

Joe lived more than 92 years. As he had wished, he was buried in the same suit he wore when he married his lifelong companion, Vera. He was laid to rest in his hometown, Milwaukee, in a ceremony both solemn and inspiring.

As Marcy said at the dedication of the Zilber hospice: "The first thing we do when we're born is we take a breath in and then we cry, and the last act of life before we leave is, we let a breath out, and everybody else cries. In between are all the joys and sorrows."

Mike Mervis
Assistant to the Chairman and
Vice President, Zilber Ltd.
Milwaukee, Wisconsin
April 17, 2010

INDEX